Library of
Davidson College

TOWARDS A POLITICAL ECONOMY OF NIGERIA

Towards a Political Economy of Nigeria
Petroleum and Politics at the (Semi-) Periphery

JULIUS O. IHONVBERE
University of Ife
Nigeria

TIMOTHY M. SHAW
Centre for African Studies
Dalhousie University

Avebury
Aldershot · Brookfield USA · Hong Kong · Singapore · Sydney

© Julius O. Ihonvbere and Timothy M. Shaw 1988

All rights reserved. No part of this publication may be reproduced, stored in a retrieval system, or transmitted in any form or by any means, electronic, mechanical, photocopying, recording, or otherwise without the prior permission of Gower Publishing Company Limited.

Published by

Avebury

Gower Publishing Company Limited
Gower House
Croft Road
Aldershot
Hants GU11 3HR

Gower Publishing Company
Old Post Road
Brookfield
Vermont 05036
USA

British Library Cataloguing in Publication Data

Ihonvbere, Julius O., *1956-*
   Towards a political economy of Nigeria : petroleum and politcs at the (semi-) Persphery.
   1. Nigeria. Economic conditions. Effects of petroleum industries & trades, 1960-1982
   I. Title   II. Shaw, Timothy, M.
   338.2'7282'09669

ISBN 0 566 05422 1

Printed and bound in Great Britain by
Athanaeum Press Ltd, Newcastle upon Tyne

Contents

Lists of Tables vii
List of Abbreviations viii
Map x
Preface xi

   1 Introduction: towards a Nigerian mode of production 1

I A (semi-) peripheral social formation

   2 Nigeria: oil production, class formation and social contradictions in a (semi-) peripheral capitalist society 21

   3 Rural Neglect in Nigeria: oil, towns, food and inequalities 67

   4 Towards a Political Economy of Ideology: planning the mixed economy 89

   5 Materialist Insights into Coups: the crisis of hegemony in the Nigerian state 119

II Nigeria in the world system

6 Resource Availability and Foreign Policy Change: affluence and influence — 139

7 The State of Nigeria: oil crises, power bases and foreign policy — 165

8 Nigeria Restrained: foreign policy under changing political and petroleum regimes — 183

References — 195

Index — 205

Tables

1	Gross Domestic Product, 1958-9 to 1985	16
2	Oil Production and Revenues in Nigeria	26
3	Nigeria's Oil Economy	28
4	Industrial Production (1972=100)	30
5	Federal Governments Actual Receipts (N Million)	70
6	Federal Governments Actual Expenditure	72
7	Exports of Major Commodities	142
8	Nigeria's External Trade by Commodity	144
9	Imports by End-Use	146
10	Oil Refineries	169
11	Nigeria's Oil Production in Million Barrels a Day	186

Abbreviations

ACP	African, Caribbean and Pacific (countries associated with EEC)
BHN	Basic Human Needs
BP	British Petroleum
CEAO	West African Economic Community
CPO	Central Planning Office
ECOWAS	Economic Community of West African States
EEC	European Economic Community
FESTAC	World Festival of Black African Arts and Culture
GDP	Gross Domestic Product
IBRD	International Bank for Reconstruction and Development (World Bank)
ILO	International Labour Organisation
IMF	International Monetary Fund
MPLA	People's Movement for the Liberation of Angola
NEPA	National Electric Power Authority
NIIA	Nigerian Institute of International Affairs
NIC	Newly Industrialising/Influential Country
NLC	Nigerian Labour Congress
NNPC	Nigerian National Petroleum Corporation
NPN	National Party of Nigeria
NYSC	National Youth Service Corps
OAU	Organisation of African Unity
OFN	Operation Feed the Nation
OPEC	Organisation of Petroleum Exporting Countries
SMC	Supreme Military Council

UN	United Nations
US	United States of America
UPE	Universal Primary Education
WAI	War Against Indiscipline
WIN	Women in Nigeria

Note on the value of the naira

Nigeria's currency, the naira, was valued at approximately US $1.5 at the beginning of the 1970s, after the devaluation of the dollar, rising to circa US $1.8 at the beginning of the 1980s because of the strong price and demand for oil. However, after floating downwards in the early-1980s reverting to about US $1.5, the naira was effectively devalued to about US $0.25 in the mid-1980s, on the introduction of the Second-Tier Foreign Exchange Market (SFEM), or just over 15 pence sterling.

Map: The Federation of Nigeria since Independence

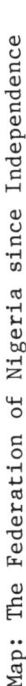

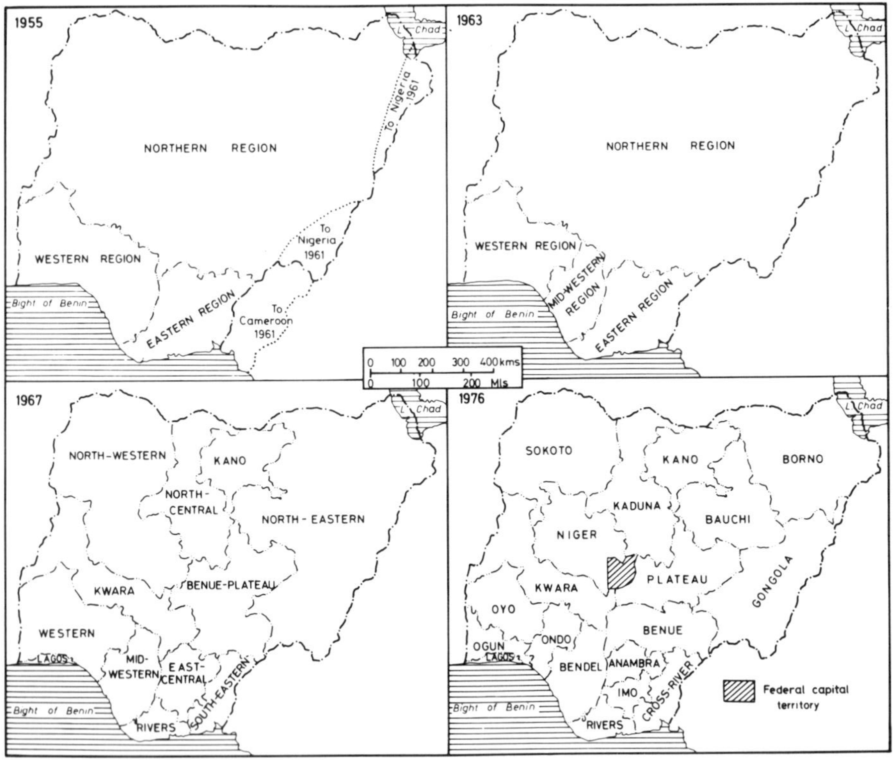

Source: K. Michael Barbour et al *Nigeria in Maps* (London: Hodder & Stoughton, 1982) p. 39 with permission

Preface

This coauthored volume is one product of a decade of collegial cooperation which began in Canada in the mid-1970s and has continued since in both Nigeria and Canada as we have both changed bases and status. Assorted professional demands and political commitments have delayed this book's appearance but despite apparent changes in the political economy of Nigeria we believe that its mode and method of analysis remain relevant. Although Ihonvbere drafted chapters 3, 4, 5 and 6 and Shaw chapters 7 and 8 we have both edited and revised each other's work in this and other manuscripts. All of the essays have been updated and compressed but some appear here by permission of original publishers: <u>Arika Spectrum</u> (#6), <u>Canadian Journal of African Studies</u> (#7) and <u>The Annals of the American Academy of Political and Social Science</u> (#8).

This volume as others would not have appeared without i) the support and tolerance of our spouses and families; ii) the skills and patience of Elfrieda Schneider and Evelyn Flynn; and iii) the encouragement and indulgence of various publishers and graduate students. Finally, Shaw acknowledges the continued financial support of the Faculty of Graduate Studies at Dalhousie and the Social Sciences and Humanities Research Council of Canada.

Halifax and Port Harcourt
September 1987

1 Introduction: towards a Nigerian mode of production

Nigerian social science like the Nigerian political economy is in a state of crisis. This crisis has been engendered not only by the belated efforts of orthodox analysts to reconceptualise their modes and tools of analysis (cf Bienen & Diejomaoh 1981), but also because of the intention of the emerging radical school of thought to raise issues of theoretical relevance and political praxis (cf Nnoli, 1978 and 1981 and Williams, 1976 and 1980). The tardy efforts exerted by the orthodox writers have become necessary in order to meet the intellectual challenges and analytical rigours of radical approaches towards the understanding of the current and future character of Nigeria's distinctive political economy: the "rentier" state (Falola & Ihonvbere, 1985).

The changing nature of Nigeria's politics and economy on the one hand and the changing role of the country in world politics as well as changes among social forces and relations on the other hand have also necessitated the need to adopt alternative approaches – those located within the radical paradigm – towards the study of Nigeria's political and economic evolution. More specifically and within the last decade a set of transitions – the advent of military rule, the recent transitions to and from civilian rule, the problematic institutional experiments, the attenuated oil binge and the current period of economic contraction – have all combined to highlight certain persistent peculiarities of the political economy where new ones have not been generated. In short, the particular "Nigerian mode of production" has produced its own problematique.

a) Analysis

The dynamics of contemporary Nigerian society — the cluster of contradictions and coalitions — have provided more than enough room and data for debates between the orthodox and radical schools of thought. The specificities of the Nigerian social formation — how these have shaped and determined the mode and relations of production: the organisation and (re)action of social classes and the peripheral state; the particular type which the "rentier" state represents; the impact of oil wealth on class relations and rural-urban interactions, particularly agriculture; and the crisis of hegemony which has faced the state and bourgeoisie since political independence (see Chapter Five) — are all central forces and factors treated in the debate. Other issues include the nature of Nigerian peripheral capitalism; the crisis generated by economic contractions in the post-OPEC boom period; the use of oil wealth in support of foreign policy objectives; the limitations of oil diplomacy (see Part Two); the introduction and negation of a new constitution; the transition to and from civilian rule; the efforts of the "new" "national" bourgeoisie to consolidate its hold on the political economy; the position of women in the political economy; the informal sector and the parallel economy; and the precariousness of the environment. These issues are covered in this introductory contribution to Nigeria's political economy and are picked up in the substantive chapters.

However, we also seek to go beyond already established orthodox-radical perspectives, even though we see our work as falling within and, we would hope, furthering the latter perspective. Our perception of the state; the nature and possibilities of capitalist development in the (semi)periphery; the nature of military intervention; and the context and direction of class struggles of contradiction and coalition are some aspects of the rentier state about which we attempt to put together ideas and materials with questions of relevance, change and continuity always in mind.

In particular, our work attempts to weigh theory against reality in order to make our criticisms and analyses relevant for policy-making in and about Nigeria and other African political economies. By this, we mean an approach which attempts to link theory and reality with policies and projections. Whilst the orthodox school has traditionally been preoccupied with "difficulties", we are primarily concerned with "dialectics". This critical perspective enables us to transcend the tendency to concentrate on and to describe the symptoms of otherwise fundamental dynamics that shape the development, demise and/or modification of social forces. Our concern with institutions, personalities, "major developments," etc., are all located within a broad conceptualisation of Nigeria's distinctive political economy. While we hold that changes and struggles within the Nigerian social formation can hardly be divorced from those occuring in the world economy, we also note that, in the first instance, not only do the peculiarities of the "local formation" determine how it is affected supposedly by "external" developments but also that local responses to such developments will depend on the intensity and direction of class struggles. In short, there is a distinctive Nigerian mode of production – the rentier state – which is based on particular relations of production, themselves being the articulation of a range of social forces.

Dramatic transitions – conjuncture? – in the Nigerian case, just like the bell-wether examples of Ivory Coast, Kenya and Tanzania (even if not yet to the same extent) (see Lubbeck, 1986), are reflective of the demise of established scholarship. This is notwithstanding the efforts of more informed and sensitive orthodox scholars to move some way from the outmoded and discredited framework represented by the "modernisation" paradigm. In fact, many traditional approaches and advocates have come to absorb such concepts as "class," "the state," "contradictions" and even "class struggles," as against elites, governments, problems and political development. Thus in general the trend established by all shades of radical scholarship – with an emphasis on inequalities, self-reliance and forms of socialism in the face of rising contradictions and class struggles – appears to have laid out a basic path for the study of underdeveloped formations. Given the growing deficiencies and difficulties of the orthodox genre, it has become increasingly necessary to subject various aspects of Nigeria's political economy to such an approach, one which concentrates on contradictions and conflicts as well as on coalitions and fractions.

This is especially so because at the level of policy it serves to present and delineate alternative development strategies broadly concerned with self-reliance and socialism. In doing so, it highlights the distinctive characteristics of each formation and therefore cautions against efforts to transplant "development" or "success" from one formation to another. At the level of theory it constitutes an alternative framework for organising and explaining data on relationships. In so doing, not only are traditional concepts and methodologies challenged at a fundamental level, but new insights which capture the essence of changes and contradictions are introduced. As Joel Samoff (1982:42-43) suggests in the case of Tanzania in particular and Africa in general:

> The transition from one paradigm to another is fundamentally a political process, and has to do with conflict and power and a particular historical moment. The moment cannot be predicted in advance. What can be clear, however, is the increasing intellectual conflict and disarray as the challenges to the prevailing paradigm mount. In that crisis of theory, that moment of paradigmatic change, there are openings for many new approaches, most of them heavily influenced by the prevailing paradigm and most of them claiming to be the new alternative. That is necessarily a chaotic moment since the ambiguities and inconsistencies of the new paradigm are not resolved until it has become the prevailing paradigm - in a period of paradigmatic change alternatives are not clearly developed - there is a good deal of borrowing among approaches, and the debate among scholars is strident and ascerbic.

Typical of such uncertain moments, the state of radical intellectual activity in Nigeria at present, encouraged by the changing nature of class fractions and coalitions within the defunct democratic experiment and the continuing economic roller-coaster can be grouped broadly into two - political economy and materialist. The <u>political economy</u> approach represents one variety of the non-materialist approach, its primary mark being serious and sustained attention to the economic as well as to the political; but within this mode "economy" is defined in terms of exchange (especially international) and institutions (especially financial) rather than production and contradictions. In the more Marxist political economy - <u>materialist</u> - the emphasis is more exclusively sub- rather than super-structural and the primary focus is on modes and relations of production. When combined these two approaches provide a comprehensive orientation to the understanding of fundamental (as against superficial) roots of contradictions as well as the dynamics of state power and class struggles: the rentier state of Nigeria (see Part One).

The importance of the materialist (political economy) approach, however, lies in its relevance and capacity to juxtapose reality with theory. Thus, as a theoretical framework that "focuses on conflict, that assumes there are systematic connections among production, power, stratification and ideas, that asserts that outcomes are neither largely structurally determined nor largely the result of individual behaviour, that regards history as dialectical and that contradictions can be understood," (Samoff, 1982:43) it provides powerful insights into the changeable patterns of exploitation and expropriation of types of regime and ideology. Efforts to employ this approach to the study of Nigeria's complex political economy, as evidenced in the works of Claude Ake (1985), Bjorn Beckman (1985), Eddie Madunagu (1982), Terisa Turner (1976a and b) and others have provided an effective challenge to the established "modernisation" school typified by Richard Sklar (1963), Anthony Kirk-Greene (1981), Billy Dudley (1982), Oyeleye Oyediran (1979), Henry Bienen and V. Diejomaoh (1981) etc. This is so in the major political science subfields concerned with Nigeria of "comparative politics" and "foreign policy" even if less so in "public administration" and "political philosophy," which are now concerned with definitions of political democracy and economic liberalism. Analysis within this mold exists in other social sciences, especially sociology, and in other disciplines, notably history (see Osoba, 1978 and 1980 and Usman, 1979).

The debates within each of these schools — political economy and political modernisation — have been equally intense. They have revolved around such issues as: Is revolutionary change possible in Nigeria? If so, when? Or is the indigenous bourgeoisie essentially "comprador" rather than "national"? What is the nature of the Nigerian state and what level of "autonomy" does it enjoy? Within the modernisation school debates have revolved around executive versus parliamentary democracy, military versus civilian rule, prospects for party proliferation and state creation, and now privatisation of state enterprises.

b) Prognostications

Taken together, elements within the radical school have highlighted contradictions which have become evident since either political independence or the oil boom or have their roots directly in the politics and economics of colonialism, decolonisation, and instability. Some of these contradictions, which tend to define the Nigerian mode of production and are treated in greater detail in this volume, include:

(i) Those arising from the <u>institutions, structures, patterns and processes implanted in the colonial period</u>, and nurtured or slightly modified in the neo-colonial period, which have continued to contribute to the reproduction of Nigeria's peripheral (later semi-peripheral?) role in the world capitalist system.

(ii) <u>Contradictions between an expanding comprador and bureaucratic class and a more national bourgeoisie interested</u> in protecting local markets for its own exploitation. The comprador and bureaucratic fractions had their hands strengthened by the inflow of billions of "petro-naira" after 1979, but were subsequently weakened by the constraints of contraction.

(iii) <u>Contradictions arising from efforts by the bourgeoisie (as a class) to unify itself</u>, to isolate "nationalist" or "radical" elements within its ranks and to suppress other non-bourgeois classes, as evidenced in the politics of the civil-war, in post-war reconstruction programmes, in the economic policies of the military such as their indigenisation decrees, in the numerous anti-labour laws and regulations, in the massive expansion of security forces and in current privatisation schemes.

(iv) <u>Efforts of the state to define clearly spheres of interest between local and foreign investors</u> through the indigenisation decrees also generated its own contradictions, for the decrees consolidated and rationalised the presence of foreign capitals, guaranteed them a place in the "commanding heights" and technologically-sophisticated sectors of the economy, and re-integrated the Nigerian formation into the world capitalist system.

(v) <u>The increasing organisation, militancy and class consciousness displayed by non-bourgeois classes, particularly the working class</u>, heightened the contradictions between labour on the one hand and the state and capital on the other; the frequent repression of workers, the proscription of trade unions, imprisonment, detention and banning of union leaders and workers, the enactment of numerous punitive labour laws and so on only served to heighten the contradictions.

(vi) <u>Efforts by the state and bourgeoisie to divert public attention from conditions of mass poverty and official ineptitude</u> through the hosting of several cultural jamborees, "dynamic" foreign policy pronouncements on Southern Africa, and initiatives such as ECOWAS, only had temporary positive effects which increased these contradictions in the long run, as the latter case clearly demonstrates; even the later expulsions of "illegal" aliens not only demonstrated to the Nigerians that something was wrong somewhere, but when it did not generate the anticipated benefits, it demonstrated that the roots of poverty, unemployment and social insecurity lay elsewhere.

(vii) <u>With the oil boom, the old contradictions between the centre and states (formerly regions) were revived</u>. Though the creation of states and the trauma of civil war were supposed to have reduced the power of the regions and strengthened the federal government, the control of the latter over oil rents on which the country became exclusively dependent in the seventies, heightened the contradictions between centre and states: the on-going "derivation" debates.

(viii) Thus contradictions were made more intense by the struggles of factions/fractions of dominant forces to control the state, particularly at the centre, and so preside over the allocation and consumption of oil revenues; the tendency to rationalise this struggle in ethnic, religious and other chauvinistic terms has not mellowed.

(ix) The oil states and non-oil states, and the public sector and private sector, were equally placed at opposing ends of the accumulative and power processes: on the one hand the local bourgeoisies in the oil states, claiming to represent their peoples, fought hard to keep a large part of oil rents basing their case on the principle of "derivation" and the destructive consequences of oil production; the non-oil bourgeoisies on the other hand fought against derivation and tried to get as much as possible from oil rents basing their arguments on equity and need; the huge budgetary allocation to the public sector in spite of its inefficiency and decay not to mention its corruption and wastefulness continued to arouse public indignation; however, its corruption, inability to initiate effective and consistent policies, double standards, competition with private investors and intrusion into several sectors hitherto controlled by either foreign or local (or both) investors, generated its own contradictions.

(x) The oil boom generated its own contradictions and deepened old ones. The rural decay and neglect of agriculture, dependence on oil wealth, the "arrogance of power" especially at the centre, inflation, dependent food policy and high cost of living, skewed distribution of social amenities, misuse of state power, displacement of peasants by inefficient state farms and the construction boom and so on, all combined to expose the fragility of the Nigerian bourgeoisie and state while simultaneously heightening class contradictions and struggles.

(xi) The coincidence of dedemocratisation and devaluation with economic contraction served to upset established social relations and assumptions: bureaucratic fractional balances as well as class relations were thrown into disarray as were popular dreams of petro-naira affluence and official projections of Nigerian power. The "conjuncture" of the mid-1980s caused a widespread "kaleidoscopic" change in which internal as well as external terms of trade were transformed along with patterns of national production and accumulation. Nigeria's always fanciful notions of being a Newly Industrial as well as Influential Country (NIC) were undermined further whilst corporatist military regimes came to demand austerity, discipline, deregulation, devaluation and "minimum government" (see Chapter Eight). And if its NIC aspirations were eroded so too were its assertions of semi-peripheral status. To be sure, a united Nigeria will always tend to be <u>primus inter pares</u> in West, even continental, Africa. But a sustained sub-imperial role – regional or continental communications, diplomatic, educational, industrial and strategic sub-centre – is likely to remain elusive other than at the whim of extra-African interests. And

(xii) <u>The exponential pressure of women at all levels to be recognised as producers, decision-makers, traders and thinkers as well as mothers, spouses and consumers; ie. demands for change in the sexual division of labour and accumulation.</u> The established Nigerian patriarchy has rarely acknowledged the crucial roles of women in households, markets and informal sectors. With economic crises, women's conferences and feminist interest groups, notably "Women in Nigeria" (<u>WIN Document</u>, 1985 and <u>Women in Nigeria</u>, 1986), the male establishment is having to reconsider its exclusion of women from power and production. Given the lacklustre performance of the male regimes before and after independence, Nigerian women clearly need not only to be integrated into national development but also to redefine it to include the Basic Human Needs of and opportunities for everyone.

c) Problematique

These contradictions among others are indicators of the distinctive peculiarities of the Nigerian political economy which facilitate comparative study among cases, periods and disciplines. In the discussion of the nature of the peripheral capitalist state, for instance, obviously there is need to go beyond the emphasis on its being "post-colonial." It is essential to recognise and treat it as a capitalist state-type, to recognise its weaknesses, note the power of other social forces and locate the roots of the state in the pre-colonial period. In the Nigerian instance, the analysis must go even further. The rentier nature of the state during the seventies – when it came to depend almost exclusively on oil rents not only to mediate internal contradictions but also to keep internal and external projects and initiatives afloat – needs to be highlighted. The extent to which this distinctive trait has affected state power, the nature of dominant forces, their relations with international forces and its internal economic/political role need to be carefully analysed: the Nigerian mode of production.

In like manner, the specific distortions and contradictions

introduced or heightened by dependence on oil revenues (and their subsequent decrease) have to be noted in the Nigerian case: What internal/external forces prompted this dramatic shift — that is, the neglect of agriculture and over seventy per cent of the near-100 million population — to dependence on a foreign capital-dominated sector which employed at its peak less than six per cent of the total number of workers in the modern sector? How has this shift affected internal power relations, non-bourgeois forces, the state and Nigeria's role in the international division of labour? What level of industrialisation has been realised with the oil boom and influx of foreign investors? Do we see a dependent capitalist developmental pattern emerging or does the fragility of the revenue base serve as an obstacle to industrialisation? To what extent were the indigenisation decrees and subsequent austerity measures helpful to the industrialisation efforts of the state? What fraction of the bourgeoisie stood to gain from these industrialisation and privatisation programmes and how have these policies and periods affected non-bourgeoisie forces especially the working class?

At the political level, the advent of military rule, the transition to civilian government and the experiment with the presidential system unleashed a spate of alignments and realignments. Obviously it will take time for the political lines to be clearly drawn after the present period of renewed military rule, particularly if a new generation of politicians does emerge after the decade's embargo on the established but discredited old guard. But factions and fractions of the bourgeoisie under the presidential system were always at "war" attempting to win access to the state and its control of oil revenues and the means of coercion. Those in power wanted to retain control irrespective of the cost, while those outside power wanted to capture it, no matter the price or means. Tactical political coalitions, which had practically little or no ideological motivations, also involved physical elimination, expulsions, deportations, dismissals, impeachments, failure to register specific political parties, the registration of other parties with "nuisance value," disqualification of others from contesting elections, and so on. While most of the political figures tried to use the masses as objects of manipulation, there were pockets of resistance and opposition to them.

Again, these tendencies, following a thirteen-year period of military government, raised interesting questions as to the possibility of divorcing political (or rather constitutional) development and sophistication from material advancement. If anything, and as the International Labour Office (ILO) (1981) demonstrated recently, not only can the contemporary Nigerian economy not be described as stronger, but the majority of Nigerians are worse-off materially than they were a decade ago. Moreover, the prospects for political instability or the emergence of an amalgam of civilian-cum-military rule – corporatism (Shaw & Ihonvbere, 1987) – or a more fascist-type military junta cannot be ruled out given the corruption, political violence, and wastefulness of the bourgeoisie, and the alienation and restlessness among non-bourgeoisie classes which came to characterise the civilian administration under Shehu Shagari, particularly in the period preceding and succeeding the farcical 1983 elections.

Focusing on specific aspects of the political economy over time – the Nigerian mode of production – certain distinctive features can be highlighted. These features are more products of class and production relations than the precipitates of state policies. Though the Nigerian state has initiated policies aimed at strengthening itself and the bourgeoisie or resolving contradictions either between it and the bourgeoisie or between it and foreign capital, the weak and unstable accumulative base of the dominant forces and the crisis of hegemony which has plagued the state since political independence have often undermined such efforts. Nigerian federalism and Nigerian capitalism have meant different things to different regimes whether they be civilian or military.

But, more importantly, the essence of federalism has varied with developments in the political economy. In the first republic, the state meant a very weak centre with very powerful and competitive regions. Under the first military decade, it meant a powerful and domineering centre and subservient regions. Under the second republic, there were struggles by the centre, in spite of constitutional provisions, to retain all the powers and privileges enjoyed by the military. The states on the other hand campaigned to employ all their constitutional rights to resist federal power and intervention. However, such efforts of the states were severely mediated by their dependence on the centre for revenues and the tendency of the "local" bourgeoisies to concentrate on gaining access to central power structures. Likewise, Nigerian Capitalism (Schatz, 1977) has evolved but not been transformed, over time; it remains expensive, dependent, extroverted and tenuous (Schatz, 1981 and 1982).

While ethnicity has continued to be a potent force in the calculations and political activities of the bourgeoisies, it has more often than not been employed as a rationalisation of efforts to win economic and political concessions from either the centre or opponents. It is important to note the declining potency of this factor in Nigerian politics, as the political elements increasingly found it difficult to meet the material needs of the majority and as alternative claims of class and gender became more salient. The mass poverty, alienation and disillusionment caused by the mismanagement of the oil economy had a contradictory effect on the emergence of viable class-based organizations and political actions.

Instead of stereotyped ethnic links, two types of patron-client relations, often not along ethnic lines, emerged in the civilian period of the second republic. In the first instance, upper middle-class elements and bureaucrats have attempted to climb the "ladder of society" into bourgeois ranks by exploiting forms of connections with established bourgeois elements. This process, which had its roots in the colonial and immediate post-colonial period, was intensified in the oil boom years as various fractions struggled to corner a share of the "national cake" or the "petro-naira" before they disappeared. The second case involves members of non-bourgeois classes organising under ethnic, community, clan, religious or cult banners to sponsor a "patron" to the centre of societal politics and through intensive lobbying and pressure ensure that he occupies a "lucrative" position. The "patron" in turn brings "home" the community's share of the "national cake" either in the form of some amenities or in the provision of jobs or contracts. (We use the male personal pronoun here deliberately: patriarchy is a further characteristic of Nigeria's, like most other, political economies) (see WIN, 1985).

The belief in the efficacy of patron-client relationships is apparently still strong and remains one of the obstacles to the development of class consciousness in Nigeria. Even in the face of i) massive neglect of agriculture and the rural areas which has necessitated migration to urban centres, and ii) the general failure to meet the basic human needs of the majority of Nigerians, the "Nigerian dream" continues to be the opium of the masses. The ideology of mixed economy and planning which is supposed to be the corollary of ideological neutrality between capitalism and communism, now redefined as privatisation and rationalisation, has come to serve as a potent weapon for incorporating and domesticating non-bourgeois forces, diverting public funds into private coffers, rationalising and subsidising private capital accumulation and providing the infrastructure which facilitates further international capitalist exploitation of the Nigerian economy.

Intra-class contradictions have also had two major effects on class struggles in Nigeria. First, they have promoted the process of crystallisation of class forces, to the extent that it has forged new coalitions and resulted in the emergence of new fractions. And the second effect arises from the first; the strategies and tactics of alignment and re-alignment have forced non-bourgeois forces to organise and re-conceptualise their relations beyond ethnic, religious and regional lines. It is against this background that one can understand the increasing number of incidents of industrial unrest both isolated or organised, the occupation of factories by workers, peasant resistance and the activities of school children and market women. Changing class differentiation within the rural areas, particularly the penetration of international capital and the emergence of "absentee and progressive farmers," based on new land distribution decrees, have also generated rural pressures which have far-reaching implications for state policies and alliances with other social forces.

The concentration on distribution rather than production in both political and intellectual circles is symptomatic of the weak accumulative base of dominant forces, the peripheralisation of the social formation within world capitalism and the dominant position occupied by vertically-integrated transnational corporations. These features have directly contributed to deepening the crisis of the Nigerian economy in the post-OPEC years with the reduction in oil production, export and revenue. The dramatic decline in foreign reserves and the cash flow problems of the state which forced it to introduce "austerity" measures exposed the weakness and unproductive nature of the bourgeoisie. The bourgeoisie was incapable of producing any of the goods either completely banned or placed on special import licence by the government. Indeed, some fractions undermined prospects of local production by facilitating large-scale smuggling. Mass media reports were full of statements by members of the bourgeois class calling on the government to allow the importation of goods that had been hitherto produced internally but had been imported in the period of the oil boom. Thus, even opportunities created for the bourgeoisie to expand its role in the local market could not be exploited immediately; an endless "war against indiscipline" is unlikely to advance domestic production without structural change. Yet these manifestations of structural and class weakness were not major campaign issues in the electioneering campaigns of the registered political parties at the fatal 1983 elections.

In fact, a close look at the six registered parties for the last vote clearly shows that they had more in common than readily meets the eye. The Unity Party of Nigeria (UPN), which during the 1979 campaigns declared that "democratic socialism" was its purpose, conveniently retreated from such a goal in 1983. The Peoples Redemption Party (PRP) was dealt a bad blow with the death of its leader, while Waziri Ibrahim of the Great Nigerian Peoples Party (GNPP) succumbed to his business inclinations rather than remaining in political opposition to the ruling National Party which controlled all major contracts and national patronage networks.

Without doubt, a large part of the economic woes of the country has been caused by the wastefulness of the discredited politicians in all the political parties, the attempt to pay political debts, misplacement of priorities and lack of attention to pressing developmental issues. This explains why all political parties conveniently ignored the fundamental causes of the crises of the economy and instead concentrated like orthodox analysts on peripheral issues, personalities, and unrealistic prophesies:

> The poor state of the Nigerian economy has inevitably developed into a major issue in the country's elections. Foreign exchange problems, import licence difficulties and import prohibition have led to production cut backs in local manufacturing plants, shortages of many consumer goods and higher prices. These developments would be god-sent news to opposition politicians anywhere. Sadly, however, the discussion of the economy's problems so far has not transcended the level of politiking. The first objective is to find a scapegoat of whom there are many; then rosy solutions are offered, which cannot stand close examination. The rhetoric then tries to confuse issues, and all too frequently succeeds in merely diverting attention from the basic problems ("Keeping Nigeria on track" West Africa 3427, 27 June 1983, 1487).

This inability of the members of the dominant political classes to raise critical issues that underscore the very survival of the nation, raises issues concerning Nigeria's future as (i) a class society, (ii) a regional sub-imperial power, (iii) a rentier state, (iv) a (semi-)peripheral capitalist society, and (v) a member of the world capitalist system.

d) Projections

Given that the distinctive feature of the materialist mode of analysis lies in its concern for the sub- rather than super-structure as well as its focus on relations and forces of production, any attempt to discuss the future of a social formation must be located within this mode; a characteristic of real materialist analysis. Perhaps in the Nigerian case, part of the projections can be drawn from the lessons which are identifiable in the distinctive political economy of Nigeria both as a peripheral capitalist society and as an oil-producing country. Such projections would, for instance, among other things raise questions relating to modes of analysis and praxis; contradictions and/or coalitions; development and/or growth; democracy or repression; and disintegration or revolution — the Nigerian mode of production.

Underlying these projections would be a particular historical experience that cannot be wished away, such as the political economy of military intervention (see Chapter Five). The Nigerian experience has shown that the military has always intervened successfully in periods of socio-economic and political disaffection when social contradictions are advanced and close to explosion; New Year's Eve 1983 confirmed this predisposition. The intervention is usually on behalf of warring fractions and/or factions of the bourgeoisie who are typically re-integrated under military rule. Essentially, while the military has to date achieved some political successes which have reduced tensions and contradictions among bourgeois forces, they have failed woefully at the economic level at least in terms of meeting the basic needs of the majority, promoting development and re-defining Nigeria's peripheral role in the international division of labour. The present period of post-Shagari military rule represents another opportunity to prove or disprove this legacy, with its emphasis on austerity, privatisation, devaluation and desubsidisation; ie. structural adjustment.

The nature and direction of Nigerian politics in the 1980s did not appear to be fundamentally different from what it was in the 1950s and 1960s until 1984. Conditions which prompted civil unrest in the first republic and forced the military to intervene on behalf of the bourgeoisie can be said to have reappeared and worsened since 1979. There was, therefore, no reason not to expect a rapid return to military rule, as happened after the 1983 elections. The crucial question then was: in the advent of a military intervention in Nigeria, what would be its nature? Alternatives include the Ethiopian, Ghanaian, Liberian or Latin American styles. However, given the nature of working class organisation, the rising level of militancy and class consciousness as well as alliances with rural forces, and the very poor economic conditions such a military would inherit, we would have expected a Latin American style: one which would repress workers, isolate nationalist elements of the bourgeoisie, and initiate an elaborate "corporatist" programme (see Chapters Seven and Eight). The march towards fascism in such instances cannot be halted if the indigeous bourgeoisie is to retain the alliance of international capital by demonstrating its control over internal social forces: the war against indiscipline may in reality be a war against the non-bourgeoisie.

e) Parables

What, then, are some of the specific lessons of the Nigerian experience? First, the contradictions and constraints of growth (not to mention development) within a distorted and peripheral economy, irrespective of human and material resources, have been clearly demonstrated. The more than two-decades experiment with (under-)development planning and efforts to sponsor the emergence of an indigenous bourgeoisie have yielded marginal and tenuous results. The ILO (1981) survey clearly demonstrates that the Nigerian economy since political independence has not succeeded in meeting any of its developmental goals! Import-substitution industrialisation, even where it generates some employment, does not readily conserve foreign exchange. The spatial consequences have also had devastating effects on rural-urban relations with the continued concentration of industries in the latter.

A second lesson relates to the natures of the state and of dominant forces. Once again, the weakness of the peripheral state and its inability either to manage effectively the societal resources or to mediate class contradictions have generated conditions of crisis and instability. Military coups, a civil war, general strikes and isolated confrontations have characterised the efforts at instituting state hegemony since political independence. The enactment of anti-labour laws and the expansions of the armed forces and bureaucracies have hardly had significant effects on the rising organisation, militancy and consciousness of non-bourgeoisie forces.

The weak and unproductive natures of the bourgeoisies have also shown that given the difficulties of forcing a comprador class to become productive, especially under the guidance of an unstable and weak peripheral state, the bourgeoisie might have to be by-passed in the developmental process. The attachment of the bourgeoisie to distribution as against production is almost religious. The Nigerian state, in its efforts to reconcile and promote the diverse interests of international capital, the bureaucrats, the compradors and national bourgeoisie works against the interests of the latter which is always in danger of being marginalised and reduced to compradors, especially if indigenisation and privatisation proposals fail to advance its factional interests.

A third lesson arises specifically from challenges in the oil boom period. The dangers of dependence on a single non-renewable export commodity, the inability to absorb effectively or manage huge rents collected from such exports and the distortive effects on several sectors which are in turn direct products of state policies and the nature of the dominant forces, demonstrate the tenuous linkage between resource availability and development. The Managing Director of the Nigerian National Petroleum Corporation (NNPC) Lawrence Amu (1982:4) captures this danger of dependence effectively:

> Clearly, it is hazardous for a country to rely on one single commodity to this extent because any reversal in the fortunes of this commodity will automatically adversely affect the country's development programme. Besides, a country that depends on a single product is also highly susceptible to political blackmail. The situation would

Table One

Gross Domestic Product, 1958–9 to 1985

	1958–9	1963–4	1968–9	1973–4	1978–9	1979–80[1]	1983	1984	1985[1]
GDP at current factor cost[2] of which in %	920	1396	1486	12118	27370	31424	27360	25854	26473
Agriculture, forestry and fishing	68	60	55	28	20	18	24	26	26
Petroleum	0.07	1	3	23	21	24	14	17	18
Other mining	1	1	1	2	2	2	2	1	1
Manufacturing	4	6	9	5	6	7	13	11	12
Distribution	12	14	13	19	20	19	18	18	18
Transport and communication	4	5	4	4	5	5	4	3	3
Construction	3	4	4	7	11	11	8	7	6
Other	8	9	12	13	14	14	17	17	16

[1]estimates [2]prices in million Nigerian pounds (1958–9 to 1968–9) and million Naira (1973–4 to 1985)

Sources: World Bank, Federal Office of Statistics, Central Bank of Nigeria

be worse for a high cost economy like ours where the industrial sector cannot be relied to produce goods at competitive export prices to generate foreign exchange and where administrative machinery calculated to check the excesses in government expenditure is very slow and almost ineffective.

The inability of the national bourgeoisie to capitalise readily on the "austerity measures" introduced by the government – by expanding its role in the domestic market at the expense of foreign capital – demonstrates the limitations imposed on it by its nature and unequal relations with the international bourgeoisie. Import-substitution industrialisation remains import-dependent and so vulnerable to any changes in the supply and price of "forex".

A fourth lesson relates to external relations. Though emboldened with oil-naira and pushed by the nationalism of a fraction of the bourgeoisie and the security problems exposed by the civil war, successive governments pursued an enlightened foreign policy in the African continent; yet the limits to a radical foreign policy irrespective of size of army, resources and population were demonstrated. ECOWAS did not reduce Nigeria's security problems in spite of its huge financial costs. In fact, ECOWAS worsened the country's internal problems and only succeeded in alerting the francophone states that had traditionally been suspicious of Nigeria. On change in Southern Africa, it is evident that credit first must go to the liberation movements and next to the Front Line States. Like Libya in the Middle East crisis, Nigeria has been a very distant and safe "noise maker" and financial contributor in the Southern region. Its double standards in dealing with the forces involved in the struggle to which it claims to be totally committed exposed the unreliability of its pronouncements. The nationalisation of British Petroleum with full compensation juxtaposed with silence over the open relations of other transnationals with South Africa is a case in point. Also, though it claims to have no dealings with Israel, scores of Israeli firms continue to do a profitable business with the government while Nigerians and Israelis have exchanged visits frequently. And finally, the fact that Nigeria's relations with the outside world, especially since the end of the civil war in 1970, have been based on its oil wealth, fluctuations in revenues and continued foreign domination of the oil sector have together imposed restrictions on the mobilisation let alone employment of the oil weapon.

A fifth and final lesson arises from Nigeria's location and role in the world capitalist system. Structural incorporation into this system has generated its own internal contradictions which impact upon and reproduce external linkages.

Essentially, while increasing the possibility of internal accumulation, import-substitution industrialisation, regional hegemony and the oil boom have pushed Nigeria from an inherited position at the classic periphery to a tenuous one at the semi-periphery; yet the vulnerability of the Nigerian economy to practically all changes at the centre has remained constant. The falling rate of profit, technological stagnation, emergence of new nodes of export, economic contraction and so on at the centre have all had far-reaching effects on the local economy. Specifically, fluctuations in a world market dominated by transnational corporations have had significant consequences on internal stability, the patterns of accumulation and relations of production. Thus, unless fundamental restructuring of inherited relations, institutions and processes takes place in peripheral economies (Nigeria included), efforts to sponsor growth with or without development will continue to reproduce underdevelopment and crises.

Increasing contradictions arising from these lessons and developments have provided the raw materials for radical analysis with clear-cut and long-term political implications: ecology as well as economy. The point may be made that while there is hardly a viable left-wing organisation let alone party in Nigeria at present, the trend is towards debates about relevance, unity, strategy and tactics. Thus, intellectual contributions which raise issues within the materialist political economy mode - from fractions and gender to environment and corporatism - contribute significantly to these debates. There is clearly no reason not to expect the contradictions discussed thus far to continue or to be intensified. The desire to keep political positions and prevent others from gaining access demands more daring measures and more political debts. These would take place in a period of dwindling revenues and increasing restlessness within the ranks of non-bourgeois forces. And since Nigeria has experienced growth without development in the past two decades, the state has to adopt stringent measures to contain popular pressures. These are facilitated, of course, by the return of the soldiers: corporatism through coercion (Shaw & Ihonvbere, 1987).

Current evidence indicates that the state might have exhausted all "rational" possibilities - the creation of states, expansion of the bureaucracy, establishment of parastatals, attempts to control workers through legislation, indigenisation decrees and austerity measures. The alternatives are not too encouraging and there are no painless or costless options. At the very heart of the options lies the survival of the democratic and capitalist experiment. The performance of the national assembly in its first term was a disappointment to a majority of Nigerians. Most parties adopted the easy way out of mass rejection at the polls by not renominating over 70 percent of those who were elected in 1979. The efforts to drag the military into taking sides in the politiking was quite tempting to certain ranks within the armed forces (see Falola & Ihonvbere, 1985).

Ultimately, the ability to contain popular pressure "rationally" will condition both short- and long-term options. But given the unlikelihood of sustained recovery in the world oil market in at least the medium term, the inability of the state to guarantee basic amenities and the problematic survival of the average citizen — for example the failure to pay workers in some states for up to six months — the tendency will surely be towards increasing organisation and revolution. Given the dialectics of such cycles, however, the praetorian state can be expected to contain and control such efforts, at least until coercion becomes irrational or communication so problematic. The (semi-)peripheral state does not give up easily despite its limited developmental ambitions or achievements, to which we turn in Part One.

2 Nigeria: oil production, class formation and social contradictions in a (semi-) peripheral capitalist society

"...Nigerian social science has rendered a disservice to the cause of Nigerian development. In its present form it is incapable of providing intellectual leadership and an adequate theory for the revolutionary tasks required by that process. Therefore, the necessary revolutionary transformation of Nigerian society must include the radicalisation of Nigerian social science."
— Okwudiba Nnoli (1981:46)

"On the level of social formations, it is not even enough to know that there are three main classes in Nigeria: the capitalists, the peasantry and the working class. It is also necessary to know that there are differentiations (often politically crucial) within each class, that the boundaries between the classes are extremely fluid, unstable and in some areas almost indeterminate, that there are several (some of them strategic) intermediate social groups and strata... in Nigeria - just as in several other parts of the world - class oppression often merges with ethnic oppression, and conversely."
— Eddie Madunagu (1982:98)

"Nigeria in 1980, at the end of its first year of restored civilian government, appears strikingly different in its politics and economics from the country in which fratricidal strife was terminated in 1970 only by the envelopment and exhaustion of the secessionists...
Nigerian society is still fissured by communal, ethnic and religious affiliations though perhaps not yet by class differences...
The good fortune that eased the soldiers' statecraft in the 1970s is likely to continue into the 1980s... A long purse will strengthen the acceptability of the civilian government as it did that of the military regimes. The common repugnance which parties and factions in Nigeria now have toward military government is also a force making for compromise and agreement among them."
— Anthony Kirk-Greene and
Douglas Rimmer (1981:153-6)

"It has been argued that political competition in Nigeria would shift from its former ethnic or communal base to a more class-orientated competition once the Nigerian Federal Republic was changed from regions into a system of 12 and then 19 states...
...However, after a civilian regime returned to power in late 1979, revenue allocation between the federal government and the states continued to be a major issue. A clear shift to class and sectoral terms of reference is neither taking place nor likely to take place in the future in Nigeria in any simple or straightforward fashion.
...In objective terms Nigeria is forming a class structure, but most Nigerians do not perceive this.
— Henry Bienen (1981:4-5)

The debate about the character and future of Nigeria's distinctive political economy has been joined as we noted in our introduction, encouraged by the transitions from military to civilian rule and back again and from economic expansion to contraction. This chapter focuses on six aspects of the national debate and data in addition to addressing en passant selected features of the continental intellectual and existential crises. First, we treat the issue of the "rentier" state and the hegemony of certain class fractions within it, going beyond established notions of the "overdevelopment". Second, we analyse the peculiar features of a (semi-)peripheral political economy dependent on i) petroleum production and exportation and ii) capital good and food importation: the rather perverse political culture of "petro-naira" (Barber, 1982). Third, we examine the interrelated policies of capital indigenisation and labour repression. Fourth, we examine the impact on and response of non-bourgeoisie classes – the workers and peasants – to state capitalism and uneven growth, a neglected area of scholarship. Fifth, we look at the reasons for and results of privatisation and devaluation. And finally, sixth, we suggest alternative futures for Nigeria given the pattern of class contradictions and coalitions. In short, this first chapter seeks to identify crucial relations in Nigeria's political economy for reasons of both explanation, projection and reaction.

a) New Dependence: towards a political economy of Nigerian oil

Foundations: the imperative of radical analysis for Africa

Whilst at the levels of super- and sub-structure the start of the 1980s was marked in Nigeria by near simultaneous transitions towards civilian rule and away from economic expansion, at the intellectual level it was marked by the appearance of significant analyses of the distinctive national political economy (see Nnoli, 1978 and 1981, Osoba, 1978 and Usman, 1979). The ensuing debates, situated as they were in a period of electoral excitement and economic collapse, served to advance further the focus on the essential characteristics of the Nigerian state which continued under the constraints of the Buhari and Babangida regimes. The established orthodox school has not remained silent nor dormant, however; rather, it has moved some way to distance itself from the outmoded and discredited framework of the "modernisation" paradigm (see Oyediran, 1979 and Kirk-Greene & Rimmer, 1981). The Nigerian case is reflective of the demise of orthodox scholarship and the promise of more radical approaches. This intellectual ferment in Africa is inseparable from i) challenges to established social scientific paradigms everywhere, ii) the ineluctable continental economic crisis, and iii) alternative political parties and policy positions.

Such a debate is important, then, for reasons of both *praxis* and analysis. At the level of policy it serves to present and delineate alternative development strategies, broadly concerned with self-reliance and socialism (see section below). And at the level of theory it constitutes an alternative framework for organising and explaining data on relationships (see next two sections). But such an intellectual "crisis", reflective in the African and Nigerian cases of broader social crises (see Shaw & Aluko, 1983 and Adedeji & Shaw, 1985) is necessarily a period of uncertainty and controversy: the excitement is almost palpable.

The confrontation between radical and orthodox perspectives has not yet advanced in the Nigerian case to the stages of those in Tanzania or Kenya, where the prevailing "paradigm" is political economy and the debates are between non-Marxist and Marxist, and <u>dependencia</u> and materialist approaches, respectively (Bernstein & Campbell, 1985). Rather, in our case, the major issue is whether political economy at all is an appropriate mode — i.e. radical or not — not (yet?) the debate within it — i.e. more or less radical, although there is the beginning of an argument about the indigenous bourgeoisie — is it national and/or comprador? — to which we hope to contribute (Beckman, 1982 and 1985).

Formations: the challenge of radical analysis for Nigeria

These relevant radical approaches are, then, of two major varieties: political economy and materialist, with the latter constituting a Marxist variety of the former. The primary mark of the political economy mode is serious and sustained attention to the economic as well as to the political; but within this mode "economy" is defined in terms of exchange (especially international) and institutions (especially financial) rather than production and contradictions. In the more Marxist, materialist mode, the emphasis is more exclusively sub- rather than super-structural and the primary focus is on modes and relations of production.

Although there is a tradition of non-materialist political economy in the Nigerian case — see especially the work of Sayre Schatz on <u>Nigerian Capitalism</u> (1977) — the more salient challenge to the prevailing paradigm comes from the more embryonic Marxist school. This is characterised by distinctive analytic level (substructural), mode (materialist) and implications (dialectic), even if, at least not always, by synthesis and socialism in the longer-term. As Joel Samoff (1982:49) argues for both country-specific and continent-wide studies:

> ...a theoretical framework that focuses on conflict, that assumes there are systematic connections among production, power, stratification, and ideas, that asserts that outcomes are neither largely structurally determined nor largely the result of behaviour, that regards history as dialectical and contradictory, and that presumes that both the dialectic and the contradictions can be understood, offers a powerful vehicle for studying Tanzanian (and African) politics.

If, in the Tanzanian case, a neo-Marxist perspective helps to explain "how a genuinely nationalist, dedicated and honest leadership can pursue policies that perpetuate poverty" (Samoff, 1982:49) then in the Nigerian case it can surely advance understanding of changeable patterns of exploitation and expropriation, of types of regime and ideology. Given the extant complexities of the Nigerian political economy it is all too easy not to look beyond established debates about military versus civilian rule, federal versus state administrations and continual fractional partisan shifts. Yet such a radical perspective is all the more necessary for a clearly capitalist state at the (semi-)periphery.

In the Nigerian case this alternative approach has been most closely associated with the work of Claude Ake (1986), Eddie Madunagu (1982), Okwudia Nnoli (1978 and 1981), Segun Osoba (1978) and Bala Usman (1979) and now Toyin Falola & Julius Ihonvbere (1985). Together they have confronted the approaches, assumptions and solutions characteristic of the established "modernisation" school, whether it be expatriate (e.g. Richard Sklar (1963) and Antony Kirk-Greene (1981)) or indigenous (e.g. Billy Dudley (1982) and Oye Oyediran (1979)) in origin. These radical Nigerian scholars have been encouraged by a group of foreign authors who share their preoccupation with substructure (e.g. Bjorn Beckman (1982 and 1985), Terisa Turner (1976 a and b) and Gavin Williams (1976 and 1980)). While the debates within each of these schools are also intense and important (e.g. is military government more or less effective than civilian, on the one hand, and is the indigenous bourgeoisie essentially "comprador" or "national"?) the major cleavage lies between radical and orthodox schools, with the latter responding with either revisionism (cf. Kirk-Greene and Rimmer (1981) but not Bienen and Diejomoah (1981)) or rhetoric (e.g. Bienen (1981:3): "Many of us have the conviction that the current emphasis in academic writing on development stemming from a concern with distribution obscures the fact that raising the standards of living in poor countries (especially for the poorest people) is more important than redistribution".)

Interestingly, the most effective recent rebuttals of the optimism (or mystification?) of the Bienen and Diejomoah (1981) collection come from two non-radical non-academic institutions: the Economist Intelligence Unit (EIU) (1982) and the International Labour Office (ILO) (1981). The former, in a monograph prepared by Christopher Stevens, provides a convincing sense of the ebullience of Nigerian capitalism, one which transcends period of regime or economy: "It is difficult to overstate the attachment of Nigerians to private enterprise" (EIU, 1982:30). The latter, in a data-laden report from the Basic Human Needs (BHN)-oriented Jobs and Skills Programme for Africa (JASPA), provides a critique of Nigerian development plans and performances asserting that successive regimes have rarely put First things First:

> There is little evidence that Nigeria's big expenditure

Table Two

Oil Production and Revenues in Nigeria

Year	Barrels (Million per Day)	Revenues (Million Naira)
1960	0.017	2.4
1961	0.046	17.0
1965	0.275	29.0
1966	0.420	45.0
1968	1.1	29.6
1970	2.1	176.4
1973	2.3	1,368.0 (billion US $)
1976	2.0	8.9
1979	2.3	—
1980	2.1	23.4
1981	1.5	16.7
1982	1.3	13.0
1983	1.2	10.1
1984	1.4	11.4
1985	1.4	11.9
1986*	2.0	7.2

* estimated

Sources: Nigeria Trade Journal (Lagos) and Petroleum Economist, March 1986, 83-84.

has made much more impact on the conditions of the majority of the population. The distortions experienced by the other oil exporters seem to have been repeated in Nigeria. The (past) Plans...attached far too much importance to economic growth per se.
To meet the country's basic needs and achieve greater self-reliance would have required a very different, indeed the opposite set of priorities (ILO, 1981:5 and 10).

Somewhat surprisingly, then, the EIU and ILO both recognise the exponential nature of inequalities in the Nigerian semi-periphery, so providing support for the radical perspective, while intellectuals like Bienen and Diejomoah eschew such data. Despite all the quantitative and circumstantial evidence to the contrary, Bienen (1981:13) can still assert at the end of the boom decade of the 1970s (a boom for the local bourgeoisie, at least) that: "In general, Nigeria does not appear to have an unequivocally and rapidly worsening income distribution situation."

Contradictions: towards the recognition of inequalities

Most observers recognise, however, that the post-independence roller-coaster has served to exacerbate established inequalities within the Nigerian political economy, especially during and after the oil boom and the Second Republic. In particular, given its experience of industrialisation and urbanisation (let alone indigenisation), class has come to join region, religion and ethnicity as a salient factor. Class formation and contradiction are not new phenomena in Nigeria but recognition of them, in both political and academic circles, has been lagard. The "rentier state" (see next part) has come, however, to stand for a distinctive form of (semi-)peripheral capitalism, one characterised by marginal progress towards self-sustaining industrial take-off yet by intense fractional disputes over the spoils of uneven growth. The concentration on distribution rather than production in both political and intellectual circles is symptomatic of benign approaches. Yet bourgeois class coalitions have been able thus far to contain or restrain proletarian pressures in politics (see section b). The intellectual bourgeoisie is increasingly less able to contain radical views, however (see section d).

The evidence of growing inequalities of several kinds in Nigeria is now incontrovertible. First things First provides powerful evidence:

> Since the overall rate of economic growth has apparently been fast in the past two decades, there should be by now signs of substantial improvements in the living conditions

Table Three

Nigeria's Oil Economy

Oil as a % of:	1970	1973	1974	1975	1976	1977	1978	1979	1980	1983	1984	1985
GDP	10	23	22	18	18	17	21	24	26	14	17	18
Government current revenue	46	67	81	79	78	74	68	82	84	69	73	73
Merchandise exports	58	85	93	93	96	96	89	94	96	96	97	97

Source: Central Bank of Nigeria

of the majority of the Nigerian people. These are not
evident. Indeed...large numbers are worse off in numerous
respects, especially in the rural areas but also in the
big new slums of the cities.
...There is growing official awareness of the importance
of basic needs and the weaknesses of the past approach to
development (ILO, 1981:v).

However, such alleged "official awareness" of a declining quality of life for the majority of Nigerians has yet to affect some academic perceptions. Despite all the quantitative, non-dialectical data in his own collection, Bienen (1981:162) still asserts that ethnicity not class is the salient factor, denying any connection between the two types of aggregation:

Insofar as Nigeria has seen its politics governed by distributional issues, these have been communally defined for the most part and have centred on allocations from the centre to regions and states in the Nigerian federation. There has been no clear development of a class-based politics in Nigeria. Neither peasant organisations nor trade unions in the industrial sector have been strong organisations pushing for redistribution of income. Nor have people in the urban informal sector constituted a force for effective radical change.

Yet peasant actions in the North have caused death and destruction and trade union activities in the major industrial cities, especially in the South, have regularly disrupted the production of goods and supply of services (see next section). And, unlike Bienen, Jon Kraus (1982:136) expects (and has already had this perspective verified) such incidence of inequalities and reactions to continue in the foreseeable future: "The urban and rural poor will suffer most, and the better organised - the urban workers and college students - will protest the most energetically." But the distribution of wealth remains less controversial and more apparent than its generation.

Conditions: the "petro-naira" nexus

The debate over income patterns represents only a small step towards a more political economy perspective: it treats the results (maldistribution or dissatisfaction of BHN) and not the causes (a distinctive capitalist mode of production at the (semi-)periphery based on petroleum): <u>the rentier state</u>. The causes, as Ake, Madunagu, Nnoli <u>et al</u> indicate, lie in the history of both Nigeria and global exchange: the incorporation of the "Nigerian" political economy into the

Table Four

Industrial Production (1972 =100)

	Manufacturing	Mining	Utilities	Total all Industry
1970	89	80	68	83
1971	93	86	88	88
1972	100	100	100	100
1973	124	113	118	116
1974	120	123	130	122
1975	148	98	154	115
1976	182	113	185	137
1977	194	115	213	144
1978	221	104	261	145
1979	238	126	345	167
1980	264	113	399	168
1981	395	79	325	186
1982	447	70	345	207
1983	319	67	353	155
1984	281	76	317	147
1985	335	82	334	167

[1]estimated
Source: Central Bank of Nigeria

world system first for slaving, then for palm oil, thence for cocoa and now for hydrocarbons. At each stage, distinctive social formations at the periphery (now the semi-periphery?), have been thrown-up to advance the integration and to resolve or contain any contradictions. And at each stage in the interface between global and national systems various contradictions and coalitions have emerged, mediated by pre-colonial, colonial or post-colonial state structures.

In the post-independence period, the successive civilian and military regimes have confronted assorted fractional challenges (e.g. "Biafra") and consisted of various class coalitions (e.g. "progressive" military regime of Mohamed/Obasango, "rentier state" of Shagari and "corporatism" of Buhari/Babangida (Shaw & Ihonvbere, 1987)).

The first half of both the Madunagu (1982:9-41) and Nnoli (1981:1-191) volumes are devoted to radical revisionism: the reconceptualisation of Nigerian history within which external interests, class struggles, developmental "ideology" and populism and repression play parts - the distinctive "mixed economy" syndrome. The multilateralisation of international capitalism - especially in the Nigerian case the displacement of British hegemony by American, European and Japanese capitalisms - and the monopoly of petroleum are the dominant features of the post-independence, especially post-civil war, political economy (<u>Economist</u>, 1984).

The rapid recovery from the ravages of war in the early-1970s was made possible not only by official amnesty and private activity; it was also accelerated through the OPEC windfall. The first half of that second post-independence decade experienced rapid, almost runaway, growth which led, of course, to the pressures which overthrew Gowon. "High life" produced new wealth and new contradictions: the rise of a <u>nouveau riche</u> bourgeois fraction within the bureaucracy. As Kraus (1982:108) notes

>...a relatively small percentage of Nigerians and foreign capital have benefitted from the patterns of government spending, while the standard of living of many Nigerians has declined. A whole new class (sic) of state-created capitalists and middlemen have been produced by government contracts, import licenses, commerce and massive corruption. Of course, many honest Nigerians labour for the common good. But the crass materialism in Nigerian life is infectious; the desire to cash in on the possibilities for wealth is pervasive and blatant.

The combination of windfall "rents", economic nationalism and technocratic preferences led, during the Mohammed/Obasanjo period of populist praetorian rule, to a massive scheme of indigenisation; essentially a risk-free licence to distribute corporate profits to the new class of professionals, politicians, bureaucrats and entrepreneurs (see also final section). A far-cry from nationalisation and a precursor of "privatisation", the indigenisation decrees "localised" formal ownership without disturbing either capitalist values or external technologies. Indeed, expatriate interests were consolidated rather than curtailed — guaranteed, as it were, by the state — and Nigerian capitalism was further entrenched. To cite Kraus (1982:108) again:

> ...the state itself has fathered a new capitalist class. In the indigenisation process...the state ordered banks to extend credit to Nigerians to purchase...shares. By mid-1979, the fortunate few — the importers, contractors, lawyers, businessmen and academics — who obtained bank loans had acquired over 500 million shares in 1,858 companies valued (actually undervalued) at $736 million. Dividends were high; the risk was negligible. The state served as the creator of large-scale domestic capital and as the intermediary between domestic and foreign private capital...

From a critical, political economy perspective, such indigenisation becomes merely restabilisation or redistribution among external and internal bourgeois fractions. As Bade Onimode argues in the Nnoli (1981:91) collection:

> ...equity participation by individuals does not really ensure effective control of foreign enterprises. It was probably not meant to do that. Consequently, indigenisation has been a petty bourgeois compromise between patriotism and puppetism, which has at best strengthened the economic base of the petty bourgeoisie without seriously challenging the neo-colonial under-development of the country.

So planning becomes an exercise in preparing ideological frameworks and guidelines for the coordination and rationalisation of external and internal interests, and fractions within them, given prevalent and projected changes in national and international cycles. In a subsequent chapter, Onimode captures well the essence of state involvement in a non-socialist milieu:

> The associated increase in the prosperity of the privileged classes with the surging development of the imperialist countries logically suggests that planning in Nigeria has been inseparable as a class category from colonial and neo-colonial policies of underdevelopment. Therefore, the conversion of planning from an

instrument of class domination and exploitation into a powerful organisational principle for liquidating underdevelopment and generating genuine development with the liberation of the masses requires continuing class struggles (Nnoli, 1981:149).

Coalitions: claims to position at the semi-periphery

Given the peculiar characteristics of class relations at the semi-periphery - in particular the contradictory roles of different factions within the local bourgeoisie - it is not too surprising that this bourgeoisie's response to inadequate development and ensuing demands for economic nationalism has been "indigenisation" rather than "nationalisation" and "privatisation" rather than "socialisation": buying into corporate branches and activities, with individual profit as the incentive, rather than taking over the economy for collective (class and/or national) gain. The Nigerian state, based as it is on continuing fractional disputes, plays a central part in this balancing of both inter-fractional and inter-class antagonisms. In the process, national fractions have been strengthened while populist demands have been restrained. Yet, as noted already, many fractions in the national bourgeoisie have been more interested in immediate consumption than future accummulation and reproduction.

As Tom Forrest (1982:337) suggests, indigenisation had political as well as economic intent - to head-off further pressures for economic nationalism - yet it may have created the base, at least, for a more independent national bourgeoisie, in association with state and foreign (but not comprador) fractions: "It has also reduced the threat to large companies of state takeover on occasions of mass nationalism. In effect, it is capitalism that has been indigenised, not through the takeover or withdrawal of foreign capital, but through higher forms of collaboration, accomodation and institutionalisation."

So the contemporary rentier state, given the distinctions of Nigeria's history of incorporation, is characterised by two striking features. First, the coexistence of certain internal and external fractions; and second, the essential "parasitism" or "consumerism" of the embryonic "national" bourgeoisie. Onimode has captured the essential contradiction within the bourgeoisie yet goes on to explain how this can be overcome so that seemingly antagonistic interests are rendered compatible within what Peter Evans (1979), in the Brazilian case has called a "triple alliance". In portraying the particular background, Onimode (Nnoli, 1981:178) asserts that classes as well as countries can exist in an intermediary position:

> The Nigerian petty bourgeoisie has historically been

ambivalent towards the imperialist bourgeoisie because of the former's divided loyalty towards the national state. On account of its material class interests and 'dual mandate' (from the national population and the imperialist bourgeoisie), the petty bourgeoisie has to fight the imperialists in order to expand its economic base in the domestic economy. But because this economy is neo-colonial under imperialist domination, the petty bourgeois class is at the same time subordinate to, and dependent on, the imperialists with whom it has to colloborate in order to maintain its power...

The continual struggle between military and civilian fractions, and within the civilian fraction – national, comprador and bureaucratic fractions primarily – constitute the stuff of Nigerian "politics", on which the orthodox school focuses almost exclusively. But such "petty-bourgeois politics" need to be situated within a distinctive and less changeable political economy. Onimode (Nnoli, 1981:188) identifies salient characteristics of past and present military regimes, their social coalitions and development directions:

...the consistent and dominant role of military regimes as ruling groups within the petty bourgeoisie has been implicit alliance with, and overt defence of, the interests of the domestic and foreign capitalists. To sustain such a role they have had to institute populist reforms which preserve the critical nature of neo-colonial capitalism and underdevelopment.

Yet indigenisation did not bring dramatic results (other than personal wealth), because of the origins and orientations of the indigenous bourgeoisie: consumption rather than accummulation. This helps to account for the dramatic laissez-faire quality of the national political economy: the priority of individual indulgence over collective goods. As Madunagu (1982:40) indicates, most members of the Nigerian bourgeoisie are distinctive and individualistic – preoccupied with personal indulgence: "Because each Nigerian bourgeois is concerned with the promotion of his or her immediate exclusive interest, he or she exploits every situation for personal benefit – even when such exploitation works against the interest of the bourgeois class as a whole, and undermines bourgeois collective comfort":

The Nigerian bourgeoisie are thus extremely irrational and underdeveloped. Their counterparts in Europe, North America and Japan have long realised that to ensure an exclusively comfortable life for themselves, they have to make some concessions to the masses. Thus a developed bourgeoisie would build good roads to their exclusive hotels, ensure good and efficient water and electricity supplies in the major industrial, commercial and administrative centres — facilities which the masses, by default, will also enjoy. But what do we see in Nigeria? Colour television sets but an unreliable and inefficient electricity supply, luxurious cars but bad roads, ultra-modern airports but extremely backward and inefficient postal and telecommunications systems, ultra-modern residential areas which are surrounded by, and approached only through, filthy slums.

And Ake (1981:1163) made rather similar and telling points in his 1981 address as president of the Nigerian Political Science Association, a lament for the deficiencies and peculiarities of the local bourgeoisie:

> Our problems are rooted in our history and in the concrete economic and social structures which it has evolved. By the very nature of the problems they cannot be solved without, at the very least, breaking our exploitative dependence on the West, and doing away with the existing relations of production...the contradictions of the present system are creating the conditions that will change it.

But such a break or delinking becomes ever more problematic as dependence is not simply an "external" or exclusive phenomenon; rather, it pervades the whole political economy. The essential class structure of the (semi-)periphery involves, as Onimode suggests above, an organic link — a division of labour — between international and indigenous fractions. In an illuminating comparison between Nigeria and Brazil — the semi-periphery <u>par excellence</u> — Evans (1979:299) indicates that the Nigerian bourgeoisie has done rather well within the context of such a "triple alliance" comprising state, local and international capitals:

> ...in Nigeria as in Brazil, the local bourgeoisie has not been left out. Given the objective weakness of local private capital in Nigeria and the low likelihood of its making a significant contribution to industrialisation, it would be reasonable to expect a dualistic battle between the state and the multinationals rather than a triple alliance. But, far from being excluded, the local private sector has done extremely well for itself. Relative to its resources, it has probably done better than local capital in Brazil.

We turn in the next two parts to the particular character of the Nigerian state and its capital. Here, however, we pause to note, along with Evans (1979:313) "that the Nigerian case appears suitable to formulations of the triple alliance at all is impressive. In fact, the prospects for Nigeria moving successfully in the direction of the triple alliance seem good."

Nigeria remains closer to the "classic" form of dependence than is Brazil, yet its political economy did seem to be moving as the 1970s became the 1980s, for reasons contained within the logic of the global capitalist system as well as within its own national system, towards the "dependent development" more characteristic of a Newly Industrialising Country (NIC):

> To call Nigeria the "Brazil of Africa" underlines the difference between the two continents as much as it does the similarities between the two countries. In an African context the structure of the Nigerian economy may appear relatively advanced; in a Latin American context it would appear anachronistic. From the role of the state to the position of the multinationals, the structure of the Nigerian elite is in many ways more suggestive of the period of classic dependence than of the current period of dependent development in Brazil and Mexico (Evans, 1979:309).

The emergence (yet not the dominance) of a national bourgeoisie in Nigeria, as in Brazil (or the Ivory Coast or Kenya (Lubbeck, 1986)) is an ineluctable process, however, one advanced somewhat by indigenisation decrees and state intervention through institutions such as the Nigerian National Petroleum Corporation (NNPC). If in Brazil Petrobras and the National Development Bank and in Kenya state marketing boards and development banks have been central then in Nigeria, particularly in the post-civil war and post-OPEC era, it has been the NNPC which has "captured" the "commanding heights" of the rentier state. However, the establishment and expansion of the parastatal system at federal and state levels does not by itself create the conditions for either accumulation or development. Indeed, the simultaneous divergence in living standards, further intensifying the prospects for both corruption and patronage, suggests that such growth may serve to intensify rather than ameliorate, inequalities.

Aside from inter- and intra-class contradictions and coalitions there is one further factor which needs to be treated in any political economy as well as political sociology of Nigeria: "ethnicity". Social relations based on ethnic identity, whether inherited or assumed, remain salient in all political systems - less and more "developed" alike - yet it is only within the modernisation genre, as indicated by

Bienen's citations above, that these are taken to overshadow all other social cleavages. And it is in the "classic" Nigerian case that they are assumed to be primary. Yet ethnic factors are not static; neither are they separable from class relations (see following sections). The two are closely interrelated, with ethnicity providing the basis for some <u>intra-class</u> fractions and class constituting one element in <u>intra-ethnic</u> disputes; they exist, then, in a dialectical relationship with each other.

The compatibility of ethnicity with the modernisation perspective lies in a common superstructural level of analysis. These are unconcerned with production, only with distribution; hence the intense wrangles over revenue distribution and service between states, cities and villages. Ethnicity was reinforced during the colonial period as a convenient mechanism by which to divide and dominate Africans. Only in the brief nationalist period were its effects contained, and then only in certain countries. In many, as in Nigeria, ethnicity determined patterns of party politics: the ideology became reality. And to maintain support and power on the one hand and to exclude and exploit "others" on the other hand ethnicity as "sectionalism" remains a handy political device for members of the political, military and bureaucratic bourgeoisies. As Nnoli (1978:30) argues in his subtle analysis of <u>Ethnic Politics in Nigeria</u>:

> ...ethnicity in Africa has a class character. Its understanding cannot be achieved in isolation from the general class struggles in society...As a result of their success in ethnic politics, the present leaders now occupy political and economic positions of power and privilege in the inherited colonial structures which gave rise to and continues to reinforce those politics. Therefore, they have an objective interest in maintaining the ethnic pattern of activities and the imperialist structures, both of which are inimical to interethnic harmony.

Ethnic identities and ideologies complicate and divert class formations and relations: "patron-client" connections cut across and ameliorate class contradictions. In Nigeria, colonial ("indirect") rule, regional polities and economies, and divided nationalists reinforced ethnicity at the levels of ideology and organisation. As Nnoli (1978:148) laments: "the search for petty bourgeois and comprador bourgeois fortunes dominated the nationalist struggle for independence. Its inevitable consequences were the regionalisation of politics and the politicisation of ethnicity."

The petro-naira boom and subsequent agitation for states were merely contemporary post-colonial, post-civil war instances of rampant ethnocentrism: the fight among different bourgeois interests for resources, not for production but for consumption. This has had the effect of restraining and diverting potential class formations and antagonisms which in turn has served to reinforce bourgeois hegemony and minimise proletarian pressures. As Nnoli (1978:177) suggests in explaining why bourgeois interests are more concerned with distribution than production:

> In Nigeria, one of the instruments for this manipulation has been ethnicity. By presenting politics as an inter-ethnic struggle for socioeconomic resources, these classes camouflage intra-class struggles for the division of the national wealth that is inimical to the interest of the underprivileged classes, the working class, and the poor farmers who constitute the vast majority of the population.

No party was more successful in both playing and simultaneously disguising ethnic politics than the "natural" ruling party – the (appropriately-styled) National Party of Nigeria – which under the aegis of "modernised" Northern aristocrat, Alhaji Shehu Shagari, followed in the footsteps of its military predecessor (and its successor) in being resistant to popular pressures. The petrol boom encouraged its inclination to Tory-style noblesse oblige during its first months in office. It essentially lost the second election with such an image and record because of dramatically different economic circumstances.

b) New Classes: contradictions and coalitions in the rentier state

The nature of the post-colonial rentier state is of primary importance in situating and comprehending the direction of class alignments, re-alignments and struggles. In addition, the crisis of hegemony, which faces the rentier state as a result of the weak base on which capital accumulation takes place in a semi-peripheral capitalist social formation like Nigeria, provides insights into the dynamics that determine or condition class struggles and the use of state power elsewhere.

The post-colonial state: overdeveloped or pre-hegemonic?

The debate on the nature of the post-colonial state has been heavily influenced by a rather mechanistic perception of social classes and state power in advanced capitalist societies. Though attempts have begun to be made to pay attention to the "historical specificities" of each state and social formation, there are still shortcomings in the general literature. The use of given social categories sometimes fails to capture the peculiarities of the underdeveloped formations in the Third World. In addition, the post-colonial state is treated as a given and attempts are made to understand its nature through an analysis of the attitudes of state functionaries. The conclusions often derived from this "straw-man" approach are that the post-colonial state is relatively autonomous and rather interventionist. Moreover, it is argued, state control over both national resources and inherited bureaucratic apparatuses make it "central" and "overdeveloped".

But "interventionism", extended bureaucracy and "relative autonomy" are not peculiar to the post-colonial state. In fact, the idea of an "overdeveloped" state tends to neglect the socio-economic dynamics which prompt such interventionism. Because colonialism is employed as a starting point, the processes of class formation and capitalist accumulation in the pre-colonial era are often neglected; and the interplay of class forces in the period of decolonisation is given insufficient attention with emphasis placed on the post-colonial era. Even then, much is made of the "power" of the state with limited attention paid either to its weaknesses or to the power of other social classes.

To be sure, the post-colonial state inherited the institutions implanted by the colonial state. However, it did not inherit its location in the international division of labour; neither did it inherit its expertise, military power, finances or metropolitan support. The tenuous relation of the dominant classes that captured state power at independence to productive activities translated into situations of characteristic "dependence" on foreign capital and food imports, plus reliance on foreign aid and foreign military protection. Thus, the world view which the custodians of state power advanced in society, the violent response of the state to opposition, and the inability of the "new" indigenous bourgeois class to constitute itself into an effective hegemonic class, all reflect the contradictions which characterise the post-colonial state.

These general problems are highlighted in a somewhat different form in the "rentier" state - a state which dominates an economy which receives substantial amounts of external "rents" on a regular yet fluctuating basis from foreign governments, institutions and agencies - particularly when it is located at the semi-periphery; ie. a concept relevant to Nigeria from the early 1970s to the early 1980s. In the case of oil, production has very little to do with the domestic economy. Four major features of the rentier state have particularly far-reaching implications for the Nigerian example. These constitute direct challenges to the presumed characteristics of the classic post-colonial state.

First, the state as the collector of huge oil rents automatically becomes the focus of capital accumulation as fractions and factions of the dominant class compete for control. This competition, as in the Nigerian case, is evidenced in i) the alignment and re-alignment of political forces, often rationalised through religious, ethnic and other chauvinistic means; ii) unbridled corruption aimed at climbing the social ladder; iii) military intervention on behalf of fractions of the dominant class; iv) constitutional and legal battles to superimpose the interests of one fraction over those of others; v) temporary alignments or coalitions with other social forces (e.g. the working class); and vi) intra-class conflicts over revenue allocation. At whatever level this competition takes place, it heightens the class contradictions and struggles in the society as a whole.

Second, the rentier state has the ability to undertake gigantic state expenditures without depending on foreign aid or internal taxation. To organise this allocation of national resources, the bureaucracy experiences a dramatic expansion. Yet spectacular growth in certain sectors of the economy does not fundamentally alter the living conditions of the majority of the people. Some dependent form of industrialisation might take place, while extensive labour control strategies are adopted. The coercive institutions are often modernised and strengthened. However, the nature and direction of these developments are conditioned by the social origins and nature of the dominant social classes operating either at the political or economic levels.

In the Nigerian situation – a particular and peculiar rentier state – the dominant classes have traditionally believed in working closely with foreign capital thus occupying either a dependent or intermediary position in the economy. Although the Nigerian state collected over US$50 billion in 25 years of oil production and marketing, the origins and orientations of the bourgeoisie have determined the rising import bill (of over N1 billion per month in the early 1980s), the initiation of a dependent food policy, the neglect of agriculture, the efforts to emerge as a dominant power in the sub-region and the initiation of fluctuating policies towards foreign capital. Federal control of oil revenues and the central direction of state expenditure transformed the techno-economic autonomy of the oil industry into the socio-economic autonomy of the state.

Such state autonomy is, however, very tenuous and unstable as indicated by Nigeria's condition in the mid-1980s. The instability arises from i) the challenges posed to the state by other social classes; ii) the peripheral location of the social formation within world capitalism; iii) the massive expansion of the commercial and distributive sectors at the expense of productive activities; iv) the fluctuation of revenues on which the state becomes almost totally dependent; and v) the intra-class conflicts which naturally accompany fluctuating revenues.

Third, new patterns of i) capital accumulation, ii) incorporation into world capitalism and iii) circulation of struggles arising from the oil boom characterise the rentier state. The expansion of the commercial and distributive sectors, as against production, means that consumption becomes geared towards imported foods, the economy is invaded by all forms of foreign corporations, and the national bourgeois class is stunted. These developments not only deepen but also consolidate the incorporation of the rentier economy into world capitalism.

And finally, fourth, the post-colonial state, despite its huge rents, is subject to the power of two major countervailing forces in addition to global-energy demand and price. First, the transnational oil corporations which dominate the production and marketing processes involved in oil, can manipulate the direction of state policies. This is possible because they realise its extensive dependence on the oil sector - the Nigerian state has depended on oil exports for over 95% of its revenue. The relations of the rentier state with foreign capital often necessitate conditions of alliance or coalition against labour. So, second, the other countervailing force confronting the oil state is the oil workers. Though few in number, the abilities of the companies to make profits and of the state to collect revenues are dependent on the sustained activity of these workers. Thus, as everything in the economy becomes linked to the oil industry any cessation of work would have spiralling negative effects on the whole political economy, as indicated by the catastrophic recession of the mid-1980s.

It is within these conditions and dynamics that an oil state like Nigeria has attempted to mediate class struggles and contradictions and to create viable class coalitions. In this section we shall focus on three salient aspects of the rentier state briefly: i) rural decay and the neglect of agriculture; ii) workers and labour control and iii) the elusiveness of state hegemony. These elements became crucial in the atmosphere of austerity, recession and instability of the mid-1980s.

Peasants and rural decay: the green non-revolution

At independence Nigeria, like most colonies, was an exporter of primary products. Food was imported to supplement local production, though emphasis was still on cash crop production - a precipitate of colonial agriculture. This system was predominantly under the control of peasants with occasional pockets of mixed capitalists and state-owned or -controlled farms. In 1960 the essential institutions and exploitative mechanisms of the colonial period were "Nigerianised" and preserved intact. The inequalities in resource allocation and power relations between the rural and urban sector were preserved; the educational system which traditionally looked down on agriculture and on farmers was not restructured. The rural people were neither involved in plan initiation nor implementation because they were seen as "ignorant and illiterate"; despite the fact that the sector in which they operated was then the mainstay of the economy in terms both of foreign exchange earnings and of food supplies to urban markets.

Prior to the 1973 Middle East crisis and oil price increases, petroleum contributed an insignificant proportion of total national revenue: in 1958/59 0.7% of the GDP. But by the <u>Third National Plan</u> of 1974/75, oil was contributing about 92%. Conversely, agriculture which had contributed 63% of GDP in 1960, declined to 23% in 1975 and has continued to decline steadily at least until the conjuncture of the mid-1980s. The export of agricultural commodities accounted for 80% of the total value of exports in 1960 but decreased to 6% in 1974 and remained below 5% for the decade until 1985.

Reflective of current widespread awareness, Nigeria's then-President refered to the oil industry as "the main source of government revenue and foreign exchange earnings". Elsewhere he noted that "the fortunes of the economy are closely linked with developments in the oil industry," (<u>News from Nigeria</u>, January 1981:8) not agriculture. And in presenting his 1982 budget to the National Assembly, he remarked that, "As you all know Nigeria's economy for many years has been heavily dependent on a single commodity, namely oil." The Managing Director of NNPC, Lawrence Amu, recently admitted that Nigeria had "totally become dependent on crude oil sales, this is a worrying development and the frightening aspect of this development is that it is likely to be a permanent feature and there is little hope for recovery in sight" (<u>News Review</u>, 1982:2).

The clear implications of these observations by prominent members of the Nigerian ruling class is that agriculture (and therefore the rural areas), which provides employment for about 70% of the population, has been neglected because it has become relatively unimportant for the rentier state. There are two major reasons for this neglect.

First, the country never had a dominant class that accumulated capital through investments in agriculture as in, say, the Ivory Coast. And second, the powerful yet unequal alliance between the dominant class and foreign capital as well as the inherited comprador nature of much of the indigenous class at independence meant the initiation of a dependent food policy as an alternative to investment in agriculture. The neglect of the rural areas following the oil boom is admitted by a former Minister for Agriculture:

> With each passing year, farming became progressively unattractive and unproductive and remains characterised by inadequate capital, lack of suitable techology, inadequate supply of farm inputs, including credit and scarcity of farm labour which has worsened in recent years by the migration of young men and women from rural areas to the cities. <u>With the advent of mineral oil, agriculture suffered an even greater neglect and was relegated to the background</u> (New Times, October 1980:35).

The post-colonial state like its colonial predecessor perceived the rural people to be incapable of feeding the productive urban population. Three major programmes were initiated as a response to the demise of agriculture.

First, a massive propaganda campaign was launched about food production as evidenced in "Operation Feed the Nation" (OFN) and the subsequent "Green Revolution". Speeches were made, vacationing university students were employed in farms, "demonstration" farms were declared "open" on television, and all sorts of leaflets were distributed. But OFN failed woefully and despite the green revolution, the oil-state has continued to import increasing amounts of food.

Second, the federal and state governments went into "direct production", either individually or in alliance with foreign capital, at least until the privatisation policies of the mid-1980s. As President Shagari put it while eulogising the achievements of the Third National Plan (1975-80): "In the agricultural sector, federal and state governments made their presence felt in the areas of direct production. No less than 147 farm centres were established by the various governments". (News from Nigeria, January 1981:5)

The net result of this policy was i) a massive displacement of rural farmers, leading to confrontation between the state and peasants; ii) the opening of avenues for "spreading the national cake" to local power elites; iii) the creation of a rural-capitalist class as well as a sub-class of "urban agricultural capitalists" - the absentee farmers; and iv) the further heightening of rural-urban migration. This policy was, in turn, accompanied by declining agricultural budgets on the federal and state levels (see table six) and by the massive involvement of the World Bank in designing and implementing Nigeria's green revolution to balance Western corporate involvement in the oil industry:

> Contrary to the World Bank's hypocritical rhetoric about concentrating resources on small farmers and aiding the

rural poor, their projects are designed to subsidize rich farmers and have created a class of absentee "overnight" farmers to take advantage of their assistance. Small farmers are specifically discriminated against in the allocation of resources or are unable to meet the cash costs of participation ("Editorial" Review of African Political Economy 13, May-August 1978:4).

These projects in themselves have yielded very limited fruits and state farm centres have not fared any better. The food import bill continued to rise as rural people i) withheld products from urban markets; ii) smuggled produce across the borders; iii) abandoned farming for urban petty trade or wage-paying jobs in the construction industry; and iv) were displaced from their farm plots.

And finally, third, the state initiated a dependent food policy, not to supplement internal production but rather to replace it. This policy was a direct manifestation of not just the role of the comprador fraction in the dominant class but also of the influence and power of foreign capital in the political economy. Thus, food imports took up to 15% of the total budget in 1973 rising to 20-25% in the 1980s (see table eight). Much of these imports consisted of basic food stuffs hitherto produced internally, thus mortgaging the socio-economic and political capital and stability of the country. In 1982 alone, the rice import level reached N400m, fish was N200m, sugar N200m and wheat was N160m. The state of course did not see this trend as alarming, at least until oil revenues declined precipitiously, the President noting blithely in 1980 that:

> Our monthly import bill which stood at a level of about six hundred million naira at the beginning of this administration (October 1979) now stands at an average of one billion naira per month... With our policy of liberalising restrictions on imports this figure is likely to rise in months ahead (Tijjani & Williams, 1981).

Thus, the response was to further liberalise restrictions on imports, recognising that certain fractions in the ruling coalition would thereby benefit.

Declining budgetary allocations to the rural areas, neglect of rural agriculture and industrialisation, failure to provide social amenities for the countryside as well as the attempts to vigorously extend capitalist relations of production and accumulation all contributed to the proceses of rural decay and the proletarianisation of peasants. The concentration of services, power and resources in urban centres as well as the massive construction boom which accompanied the oil windfall -

airports, expressways, army quarters, luxury hotels, ministries and so on — served to attract people from the decaying countryside both in Nigeria and in neighbouring states. An inability to cater for internal migration especially in terms of employment, meant that the ranks of the "lumpen-proletariat" swelled considerably leading to more crime, crises, pressures on services and conflicts in the urban centres. These problems and others, were, of course, blamed on "illegal" foreign migrants rather than domestic ones.

Finally, the admission contained in the <u>Third National Development Plan 1975-80</u> (1975:35), that the "rural areas in general would also require a new deal in the provision of social services" and that in "almost every state sizeable communities still exist without basic amenities, like clean water supply, hospital and health centres, schools and electricity" is still true. In fact the <u>Third Plan</u> (1975:35) admits that the existence of these conditions of unmet BHN inspite of the oil boom, "contributes to the low level of rural productivity, and strengthens the pull exerted on rural dwellers by higher urban incomes".

While this is so — BHN are not being met in either the cities or villages — such conditions are not "natural" or inevitable: they are the products of state policies with their urban bias. They are also the precipitate of the intensifying integration of Nigeria into the world capitalist system, a participant in the recycling of oil revenues and victim of OPEC cycles. The implication of these developments for the national political economy will be further discussed below.

Workers, the state and labour control

The rural decay that accompanied the oil boom in Nigeria intensified the radicalisation of rural producers, increased migration to the urban centres and reinforced pressures on urban workers from familial dependents. The latter, in turn, further increased the alienation and discontent of urban workers thus intensifying their militancy. Many of the peasants displaced by the activities of the World Bank, state farm projects and the construction boom, collected their compensation and migrated to the urban centres. Those who had no relatives joined the slum dwellers and created networks of survival in a harsh environment. The Director of the NNPC admitted recently that, "the oil industry has generated vast revenues but these have been so managed as to generate rapid inflation and the aspects of the industry that could actually transform the economy have been neglected" (<u>News Review</u>, 1982:3).

Moreover, the food import policy of the state has been unable to satisfy urban demands. The activities of commercial capitalists have led to higher living costs far beyond the reach of urban workers. The elitist and urban-biased planning methodology has continued to concentrate services in selected parts of cities. Meanwhile, the state has involved itself in numerous prestige projects from cultural jamborees such as FESTAC 77 to ECOWAS. The latter encouraged the inflow of foreigners especially Ghanaians in the "Spirit of ECOWAS" leading to more crime, pressure on services and competition for limited jobs (Ihonybere and Ojo, 1980).

Crises and contradictions multiplied as the semi-populist educational system which embraced Universal Primary Education (UPE) began to turn out more products into the saturated job market. "Contractmania" which characterised oil-rich Nigeria, a situation in which virtually all services were contracted out, led to uncontrollable inflation and corruption. A process of "de-industrialisation" gradually set in during the 1970s as the emphasis shifted from production to importation reflecting a shift from national back to comprador fractional dominance. For instance, in May 1978 the Lagos port alone was doing 97% of its business in imports and only 3% in exports. Smuggling became a national problem. And the cost of living index rose considerably in all urban centres; with a base 100 established in 1960, it rose from 151 in 1970 to 215 in 1974, 377 in January 1977 and 493 in January 1978. For a while, the wage increases allowed by the state to coopt the workers, widened the gap between the salaried rich and the unemployed poor; and inflation reached 45% in 1978.

The general pre-glut crisis generated by the mismanagement of oil wealth and the misplacement of national priorities was evidenced in the statement by the President in 1980 that the oil boom had

> ...brought about rapid increases in domestic prices and the level of imports. Consequently, public spending has consistently outstripped revenue since 1975, resulting in overall budget deficits and necessitating increased borrowing internally and externally... As at September 1979... the overall financial position of the Federal Government showed a deficit of ₦1.4 billion. The state governments were in the same predicament and were likewise unable to meet their contractual obligation...On the external front our debt rose sharply from about ₦54 million in 1975/76 to ₦364 million in 1978/79 (<u>Nigeria Trade Journal</u> March-April 1980:10).

It was within these conditions that the state employed its control over the means of coercion (particularly under the military before and after Shagari) to i) initiate numerous primitive labour laws and regulations, and ii) attempt to indigenise the peripheral capitalist economy without altering the relations of production, but reflective of the emergence of a national bourgeois fraction. The state put the means of coercion at the disposal of capital and shifted the blame for the economic crisis away from "external" dependence onto the "lazy and unproductive" farmers and workers. Where attempts to bribe workers through wage increases failed, ethnic chauvinism, religious fanaticism and other extra-legal measures were adopted to divert the direction of worker consciousness and militancy.

The Nigerian state promulgated several decrees specifically directed at controlling labour (Ihonvbere & Shaw, 1987). Examples include the Trade Dispute Decree No. 7 of 1976 which consolidated the Punitive Trade Disputes (Arbitration and Inquiry) Act of 1958 and the Trade Disputes (Emergency Provisions) Decree No. 21 of 1969. Further, the creation of an Industrial Arbitration Panel, a National Industrial Court, the prohibition of strikes, the imprisonment of union leaders, the proscription of unions (such as the National Union of Bank Employees and the Shell - BP and Allied Workers Union in 1977) and, finally, the banning of certain unionists from trade union activities are all aspects of a general policy of labour control.

Decree No. 23 of 1976, the Trade Disputes (Essential Services) Decree was the most far-reaching attempt to control workers. Because the fortunes of the economy had come to rely on "developments in the oil industry", the initiation of regulations to cover all aspects of society was an imperative. The Decree so defined "essential services" to include virtually every human activity in Nigeria. As Tayo Fashoyin (1981b:209) has observed, this Decree was passed because "the consequences of widespread industrial unrest in the country - particularly in major economic sectors such as petroleum, banking and manufacturing could be disastrous on the economy". Popular thinking now recognises that "everything that concerns oil concerns our vital national interest". So, in particular, the state was not prepared to accommodate any form of protest in the oil sector. While, as a reflection of the triple alliance in this strategic sector, the oil companies initiated and implemented worker domestication policies within the industry - e.g. through the payment of high wages, provision of extensive benefits and sending workers abroad on all kinds of courses - the state responded swiftly to the 1977 strike of Shell - BP workers by prescribing their union. The government declared that this strike had been,

> Calculated not only to obstruct and disrupt the smooth running of the operations of Shell-BP Petroleum Development Company of Nigeria but also to disrupt the economy

of the nation (<u>Nigerian Observer</u> 31 October 1977:13).

The state's interest in protecting the oil companies and its own revenues is evident in this statement and other actions. Under the guise of stamping out "racketeering, abuse of office, personality cults, politicisation, corruption, conflict of interests and similar malpractices" from the trade union movement, since independence and more so since the oil boom, the state has intervened in the activities of trade unions. This culminated in the abolition of all hitherto existing labour centres, the restructuring of all industrial unions into 43, the banning of certain union leaders and the creation of the Nigeria Labour Congress (NLC) through Decree No. 21 of 1978. The state allocated one million naira to this Congress and attempted to impose pro-establishment leaders on it. But the workers rejected compliant leaders whilst the state rejected activist leaders.

In February 1980, the NLC published the <u>Workers Charter of Demands</u>, a fundamentally populist document which nonetheless reflected the objective problems confronting Nigerian workers. It provided them with an alternative way of perceiving the nature and complex dimension of class struggle in a (semi-) peripheral capitalist society. This <u>Charter</u> (1980:23) called for "structural change" that would lead to "bringing the economy under the ownership and control of the workers and the masses". And it was against the pressures and contradictions deepened by the oil boom and the labour control policies of the state, that the Congress called a general strike in May 1981. Given intensifying contradictions, the NLC president subsequently observed that "the drift of trade unionists, and other intellectuals into the Marxist camp is due, among other things, to frustration with the way democracy is being practiced and the sight of misery, squalor and want in the midst of plenty" (<u>West Africa</u> 23 June 1980:1108).

The inability of federal and state governments to meet their contractual obligations, to pay workers and to keep development projects afloat has heightened the contradictions among the state, labour and capital. Though since the 1980 general strike, reflected in the repressive June 1986 anti-NLC moves, the state has strived to deprive the Congress of funds, polarize it by sponsoring rural factions and making membership voluntary, there is no reason not to expect increasing militancy, organisation and rising class consciousness in the cities. Likewise, in the rural areas, the resistance of peasants, refusal to pay taxes, rejection of prominent politicians by voters, attacks on agents of the state and "invasion" of houses of assembly by market women and school children are all manifestations of discontent.

In fact, the first nine months of civilian rule after October 1979 witnessed 247 officially-registered trade disputes involving 144,886 workers and resulting in the loss of more than one million person days (Financial Times 29 September 1980:xxi). However, for the NLC to serve as the vanguard organisation of the working class, it must begin to develop a political programme aimed at capturing state power. Until this occurs, it cannot pursue a radical proletarian cause. It, like Nigerian intellectuals, needs a sense of central contradictions in the (semi-)peripheral political economy and how to mobilise and generalise these.

Finally, the confrontation between labour on the one hand and the state and capital on the other, can be seen to have increased since the early-1970s with the oil boom and subsequent glut. The "arrogance of power" which accompanied the relative financial independence of the state, has witnessed a deepening of the alliance between it and capital against labour (see first and final sections of this chapter on the triple alliance). However, the numerous labour control policies have not prevented industrial unrest. The fluctuation of state revenues, the massive corruption and the gross inefficiency of the system — arising from the instability of the fractional coalitions within the bourgeois class among other reasons — have continued to lay bare the fragile and shifting bases of bourgeois power in Nigeria.

The elusiveness of state hegemony

One of the major weaknesses of the established radical perspective on the nature of the post-colonial state is the tendency to present the state as i) a homogenous actor which is ii) so powerful that no other social force has ever or can ever challenge it. This is the result of a concentration on the nature of state institutions and functionaries rather than on the social relations and coalitions which underlie them. The fragile and fluctuating alliance between dominant domestic fractions and foreign capital — the erstwhile "triple alliance" — the tenuous relations of indigenous classes to productive activities, the peripheralisation of the social formation in the world division of labour, the content and direction of class struggles and, more importantly, the consciousness, organisation and power of non-bourgeois social groups especially women are given limited attention. Yet it is these very aspects which create the actual conditions that make state hegemony so elusive in the semi-periphery.

In an oil-economy such as Nigeria's has been, inability to either predict or control conditions in the world market and the domination of the oil industry by foreign capital combine to make dependence on oil revenues a source of insecurity, contradictions and conflict, particularly in times of economic contraction.

Although the Nigerian state has remained to a large extent supreme at the level of political control over the coercive instruments of society, it has lacked the moral and intellectual cohesion and direction which would enable it to impose and sustain its will and world-view on society without the use of force. In other words, the state is fragile in "civil society". The hollowness of its national development plans, the domination of the world-view of the metropolitan bourgeoisie – the prevalence of the "developmentalist" paradigm – the frequent resort to violence to contain popular pressures, the inefficiency of state institutions and the massive wastefulness and corruption of the dominant classes, all these have combined to create conditions of instability and the erosion of hegemony. Hence the call of the President for a social as well as green revolution in early 1983 and the mid-1986 transition from War Against Indiscipline to National Orientation Programme.

The workers and peasants in Nigeria have historically declined to sanction the dominant social classes in alliance with their international allies to establish, maintain and reproduce their "hegemonic" position in the social formation; i.e. the triple alliance remains tenuous. In turn, the bourgeois classes have been incapable of permeating in any systematic fashion the educational, religious, social and cultural aspects of society. Neither have they succeeded in advancing any moral value, taste, culture, custom or principle, that would enable them to integrate other social classes, eliminate or drastically reduce opposition, and reproduce bourgeois domination through popular consent (see first and final parts of this chapter).

Despite control over huge oil revenues, the Nigerian state has, then, been characterised by fractional and factional coalitions (see parts a and d), political confusion and prostitution, corruption and all forms of infantile behaviour by elected representatives. And it is only this superstructural level which the established paradigm recognises and treats; hence the inadequacy of its findings and explanations: Nigerian culture rather than capitalism.

The weakness of the bourgeois class is revealed not only in its continued coexistence with and subordination to foreign capital but also in its inability to regulate and innovate, in part a reflection of contradictory fractional interests. At the start of the 1980s, the Nigerian government had to hand the national railways to the Indians, the national airlines to the Dutch, the Nkalagu cement factory to the Swiss and the problem of smuggling also the Swiss, because it could not manage them itself.

Meanwhile, the class war declared upon the workers and peasants has generated counter strategies of struggle and challenges to state power. These are also direct or indirect precipitates of the misuse of oil wealth and the arrogance of power – reflected in both military and civilian regimes – which accompanied the oil boom. The massacres of students who articulate populist demands (most recently in mid-1986), the proscription of trade unions, the banning of trade union leaders (also in mid-1986), the massacre of peasants and the promulgations of the death penalty and primitive labour laws have all demonstrated to other social classes the extent to which the Nigerian state is willing to go in order to advance and reproduce itself. In addition, the refusal to adopt a mass-based development strategy, the continued use of colonial institutions to exploit farmers, the politicisation of ethnic, religious and regional differences (see final part) and the victimisation of journalists, intellectuals and other professionals, have only culminated in the intensification of challenges to state power in Nigeria.

Meanwhile, the state has not attempted to sell itself to the masses. It has continued to repeat past mistakes and to heighten social contradictions. The inability of some state governments to pay workers for over six months in the early 1980s, the distribution of national honours to disgraced and discredited individuals, have not helped to broaden the level of popular support. Thus, it has been incapable of creating a noble national goal, national spirit or sense of commitment among millions of neglected, unemployed, marginalised and exploited Nigerians, despite change in regime, decree and motif.

The general strikes of 1945, 1964 and 1981, the myriad instances of industrial unrest and peasant-state confrontation inspite of the decrees banning such protests (<u>pace</u> Bienen) as well as the increasing number of popular protests by students, market women and school children to post-colonial regimes (civilian and military alike), all serve to demonstrate that with or without the oil boom, the state has been unable to secure hegemony in Nigeria (see chapter five below).

Finally, we suggest that several objective and subjective factors have continued to make state hegemony an elusive phenomenon in this case. To comprehend the origins of this fragility and weakness, it is essential to study the Nigerian situation historically as Madunagu, Nnoli <u>et al</u> indicate but orthodox scholars eschew. The pattern of class formation and relations of power and accumulation in the pre-colonial period, the distortion of the social formation in the colonial era, the structural incorporation of the country into the world capitalist system as a (semi-)periphery, and the relegation of dominant social forces to exchange and commercial activities have contributed to its weakness. In addition, the domination of the "commanding heights" of the economy by international capital – despite indigenisation and the creation of NNPC – and the inability of the technocratic fraction to impose an alternative strategy or resolve contradictions within the bourgeoisie following political independence have also heightened its fragility. The deliberate exclusion of the majority of the people from plan initiation and implementation and assorted social aberrations have only spurred other social forces to challenge bourgeois power rather than to accept the status quo.

Ultimately, the most formidable obstacle to the infraction of bourgeois hegemony has been the abject poverty in which the majority of Nigerians live. This condition of unmet BHN (see ILO, 1981) has been exacerbated by the unproductiveness, inefficiency, and corruption of the dominant social forces. Volatile and dwindling oil wealth has only deepened the crisis of hegemony as austerity measures are adopted in the face of bourgeois panic and popular pressures (see Osoba, 1978).

c) New Problems: peripheral capitalism in a protectionist world

Peripheral capitalism in Nigeria as elsewhere generates its own specificities which cannot be divorced from the extant class configuration of the social formation but, more importantly, from the historical origins of these classes. Neither can the role of the state in the Third World in mediating class contradictions and struggles as well as in presiding over resource allocation be divorced from the whole system of capitalist underdevelopment. Thus, to understand the role of the state under peripheral capitalism, it is essential to understand the relations both of production and of class as primary aspects of analysis by contrast to either orthodox developmental or orthodox radical positions.

The development of state capitalism in peripheral (and semi-peripheral) societies is one integral part of such specific contradictions, the peripheralisation of the social formation within world capitalism, and the peripheral nature of the accumulation process. World capitalism itself is polarised between, on the one hand, the owners of means of production and subsistence and, on the other hand, the owners of labour power. This polarisation is reproduced internally, with the representatives of the owners of the means of production — international capital — dominating the "commanding heights" of the economy along with the post-colonial state. The historical relegation of dominant classes to peripheral sectors of the accumulation process compels the state to take up the task of regulating relations between foreign capital and domestic capital — economic nationalism — while at the same time participating or competing with foreign capital — the dialectic of the triple alliance. This is not the only scenario that is possible under conditions of state capitalism, however.

The above scenario of "classic" dependence could be deepened, second, to a level of active collaboration or alliance between the state, foreign capital and the local bourgeoisie with the state serving as guarantor — the triple alliance of "dependent development". Third, it is also possible for one fraction or faction of the dominant class to capture state power and adopt a so-called "non-capitalist road" to socialism. Thus, a "bureaucratic bourgeoisie" could emerge to reproduce its power and the system through control over state institutions, a not unfamiliar situation in Africa in the 1970s. Fourth, another alternative is for a nationalist or technocratic fraction of the dominant class to capitalise on periods of crisis in world capitalism to win concessions from imperialist countries, expand their participation within the economy and attempt to emerge as a viable and autonomous capitalist system, a scenario favoured by the IMF and IBRD in the 1980s. This approach — which some Nigerian fractions now advocate rather than "austerity" alone — has to contend with the depth and duration of the crisis. Finally, fifth, a military fraction could take power and repress, if not eliminate, alternative fractions, classes and pressures.

While varieties of these five possibilities exist within the Third World, each case being mediated by the specificities of the social formation, and global situation, state capitalism in oil economies takes on a different dimension. This difference lies in the fact that the semi-peripheral state has presided over huge oil rents. So the conditions which determine the pattern of state expenditure, relations to foreign capital, expansion of state institutions and efforts to protect the local market, are dependent on the particular nature of dominant social forces: the underlying dynamic is to use state power and resources directly and/or indirectly to facilitate the emergence of a strong and productive national bourgeois class or fraction. Where the semi-peripheral state is of "strategic" importance to imperialism, the metropole can, despite some of its own class interests, assist with this process, Taiwan and South Korea being examples.

Where internal problems, dynamics and class struggles prompt a version of state capitalism in the periphery, its immediate manifestation is the nationalisation or indigenisation of foreign enclaves with the goal of a greater appropriation of surpluses by the dominant class. The development of new export sectors, protection of the internal market, an aggressive participation in the world capitalist market and efforts to contain internal social contradictions are other features of such state capitalism. Of course, the creation of parastatals and the expansion of the public sector inevitably accompanies this process, or at least did until the current era of structural adjustment. Given such a framework, one which is quite distinctive from both established developmentalist and established radical perspectives, what has happened in Nigeria since independence and more specifically since the oil boom?

The reality of the Nigerian political economy

During the first republic, a Nigerian senator was moved to complain that the "trend now is to call every company a Nigerian company. That is, somebody is appointed from the outside, a Nigerian, one foolish man, who is usually given a big salary so that they can call the company Nigerian. He has nothing to do with the company"(cited in Osoba, 1977:369). Similarly in response to calls for nationalisation by Mokwugo Okoye of "enterprises exercising a dominant influence over the peoples' livelihood" and by Obafemi Awolowo of "basic industries and commercial undertaking of vital importance to the economy of Nigeria," the premier of the Eastern Region M.I. Okpara replied:

> Those who are advocating nationalisation are communists and they should have the moral courage to say so... Every member of the NCNC should stop saying or doing anything contrary to our policy of working in association and partnership with foreign capital (cited in Osoba, 1972:99).

This general idea of partnership - the ideology of "mixed economy" - has guided state policies towards foreign capital since 1960. Thus, given the relations of production and accumulation which were "Nigerianised" at independence, the failure to adopt policies that would create avenues for rapid capital accumulation by indigenous bourgeois interests has meant the continued, albeit eroded, domination of the economy by international capital.

Although with the oil boom the public sector has witnessed a tremendous expansion - advancing bureaucratic and nationalist fractions within the indigenous bourgeoisie - the state has refrained even from considering the nationalisation of the oil industry on which it is so dependent for revenues. Rather, it set up a national oil corporation to facilitate participation in the industry, and has since encouraged small- as well as large-scale oil ventures. And as already indicated, the indigenisation decrees passed by the military regimes only served to rationalise and legitimise foreign participation as well as to define spheres of influence and participation between international and indigenous capital: the basis of the "triple alliance". Ake (1978:48) has concluded that the decrees "hardly constitute a serious attack on dependence. The spheres of economic activity reserved for Nigerians are quite insignificant in terms of their share of GNP; e.g. hairdressing. In reserving Schedule I for Nigerians the decree merely preserved the status quo." Moreover, the second half of the Shagari civilian period and the current military administrations have reduced many prevailing restrictions on foreign capital.

If the Nigerian state has not expanded its direct interests in the economy, or employed state power to expand the interest of the bourgeoisie (indeed, in the current privatisation atmosphere it can hardly do either), what has it done with the oil revenues? And why? These are relatively easy questions to answer. The state has (had?) become quite independent financially both internally and externally. Thus, it came to believe that the solution to glaring social problems could be solved through massive imports − food, luxury items, building materials, clothing and so on − at least until "forex" ran out in the early 1980s. This process, a kind of "triangular" relationship (see Turner 1976 a and b) involves the state as contractor, the comprador/commercial bourgeoisie as middleman, and foreign capitalists as suppliers. This is why the monthly import bill stood at ₦ 1 billion in 1980 and "restrictions on imports were relaxed".

The massive corruption that accompanied the oil boom along with the arrogance of power led to the commencement (but rarely completion) of numerous prestige projects and an over-extension of regional and continental responsibilities. Millions of naira went into a haphazardly organised educational programme, to generous donations to liberation movements in Southern Africa and towards the creation of the Economic Community of West African States (ECOWAS) which was dominated from its inception by foreign capital through Chambers of Commerce.

Such policies were adopted because the state was and is dominated by a techno-comprador fractional alliance (now associated with military officers). Only a crisis of accumulation not affluence, could force it to take production seriously. Its middleman position in the accumulation process, like its intermediary role in global exchange, has always been very lucrative; but it is also inherently unstable and unproductive as the beginning of the post-OPEC era suggests. Thus, state policies created conditions of homelessness, unemployment, hunger and insecurity for the masses and affluence for the few. Some state agencies and parastatals, as already noted, had to be handed over to foreigners due to their unprofitability and inefficiency. Others, such as the NNPC − apex of the rentier state − were rocked by successive scandals.

Finally, the oil boom has intensified contradictions within as well as around the ranks of the dominant classes. The successive alignment and re-alignment of political forces have provided only temporary solutions to a deepening structural crisis. The crisis has been generated through three major elements in the political economy.

First, the changing role of foreign capital, which has continued to restrict or coopt weak, nascent national bourgeois elements. The latter are in an ambiguous position, still in danger of being converted back into compradors. The higher institutions and numerous contracts create their own <u>nouveaux riches</u> who serve the ranks of the technocrats and compradors. The net result is a deepening crisis within the bourgeoisie. As Forrest (1982:339) asserts, in reference to the national/comprador bourgeoisie debate:

> ...the sphere of foreign capital accumulation has not been greatly affected by the growth of the Nigerian bourgeoisie, by indigenisation, or by the extension of the state sector. The particular class structures of accumulation that have emerged in Nigeria provide little support for Ley's Kenyan view of an indigenous industrial bourgeoisie that is antagonistic to foreign capital. State intervention has greatly favoured large scale foreign enterprise, the indigenisation exercise notwithstanding.

Nevertheless, in countless new light manufacturing plants and through the imperatives of the indigenisation exercise, the national fraction has, in collaboration with both state and foreign capital, enhanced its position (Beckman, 1982 and 1985). This is especially so in the burgeoning "service" sector, despite the rather contradictory comment of Forrest (1982:339): "The big commercial bourgeoisie (Henry Stephens, Ibru, Folawiyo, Fanz) has extended its intermediary and property interests with little movement into manufacture. In the case of Kano there is some evidence of a shift from commerce to manufacture (Dantata, Gashash, Rabiu). Although one can detect, since the 1960s, a group of Nigerian entrepreneurs who have established larger-scale industries usually in association with foreign technical partners and state capital, they themselves have not provided a challenge to foreign capital..."

Second, is the struggle by fractions of the bourgeoisie to take control of the state or elements of the state which have direct and indirect connections to the oil industry. Legal and extra-legal measures are adopted in this struggle with a not-too-frequent alliance with exploited social classes in "patron-client" ethnic-type arrangements. The net impact is the continued elusiveness of state hegemony and the inability to expand and consolidate the power of any fraction of the bourgeoisie; hence the need for inter-fractional coalitions and co-existence. The intra-class competition also renders ineffective any attempt to domesticate labour beyond the levels executed by capital within the work place.

And third, finally, there are efforts to eliminate and/or isolate populist or radical elements within the state. This is manifested in the impeachment of state governors, the dismissal of state commissioners and "resignation" of federal ministers, the detention and/or deportation of prominent politicians, the non-registration of certain political parties, and the inclusion of a few token radicals on military councils and commissions. Given the fact that fractions of the bourgeoisie are constantly under popular pressure and attack, there is no reason to expect a resolution to this contradiction in the near future. Declining oil wealth, institutional decay and austerity measures have all increased pressures on the ruling class. In such a circumstance, the tenuous relation of bourgeoisie fractions to productive activities, has prevented them from providing any viable solution, even of a temporary nature. And the series of crises of the early 1980s are unlikely to end given the combination of global recession and national restraint. The balance of fractional forces along with non-bourgeois demands and linkages will largely determine whether crisis becomes conjuncture or not; ie. the continuing articulation of oil crisis in terms of political economy.

d) New Dialectics: what future for capitalism for Nigeria?

The place of the established semi-periphery like Brazil and South Korea in the global economy of the 1980s is problematic given conflicting pressures from both centre and periphery (Carlsson & Shaw, 1987); the position is even more so for the embryonic semi-periphery such as Nigeria. For the new dependence on petroleum in many ways made Nigeria more and not less vulnerable to the vicissitudes of the global marketplace. Moreover, a massive state structure has been constructed on OPEC/NNPC rents, one which is central to the survival of certain bourgeois fractions. Hence the prevasive nervousness of the rentier state occasioned by the demise of OPEC, as revealed in the expulsions of ECOWAS aliens and the OIC debacle, despite some positive by-products, such as less dependence. Austerity also has differential implications for different classes.

The dramatic decline in national income and foreign exchange in the first half of the 1980s - the beginning of the post-OPEC era? - served to intensify growing debates about infrastructure, industrialisation, privatisation, technology and exchange rates as well as indigenisation and constitution. It transformed difficulty into crisis. Will it yet turn crisis into conjuncture? The mid-term futures projected by orthodox and radical scholars are quite different: growth versus underdevelopment, respectively. Nigeria represents an important test case of development ideas for the African (semi-) periphery in the 1980s - will export-oriented industrial and commodity production work? - otherwise repression or socialism may arise in their stead.

The rentier state: the final stage of Nigerian capitalism?

Perhaps the most optimistic preview - conceived largely within the orthodox mold - is that of Schatz in <u>Nigerian Capitalism</u> (1977) who anticipated, as did Nigerian regime and bourgeoisie, continued growth towards industrialisation and agribusiness along with with minimal social tensions. Mid-way through the OPEC-induced boom and before the vicissitudes of civilian rule, Schatz (1977:ix) reflected a widespread feeling: "Nigeria at this writing is one of Africa's most optimistic countries. Buoyed up by a great surge in oil revenues, it has high hopes of entering a new era of rapid economic development." Schatz (1977:257), rather like Elliot Berg in his World Bank report, praised Nigeria's long-run strategy (orientation?) because it deals "specifically with policies for generating the successful modern-economy investment needed for accelerated development." And during the Mohammed/Obasanjo period he identified a trend, since largely abandoned but one which may yet be revived by dint of circumstance, towards state capitalism: a transition from "guided internationalist nurture-capitalism with a welfare tendency" to "a nationalist nurture-capitalism with state-capitalist, welfare and accelerated-development tendencies."(Schatz, 1977:7).

Schatz (1977) placed confidence, then, in the combined abilities of the regime and market-place to contain assorted social pressures such as region, religion, ethnicity and class, even if he subsequently moderated his enthusiasm (Schatz, 1981 and 1982). By contrast, more critical voices see the latter set of tensions in particular as influencing state policies and practices, further retarding development and intensifying contradictions.

Given the range of class contradictions which have emerged within and around this post-colonial state - between national and international bourgeois fractions; among indigenous military, comprador, bureaucratic and national fractions; and between bourgeois and non-bourgeois (peasant and proletarian) forces inside Nigeria - the future would seem to be full of dialectical possibilities. These are exacerbated by dramatic swings in the country's economic fortunes yet restrained by nationalist sentiments and repressive potentials. As Ake (1981:179) cautions, the failure of development strategy:

...poses grave dangers for the ruling class in Africa. The danger lies in the crisis of legitimacy which it has precipitated, and in the fact that it is generating revolutionary pressures in Africa by rapidly advancing the development of class contradictions.

In response, the ruling class, in rentier and other states, engages in what Ake (1981:180-184) characterises as ideological (populism), political (depoliticisation) and economic (growth through capitalism) "containment". Yet such pressures for and against change will not necessarily, contrary to orthodox Marxist optimism and naivety, produce decisive conjunctures or syntheses. Instead, Ake (1981:187) warns that fascism is as likely as socialism in response to stagnation and stalemate, at least in the mid-term future:

> In most of Africa the legitimacy of the ruling class and the social order are in question, governmental instability is rampant, the ideology of the subordinate class is becoming increasingly assertive, and the ruling class has little confidence in itself. One must conclude that a revolutionary situation exists in Africa. Whether this revolutionary situation will yield to revolutions is another matter.

Such internal pressures, exacerbated by external cycles of recession and expansion, may yet serve to transform the character of the state in Nigeria. But whether the change is "progressive" or not depends on the balance and mixture of internal and external forces.

The rentier state, like the Kenyan case characterised by Gavin Kitching (1980:413) as "the state as merchant capital," has played a crucial role in this external-internal nexus. As in Kenya, so in Nigeria (see Bernstein & Campbell (eds), 1985):

> The state in Kenya stands at the focal point of a network of exchanges between commodities and money which link together producers and consumers within Kenya and the Kenyan sub-system of world capitalism to that world system (Kitching, 1980:413).

Given Nigeria's position at the (semi-)periphery and the indigenous bourgeoisie's position within Nigeria, indigenisation neither could, nor was intended to, transform either internal or external relations. Rather, as in Kenya, it represented a new balance in the ever-changing "bargain" among bourgeois fractions, particularly indigenous and international capital, with the state serving as intermediary and mediator. As Ake (1981:116) notes, indigenisation as reform

...does not address itself to the fundamental causes of dependence. The approach concentrates on the redistribution of ownership and not on the widening of the resource base of the economy, nor even on changing the conditions and relations of production. Finally, the approach does not come to grips with the structural links of the economy to the metropole...the strategy...reinforc(es) the dependence of the Nigerian economy...in the face of economic nationalism. While indigenising capitalism, this strategy also promotes accommodation between indigenous capital and foreign capital.

The imbalance between class contradictions and coalitions

But accommodation does not mean ready agreement: there remain continuing tensions, especially at times of economic contraction, among different bourgeois fractions which accumulate through distribution if not production in Nigeria. Bjorn Beckman (1982 and 1985) has performed a signal service by comparing and debating the "neo-colonial" versus the "national" state issue in the case of African capitalist systems like Kenya and Nigeria. He concludes that the "rentier" state acts in the interest of capital as a whole, successfully advancing the national fraction while reassuring external and comprador interests. Beckman (1981:17) points to the "coming of age" of the African bourgeoisie and its ability to extract superior arrangements from established corporate capital. Given growing contradictions in Africa "Imperialism needs a domestic bourgeoisie." Yet contradictions, albeit of a non-antagonistic kind, remain within the embryonic "triple alliance" to be mediated by state institutions.

Such a state is, then, neither comprador nor national but rather "bourgeois", standing in opposition to workers and peasants if not to multinational corporations: "The state is an organ of the domestic bourgeoisie, not because of the sectional rivalries between national and foreign capital (which do exist), but because of the strategic role of this class in bringing about the subordination of 'its' territory to the rules of international accumulation. It grows in strength in step with its success in internalising these rules" (Beckman, 1982:49). In short, the rentier state in Nigeria orchestrates the politics of accumulation based on the emerging triple alliance:

> First...the state serves as an organ of foreign capital in Nigeria as it expands its operations and entrenches itself more deeply. Second...the Nigerian state is simultaneously engaged in fostering a domestic bourgeoisie. Third... the most significant functions performed by the state in support of capitalist development cannot be reduced to the

interests of such sections of capital, Nigerian or foreign. Instead, they need to be seen as performed in the interest of capital in general (Beckman, 1982:48).

This rather nuanced conceptualisation of the Nigerian state takes us some way beyond the relatively simplistic notions of either an "overdeveloped state" or that of a "comprador state" as advanced by Terisa Turner (1980:211), the latter being compatible with <u>dependencia</u> or "nationalist" approaches. To be sure, the balance of fractional forces within the triple alliance – in her terms the "commercial triangle", "a triad of state comprador, Nigerian middleman and foreign supplier" – has changed since the first appearance of her essay in the mid-seventies. Yet the very forces which she identifies as strengthening the state's role – the "technocrats" then in the oil ministry and now in the oil parastatal – she conceives as neo-compradors. Certainly the phalanx of middlemen-cum-agents continue to divert or subvert nationalistic sentiments of this fraction particularly in periods of growth through external exchange.

However, it is surely no longer accurate to argue that "The comprador nature of the Nigerian state prevents it from organising the transfer of oil technology and, more broadly, from initiating the development of capitalist production...The middleman-comprador alliance has thus far been successful in suppressing the technocratic faction within the state" (Turner, 1980:217 and 219). In her "postscript", Turner (1980:219) admits that the technocratic or bureaucratic fraction has been strengthened by i) the creation of NNPC; ii) the support of international companies (e.g. oil MNCs) and institutions (e.g. IBRD); and iii) general "external support for state capitalists over compradors...(because of the) world recession." Nevertheless she still sees the scramble for electoral office as serving to reinforce the comprador element despite other salient strands in the post-OPEC crisis, such as reduced foreign exchange and slashed imports. In short, the "liquidity"-cum-"austerity" crunch of the early-1980s has reinforced state functionaries in their conflict with the compradors, leading to a restatement of and recommitment to import-substitution industrialism. Even Forrest (1982:341) admits to change, even if he is reluctant to accept the longer-term implications of indigenisation, namely its effect on future policy:

> ...highly profitable, low-risk intermediary activities, which depend on imported goods and technology and on access to state and foreign corporate decisions, have expanded in harness with the rentier oil state. A class alliance has been formed between foreign capital and bureaucratic and managerial elements of the bourgeoisie.

These class forces may be weakened and obscured by sectional and distributional conflicts, but it is they, in the absence of any independent industrial bourgeoisie, which largely determine the character, effectiveness and limits of state policy.

Following the post-OPEC windfall, Nigeria can no longer afford an indulgent comprador class: the economic crisis of the first part of the new decade may serve to strengthen the state-national bourgeois coalition within the triple alliance to the cost of the international-comprador association. The immodest rentier state may yield to a chastened national-conservationist regime yet the place of the national bourgeoisie, unlike that of the comprador fraction, seems to be quite secure.

The future for Nigerian capitalism: repression and/or revolution?

The potential demise of the Nigerian mix of industrialisation through indigenisation and import-substitution lies, then, in "internal" economic limitations rather than in "external" social contradictions; hence our focus on the character of the rentier state. Long before anti-bourgeois forces are organised the import-substitution bonanza, based to a large degree on petrol rents, is likely to have run its course. As Steven Langdon and Lynn Mytelka have revealed in the analagous cases of Kenya and the Ivory Coast (Shaw & Aluko (eds) 1984), such import-substitution and export-expansion strategies have limited life-spans, especially during a global recession. Instead, Nnoli (1981:252) and others advocate disengagement and socialism rather than indigenisation and regional integration:

> ...the Nigerian economy will reach the inevitable dead-end of expansion. This has been the experience of the Latin American countries, India, Egypt, and other Third World nations which have a longer history of peripheral capitalist development than Nigeria. Regional integration will only delay the time of arrival to the dead-end, but will not be able to by-pass it...Only a development strategy that is fundamentally antagonistic to economic dependence and external control will break the grip of this inevitable stagnation.

But the social and political bases of socialism in Nigeria remain weak: party politics are persistently intra-bourgeois- and inter-ethnic in character. Repression based on various forms of chauvinism as already indicated is more likely in the foreseeable future than revolution.

Aside from continued expansion — a highly unlikely prospect given Nigeria's new vulnerabilities and continued global uncertainties — two major futures are thus discernible for the national political economy: repression or revolution (or, of course, some mix of the two). Ake attempts to evaluate the forces producing these divergent futures, recognising, on the one hand, the strength of interests containing social protest whilst, on the other hand, appreciating the resistance mounted by anti-bourgeois forces as indicated in the previous two parts. However, he concludes, hopefully, by suggesting that reactionary movements will be exhausted earlier than radical pressures:

> The indications are that for the vast majority of African socio-economic formations there will be neither significant capitalist development nor socialist development. The present state of economic stagnation will continue, deepening class contradictions and causing governmental instability but not necessarily sparking off revolution in the foreseeable future...the politics of anxiety will become institutionalised...Enemies of society will be found all too ubiquitously and will be dealt with summarily. Fascism — that is the reality staring us in the face in most of Africa. The fascist option cannot really be called a resolution of the contradictions. It is only a 'stalemate' which may be very protracted but nevertheless transitional. In the long run objective conditions are more likely to move Africa towards socialism (Ake, 1981:189).

This transition is the one preferred by Madunagu, Nnoli et al to overcome both underdevelopment and ethnicity. Nnoli (1978:176-255), in Ethnic Politics in Nigeria is critical about the continued exploitation of ethnicity by different and competitive fractions within the ruling class for their own accumulative ends, criticising the concentration on distribution (e.g. "state creation") rather than on production (i.e. mode or relations of production). Elsewhere, he has advocated nationalisation and the satisfaction of BHN as necessary steps towards socialism, seeing both as economically rational for the Nigerian population as a whole. He insists that these be realised through open and democratic processes, guaranteed by worker consciousness and participation, unlike contemporary "elitist" and exclusive politics:

> Thus, nationalisation for socialist development must go hand in hand with an egalitarian democratic policy in the nationalised enterprises, the political system, and in social life in general in order to reverse the existing neo-colonial relationship between labour and capital,

ensure national economic independence, and engender the growth of the productive forces on a self-sustained basis. Far from being passive in this process, the masses must participate actively in these national tasks, serving at least to hold the fort against any attempt by the leaders to shrink back from their accomplishment. Therefore, further discussion of Nigerian development must concentrate on the details of strategy and tactics for bringing about the necessary socialist transformation (Nnoli, 1978:262).

The latter concern constitutes the final three chapters in Madunagu's book: what is to be done? He identifies four views on how to go beyond nationalisation and a popular, anti-bourgeois alliance, indicating that the struggle in Nigeria will be protracted, frustrating and indeterminate. Given all the contradictions within the Nigerian "left", reflective of those within the political economy as a whole, Madunagu (1982:91-112) calls for a revolutionary "centre" through which to organise. He ends his "tract" where he started it: a call for critical instead of benign analysis at all levels, political, organisational and personal:

> For the socialist movement in Nigeria the need for self-clarification is urgent. For more than a decade, continuous attempts have been made to unite the various localised and backward socialist/Marxist groups in the country. The equally persistent abortion of these attempts has become almost a tradition and a culture...the present conjuncture opens up possibilities for meaningful political action... Although...pessimism is real in Nigeria, it is not our intention to perpetuate it. Instead we believe that a clear admission of our political tragedy is a necessary condition for transcending it (Madunagu, 1982:3-4).

Radical scholars-cum-activists in Nigeria have begun this courageous, arduous and uncertain task of recognition, preparatory to transcendence, although their personal and professional skills may be more appropriate to the former than to the latter. Certainly they have advanced the reconceptualisation of the Nigerian political economy - the prerequisite for appropriate and postive action - as well as raised questions about the degree of "over-development" and "autonomy" of the state.

In this spirit, we have proposed notions of a rentier state and class coalitions, as well as containment and corporatism, not to exclude alternative formulations but in the quest for clarification, recognising that the Nigerian state, like other political economies, evolves over time. As Samoff (1982:50) concludes in his own defence of the alternative radical "paradigm":

> Far from being distant or deterministic, used creatively and carefully, this framework permits a much more nuanced understanding of Tanzanian politics, precisely because it insists that there are connections among different structures, disparate events, and distant arenas, and that those connections can, and must, be studied.
> ...A critical social science, as it develops its critique of ideas that are widely accepted, both transcends and draws on the insights of those ideas and the wisdom and tools of its practitioners...a critical social science incorporates the intellectual mainstream as it transcends it...

Onimode's nuanced work on "Class struggles in Nigerian development" (Nnoli, 1981:188-189) is illustrative of the power in our case of such an alternative, radical mode for reasons of both analysis and <u>praxis</u> (although we might prefer a formulation closer to the "triple alliance" than a classic "bilateral" dialectic):

> After 1960 a two-cornered struggle emerged essentially between the now multilateral imperialist bourgeoisie and the Nigerian petty bourgeoisie (led by the bureaucratic bourgeoisie), and between this petty bourgeoisie and the working class. Both struggles were fought simultaneously, while there were also ancilliary intra-class conflicts, especially within the petty bourgeoisie.
> ...class struggles have dialectically resulted in changing patterns of ownership of productive forces and changes in the distribution of surplus. But because such reforms have fallen short of revolutionary or complete structural transformation...the ruling groups...have had to institute populist reforms which preserve the critical nature of neo-colonial capitalism and underdevelopment. For the future, the possibilities of a class alliance of workers, peasants, students and others, the increasing weakness of the international capitalist system as well as the growing consciousness of the masses, are going to be critical for the direction of national economic development in Nigeria.

3 Rural neglect in Nigeria: oil, towns, food and inequalities

a) Introduction

In order to fully comprehend the impact of the decade-long oil boom on the Nigerian economy and the distortions it introduced into the political economy, one has to look back to the pre- and post-independence periods. This is because the structures, institutions and social forces accentuated and consolidated by the 1973 and subsequent oil windfalls were established in these times.

At independence in 1960, Nigeria was a major exporter of agricultural products - mainly cocoa, palm produce and groundnuts. Most of these were produced by peasants on individual farms and small holders working in cooperatives. The post-colonial state (like the colonial state) relied on marketing boards to carry out the collection and marketing of the agricultural products at least until their demise in the mid-1980s. Revenue derived from the export of these primary products was used to sponsor projects mainly in the urban centres and to enhance private capital accumulation. Planning was used as a cover for rationalising state initiatives in subsidising capital accumulation by the dominant class. In order to extract surpluses from the peasants with which to subsidise this class, the state's marketing boards through their agents underpaid the producers and invested an insignificant proportion of the surplus in the social environment.

This process of uneven development generated some

unfavourable pressures in the countryside occasionally leading to revolts and migration to the cities. The established class structure in Nigeria did not encourage the initiation of policies that would encourage agricultural development. This was because there was no planter bourgeoisie as in the Ivory Coast or Kenya (Lubbeck, 1986). However, after 1973, the Nigerian state found itself receiving substantial revenues or rents from the marketing of oil and thus the dominant class found a new avenue for capital accumulation other than agriculture. The direct impulse of this was the neglect of agriculture and thus the rural areas. This also meant having to run a dependent food policy like other OPEC states. Where agricultural investment was undertaken at all, it was aimed at displacing the peasant mode of production, and it was large-scale and capital-intensive. The displaced farmers who migrated to the urban centres formed a large reservoir of labour to service the industries. The problem of rural-urban migration in Nigeria must therefore be understood within the framework of a dependent capitalist structure. Capital accumulation in agriculture through the extraction of surpluses from peasants has historically made a considerable contribution to the development of capitalist production, especially where a dynamic link was formed with industry as between cotton and textiles. How does one then explain the subsequent neglect of agriculture in Nigeria?

The answer to this question must be understood as the result of the discovery of an alternative source of capital accumulation. It must also be seen in terms of the class position of the custodians of state power. This class position (initially comprador but gradually becoming more national) has led to the continuous reproduction of a system which concentrates projects in selected urban centres, and sees the rural areas as places for re-charging elite status and showing off wealth acquired in the cities. This class position also explains why oil revenue was not seen as a means of promoting agriculture and forming a dynamic link with industry to promote continued growth and development.

This situation creates a particular problem: the youths abandon the rural areas and migrate to the urban centres, thus abandoning the villages and agriculture to the weak and old. This "abandonment" of the rural areas and all they represent is in fact encouraged by the neo-colonial educational system which hails Western virtues and presents agriculture as a degrading occupation. The panicky agricultural measures of successive governments – from River Basin Development Authorities to green revolution – confuse rather than solve the problems created by the manifest contradictions of the neo-colonial economy.

This chapter begins with a brief review of the features of the rentier state and their impact on development. Next it examines the development controversy and connects this with Nigerian development strategy since 1945. This is done in order to explore the trends and social direction of planning before and after independence. Following these, we look at the impact or role of oil in the political economy of Nigeria in order to show how this has enhanced rather than reduced the distortions in the Nigerian society. We end by looking at the critical factors involved in the drift of the rural population in Nigeria to the urban centres.

b) The Rentier State and Development

The oil economy arises out of the conditions of the rentier state — ie. an economy which has received substantial amounts of external rents on a regular basis, largely paid by foreign concerns. The oil revenues received by countries producing and exporting oil have very little to do with the production processes of their domestic economies; i.e. domestic inputs other than location are insignificant.

However, rents received from the sale of oil enable the rentier state to undertake gigantic expenditures internally. These led to spectacular growth in certain sectors of the economy, an increase in GDP often accompanied by few positive changes in the society at large. This is possible because the state does not feel at all obliged to a large proportion of the working class (oil workers in Nigeria constitute only 6% of all workers in the modern sector so a lot less of the whole labour force!)

A direct consequence of this change is that the government's ability to spend or act gradually becomes dependent on the oil sector and the revenue it generates. Consumption also becomes geared to imported goods. The reason for this is the neglect of agriculture which hitherto occupied a very prominent position. Put simply, the rentier state appears unable to outspend itself in the belief that it could purchase anything on sale. Thus while the rentier state experiences dramatic increases in GNP per capita, without experiencing the problems of 'normal' economic growth, a lot of distortions are also introduced into the economy. The pattern and context of these distortions are conditioned by the origin, composition, nature and power of the rentier state and dominant classes. Thus the situation is more intense if the rentier state is underdeveloped with weak institutions and social classes. Thus an underdeveloped rentier state, dominated by a comprador or petty bourgeoisie, overcomes (or postpones) its problems through massive contracting. Such a state contracts everything out, usually to foreign firms, recruiting, marketing, exploration, processing, training, servicing, accounting and anything it sees fit. This process subjects the mass of the

Table Five

Federal Governments Actual Receipts
(N million)

	Provisional			As percentage of total		
	1983 (1)	1984 (2)	1985 (3)	1983	1984	1985
Oil Revenue	7,253.0	8,209.7	10,915.1	69.0	73.3	72.6
Petroleum Profit tax (PPT)....	3,746.9	4,761.4	6,711.0	35.6	42.5	44.6
Mining Rent, Royalties and NNPC earnings................	3,506.1	3,448.3	4,204.1	33.3	30.8	28.0
Non-Oil Revenues	3,255.7	2,984.1	4,126.7	31.0	26.7	27.4
Customs and Excise Duties.....	1,984.1	1,616.0	2,183.5	18.9	14.5	14.5
Others........................	1,271.6	1,368.1	1,943.2	12.1	12.2	12.9
Total Federally-Collected Revenue......	10,508.7	11,193.8	15,041.8	100.0	100.0	100.0

Less:
Statutory Allocations to State and

Local Governments (Net)............	4,236.7	3,926.6	4,671.7
Federal Government Retained Receipts...	6,272.0	7,267.2	10,370.1

Source: Central Bank of Nigeria

population to "double-exploitation" from foreign firms and internal factions of the transnational bourgeoisie (see Nore & Turner, 1986).

Oil wealth creates a mirage for the casual observer. Gigantic buildings, beautiful universities, well-equipped armies, wide tarred roads, a booming business or commercial sector and a big voice in foreign affairs all tend to give the impression that things are going well. Beneath these surfaces, however, are very tense pressures and contradictions arising from the neglect of the vast majority of the people. These are the farmers, artisans, women and youth, particularly those in the rural areas. With the creation of modern infrastructures, expansion of the service sector, a booming commercial sector and massive injection of "fast" money into the economy, labour is attracted to the urban centres. Workers are needed for the roads, universities, industries, houses and other institutions being constructed. They are required to work at the docks, offices, hotels, etc. Quick money could be made in the cities during the boom, or at least, that was the mythology.

Moreover, the rentier state must satisfy not only other rentier states and traders but also the MNCs. The latter of course struggle to maintain their vantaged position in the economy in order to take advantage of the "oil boom". Bill Freund (1978:97) gives a graphic description of the Nigerian scene in the mid-1970s thus:

> As the oil boom gathered momentum the cities of Nigeria took on the character of gold rush towns. Foreigners flocked to cash in on the bonanza. Greek merchants and Arab doctors, Filipino nurses and Indian school teachers, Italian construction workers and German lorry salesmen, American bankers and British lecturers jostled one another on the streets all attempting to sell services of good, bad or indifferent quality. Firms reckoned to retrieve their initial investment in two to three years.

The rentier state usually undertakes a massive face lift of the urban centres so as to impress these foreigners as well as its own constituents. The bright lights and false image of success attract rural dwellers to these cities. Agriculture output declines seriously; food is imported to meet the demands of the growing urban population; and large-scale capital-intensive agriculture follows where possible. Since rural migrants need accommodation, shanty towns for the unemployed and poor emerge in the cities. Farmlands close to these urban centres are used for housing projects for the middle class and real estate speculators displace other farmers and erect apartments for the "modern" workers with minimal planning controls. Displaced peasants joined the rush to the urban centres to sell their own labour for wages: the petro-

Table Six Federal Governments Actual Expenditure (Provisional)
(N million)

	Actual 1983 (1)	Provisional 1984 (2)	Provisional 1985 (3)	As percentage of total 1983	As percentage of total 1984	As percentage of total 1985
A. Administration	3,643.7	4,103.6	5,047.7	31.6	41.3	41.8
General Administration	1,922.2	2,214.2	1,914.6	16.7	22.3	15.9
Defence	1,165.9	1,290.1	2,525.3	10.1	13.0	20.9
Internal Security	555.6	599.3	607.8	4.8	6.0	5.0
B. Economic Services	2,874.4	1,625.3	2,283.9	24.9	16.4	18.9
Agriculture and Water Resources	767.3	376.1	498.6	6.6	3.8	4.1
Construction, manufacturing and crafts, mining Quarrying	1,105.0			9.6		
Transport and Communications	818.0	350.1	567.1	7.1	3.6	4.7
Other	184.1	428.3	771.7	1.6	4.3	6.4
C. Social and Community Services	1,162.7	493.4	1,337.7	10.1	5.0	11.1
Education	440.3	274.4	991.3	3.8	2.8	8.2
Health	254.5	131.2	199.4	2.2	1.3	1.7
Other	467.9	87.8	147.0	4.1	0.9	1.2
D. Transfers	3,844.6	3,705.3	3,409.7	33.4	37.3	28.2
Pension and Gratuities	67.8		276.0	0.6		2.3
Public Debt Charges	1,525.8	1,772.5	2,484.3	13.2	17.8	20.6
Grants and Subventions	388.4	695.0	649.4	3.4	7.0	5.3
Loans to States	1,834.9	690.9	—	16.0	7.0	—
Loans to Parastatals	—	546.9	—	—	5.5	—
Other	27.7			0.2		
Total	11,525.4	9,927.6	12,079.0	100.0	100.0	100.0

Source: Central Bank of Nigeria

naira dream cannot be contained.

The questions that should arise under these conditions should not be why people move from rural to urban areas as people move towards comforts and opportunities under normal conditions. Rather the questions should concern attempts to locate the rentier state in the international division of labour: identify the dominant classes and bases of capital accumulation within this division of labour. This process will require, of course, an examination of the process of class formation, consolidation and cooperation. It will also require an examination of patterns and levels of capitalist penetration and contradictions between capitalist and pre-capitalist modes of production on the one hand and bourgeois and non-bourgeois classes on the other. These will provide explanations for actions of the rentier state: for instance, why it neglects the vast majority of its citizens and appears to be more concerned with things than people.

Thus the only way to comprehend rural-urban migration is not only to analyse the obvious reasons why people move but also to examine the socio-economic system which underscores the perceptions and policies of the dominant class vis-a-vis their location and role in the world capitalist system. Thus, in an underdeveloped capitalist state like Nigeria, the questions should concentrate on national and international capitalism and the process of capital accumulation which necessitates a confrontation with the peasants and consequently the displacement of the latter. How do these conditions influence the nature and role of the state, social classes and policy outputs and in what way does international finance capital contribute to altering or perpetuating historically-determined social relations of production?

c) **The Development Controversy**

The debate over development strategies in developing countries, particularly over responses to Africa's "crisis" of the early 1980s (Adedeji & Shaw (eds) 1985), has been very intense, leading to a lack of clarity and consensus on fundamental issues. The dependency literature did no more than sensitise us to some of the general issues involved without actually addressing in concrete terms the internal dynamics of class formation, accumulation and struggle. An unfortunate aspect of this debate has been the failure to define clearly what kind of "development" is being discussed and anticipated – capitalist or socialist, industrial or rural, concentrated or dispersed development? The assumption of some in the optimistic modernisation mold has been that peripheral capitalist states can through growth and planning not only redress rural-urban distortions but also succeed in developing institutions and structures that would ensure equity and sustained development. This has not happened, however, and even where the dominant classes have "voluntarily" gone socialist, reliance on external support to survive has been substantial. In an era of "structural adjustment", dependence on international forces is even more crucial for states attempting to implement devaluation, privatisation, desubsidisation and revival of commodity and other exports.

This chapter does not intend to provide a comprehensive critique of established views on planning and development. Suffice it to say that most make the mistake of conceiving of planning for development as a neutral rather than a social issue which cannot be divorced from internal and external class relations and alliances. The application of these prescriptions in developing countries evidently increased rather than decreased inequalities, for the sectors in which resources are initially concentrated to benefit certain social classes are the same sectors that manipulate the state to prevent subsequent redistribution. Finally, as even ex-IBRD President, Robert McNamara, has observed, "the trickle-down theory of growth is an insufficient basis on which to expect human needs to be met in a reasonable period of time". (New York Times 2 April 1978).

However, a new approach has been articulated in development circles and is gaining some popularity. This is the "bottom-up" approach to planning. This emphasises the need to create networks of growth centres and linkages in order to promote commercialisation of agriculture, savings and investment in productive activities. Stohr and Taylor (1981:454) maintain that such development from below has certain basic values:

> It is a development determined from within by the people of that society themselves, based on their own resources — human, physical and institutional. Each strategy is therefore unique to the society in which it evolves. Secondly, it is egalitarian and self-reliant in nature, emphasising the meeting of basic needs of all members of the society. It is therefore communalist in nature. The ultimate aim of such a strategy is an improvement of both the quantitative and qualitative type in the life style of all members of society. It involves selective growth, distribution, self-reliance, employment creation and above all respects human dignity. It is at one and the same time a new development strategy and a new development ideology.

However, we must be very careful in accepting this approach, appealing as it may be. While it may represent an improvement on past theories it neglects some fundamental issues and falls into the trap of conceiving the present situation to be devoid of class interests. Thus it engages in "moralising" as if dominant classes will decide to undertake a "bottom-up" approach even if it is against their interests. This reduces the approach to a "theory of advice" for dominant classes and not a critical theory of rural development. It thus appears ultimately to be an attempt to rationalise the <u>status quo</u>.

The idea of a "bottom-up" strategy, encompassing egalitarianism and self-reliance, overlooks class struggle in society, the location and role of political economies in the international division of labour, and domestic and external class alliances. It also assumes that the impact of dominant classes is not strong enough to condition policy output and thus the pattern of development. Surely the pattern of development in any society is a product of its ideology, classes and social relations of production.

The intent to go "top-down" or "bottom-up" in reality makes little difference in peripheral capitalist societies. This is because the latter can be a very effective strategy to penetrate the rural areas and restructure peasant organisations and production in order to extract more surplus. Thus it can be an effective strategy to open up these areas to full capitalist or state-capitalist exploitation. It is only when we look at the dynamics and dialectics of peasantisation and proletarianisation that we can comprehend policy outputs and therefore massive migration to urban centres.

d) Nigerian Development Strategy 1945-1980

It is important to examine the context and content of development strategy in Nigeria since 1945 because it is precisely these strategies that have determined the continuous evolution and reproduction of the Nigerian social system: from colonial, to post- or neo-colonial, and now post-neo-colonial development.

Urbanisation is not new to Nigeria, which has had cities like Ibadan and Kano for centuries. But the function of urban centres, their sizes and structures were profoundly affected by the advent of colonialism. Not only did they become parasites on the rural areas sucking surplus from the latter, but the urban-biased colonial system of resource allocation accelerated the rate of rural-urban differentiation and therefore migration.

The first development plan was initiated in 1946 by the colonial government - the Ten Year Plan for Development and Welfare - with the colonial government contributing less than half of a total expenditure of £110 million. Concentrating on the development of a very limited range of export crops, mainly for the benefit of British industries, infrastructures and services were concentrated in the urban centres. There was little regard for the spatial consequences of economic investments; no attempt was made to form a dynamic link between industry or agriculture; planning was basically centre-down with heavy centralisation in the capital, Lagos. Finally, all the first Plan did was to undertake and legitimise measures to enhance the accumulative capacities of the British bourgeoisie and its local partners.

The creation of a federal system and subsequent adoption of a federal constitution in 1955 with relatively autonomous regions did not advance decentralisation as the regional power-elite came up with divergent plans to protect their own accumulative positions and exclude others. Independence in 1960 did not generate a challenge to existing institutions and structures established by the colonial authorities.

The first post-colonial Plan, 1962-68, inherited this rural-urban inequity in terms of space, services and planning. Because these features facilitated capital accumulation by the dominant classes, the post-colonial regime saw no urgent reason for change. The neocolonial economy was preserved with all its distortions and mechanisms of administration and exploitation. Initial over-dependence on external aid meant having to compromise the pattern of development. Pre-oil boom elite competition for power, status and capital finally led to the civil war, 1967-1970.

The Plan had concentrated on chasing the goddess of GDP and creating growth centres in the belief that "trickle down" would follow. Following a two-year Plan holiday, 1968-70 in the civil war, during which the federal government strengthened itself, professionals from the universities, private sectors and Chambers of Commerce (but no rural people including women) were brought together in a new centralised National Economic Advisory Board. This Board was to advise the Joint Planning Board which formulated the Second National Plan, 1970-74, for "Reconstruction and Development".

The Second Plan aimed at a united, strong and self-reliant nation with a dynamic economy, a just society, full opportunities and democratic polity. Oil was just beginning to play a substantial part in the nation's economy, yet this Plan achieved little in terms of meeting its objectives. Excessive concentration of power at the centre led to very limited mobilisation of the people and increases in oil revenues led to neglect of the agricultural sector. Rural-urban migration increased as conditions of life in the rural areas steadily deteriorated. By the time the Third Plan was initiated, things had reached alarming proportions: the "new wealth" made Nigeria, like other OPEC states, abandon agriculture and the rural areas, though over 80 per cent of the population still lived there.

This situation of neglect did not prevent one of the architects of the Third Plan, 1975-1980, Professor Ojetunji Aboyade from arguing that

> it is the task of Planners to plan according to the established political-economic structure, otherwise such plans cannot be realistic (cited in Oni, 1975:89).

The Third Plan itself admits the failure of past plans when it states in Section 6 that

> The rural areas in general would also require a new deal in the provision of social services. In almost every state sizeable communities still exist without basic amenities, like clean water supply, hospital and health centres, schools and electricity. The absence of such services obviously contributes to the low level of rural productivity and strengthens the pull exerted on rural dwellers by higher urban incomes (p. 35).

To redress this situation, however, required not only a rural development strategy but also a comprehensive policy directed at changing social relations of production which are biased against rural producers. These reduce opportunities available to rural people and lead to panicky and haphazard measures like the Operation Feed the Nation (OFN) and aimless propaganda. Moralising about the distortions cannot rectify them and as Ola Oni (1975:88) notes:

> Planning of this type is an organised effort to promote growth by creating stable conditions for the gradual emergence of capitalism from pre-capitalist structures under the cover of the world imperialist system. A development plan based on this strategy is a neo-colonial capitalist plan.

While neither capitalist nor socialist planning can challenge the domination of exploiting classes, the Third Plan, despite increased revenues did not alter the status quo. Rather the prerogative of the state was to mobilise and allocate national surplus or investible funds in ways that directly and indirectly increase private capital accumulation. This is done in the name of strengthening the private sector which has been dominated by foreign capital.

There is no doubt that Nigeria has experienced some economic growth and change since independence in certain sectors. GDP increased and so did GNP per capita and foreign reserves until the early 1980s. But these do not really indicate the quality of life and condition of the masses. As long as planning is neo-colonial and capitalist, the masses will only get the crumbs. This is because planning is employed by the dominant factions to consolidate their positions and enhance capital accumulation. Thus the Third Plan also failed to negotiate any "new deal" for the rural areas.

Finally, as Onimode (1977:301) notes, the impact of elitist conceptions of planning involving bureaucrats and bourgeois economists alone, coupled with a grossly unequal distribution of any gains of development, has been the inability of Nigeria to mobilise a mass base for planning implementation. He argues further that, in spite of propaganda anticipating a new deal for the rural areas, planning from the grass roots, etc., the masses of Nigerian peasants, workers, youths, artisans, women and patriotic professionals have never been involved actively in national planning. The consequence of this is that post-colonial capitalist planning has done a lot to Nigerians but very little for them (see next chapter).

e) Oil in the Political Economy of Nigeria

Exploration for oil started initially in Nigeria in 1938. Though World War II led temporarily to a suspension of production, 1951 saw a renewed effort by foreign capital and the colonial authority to explore for oil. The first deep exploration well was sunk in the Niger Delta that year. By 1958, the country had started to export petroleum. Historically, the development of the Nigerian petroleum industry was carried out by foreign concessionaries. Production gradually increased from a few thousand barrels to over 2 million barrels per day in the late-1970s and early-1980s (see table one). As production increased, revenue accruing to the state also increased, taking a dramatic turn upwards in 1973 because of global oil "shocks". At the same time, state control was gradually extended over the oil sector, up to 55%.

The production of high quality, low sulphur oil and the apparently growing need for energy by international capital meant an increase in revenues which enabled the state to diversify its activities further. This did not in any way radicalise state oil policy, however, because technology and high level manpower in the oil sector was and is still dominated by multinational oil corporations (Turner, 1976 a and b). But increased national revenue did reduce the nation's dependence on external aid to finance development projects unlike most African states. The development budget shot up from $4.5 billion in 1962 to $175 billion in 1980. However, while oil enabled the state to spend more on prestige projects, the immediate consequence was a decline in the contribution of agriculture to GDP, though it continued to provide employment for "about 70% of the country's labour force"

(Second Plan:103). This in turn led to a serious dependence on the contribution of oil wealth up to the tune of 85 per cent of total government revenue. Stephen Wright (Shaw & Aluko (eds) 1983:97) notes in relation to this dependence that:

> Agriculture provides an occupation for two-thirds of the population and was until recently the mainstay of the economy. Its contribution to GDP fell from 63 per cent in 1960 to 23 per cent in 1975, while exports of commodities accounted for 80 per cent of the total value of exports in 1960 but fell to a mere 6 per cent in 1974.

Wright attributes this decline in the contribution of agriculture to GDP to several reasons, the most important being the export of oil; by 1978 "oil exports accounted for some 90 per cent of total export earnings" (Shaw & Aluko (eds):98).

Claude Ake (1978:49) writing on the same issue notes that in the fiscal year 1970/71 oil accounted for only 27% of the federal governments' revenue while the share of revenue from sources other than oil was 73%. By the fiscal year 1974/75, however, there was a drastic reversal. By then oil accounted for 85% while that from non-oil sources was only 15%.

The reason for emphasising this contemporary dependence on oil is that it enables us to comprehend the neglect of agriculture which occupies 80 per cent of the 100 million or so people in Nigeria. This neglect is a product of the fact that there is no dominant social class in Nigeria that is fundamentally agriculture-based. Because of extra-agricultural bases, neglect of the primary profession of the mass of the people by successive regimes has led to a decline in government input and an absence of price incentives, which in turn directly contribute to the drift to the urban centres. Those who could no longer survive through the cultivation and sale of primary products left for the apparently booming commercial sectors in the cities.

The Nigerian situation has not been one where the state has lacked resources to stimulate production in the rural areas. This raises one of the major problems of peripheral capitalism: in what directions should dominant classes direct their accumulative powers? Peripheral bourgeoisies tend to be pre-occupied with investing in real estate and commerce, sectors that yield "instant" revenues and where the risks can be "controlled". Thus with an alternative and less risky path available to capital accumulation, little attention was paid to agriculture. In the mid-1970s, oil rapidly became the main engine of growth in the economy and virtually the only export. In 1958/59 this sector contributed only .07% to total federal revenue. But by 1980, federal revenue was N11.859 billion, of which oil alone accounted for N9.918 billion. Thus everything

in Nigeria came to revolve around oil not agriculture.
Rather than use these massive revenues to effect a comprehensive development policy aimed at redressing various historically-determined distortions, the Nigerian state did otherwise. Planning remained elitist and was conceived as a path for patronage, for diverting funds to foreign banks and for undertaking prestige projects. The neglect of agriculture (particularly food production) was compensated for through the subsidised importation of cheap food to meet urban demands. And while rural-urban migration continued to grow and unemployment and inflation increased, the Nigerian state was concerned with "going nuclear" because

> Nigeria is a great country and it needs a strong invincible and unassailable defence capability. It is only when she becomes a nuclear power that she can boast of that status (West Africa 10 November 1980:2222).

f) Drift to Urban Centres

As indicated earlier the problem of rural-urban migration can no longer be explained simply in terms of "push" and "pull" factors. Even where natural disasters occur, the desire of a people to rebuild from scratch is dependent on the level of mobilisation in a society. The "pull" factors are, of course, direct consequences of the bias against rural people in the location of services, institutions and opportunities. But this "bias" does not exist in a vacuum. Rather, it is tied to the underlying ideology of the indigenous ruling class and is specifically influenced by their perceptions of the possibilities of accumulation in and reproduction of the status quo.

Concrete data on rural-urban migration in Nigeria are not available. Though the World Bank does provide some data, observation of the dynamics of displacement of rural people which has taken place all over the country can provide estimates of migration to the cities. At independence, agriculture was the principal source of revenue. As Nigeria had not experienced settler colonialism, production of cash crops was left in the hands of independent producers though, like the colonial state, the new state extracted surpluses through taxation, administrative manipulations and the use of marketing boards. As the Minister for Agriculture noted in 1980:

> with each passing year, farming became progressively unattractive and unproductive and remains characterized by inadequate capital, lack of suitable technology, inadequate supply of farm inputs including credit and scarcity of farm labour which has been worsened in recent years by the migration of young men and women from rural areas to

the cities. With the advent of mineral oil, agriculture suffered an even greater neglect and was relegated to the background by previous administrations (<u>New Times</u> October 1980:35).

The 1980 <u>World Development Report</u> showed that while in 1960 only 13 per cent of Nigeria's population lived in urban areas by 1980 this had reached 20 per cent, an underestimation if temporary migrants are included. This <u>Report</u> also showed a 4.9 per cent average annual growth rate for urban centres. Moreover, while Nigeria had only 22 per cent of its population in cities with over 500,000 persons in 1960, by 1980 it had 57 per cent. And while only two cities existed with over 500,000 persons in 1960, by 1980 this had increased to nine. The same <u>Report</u> showed a decrease from 71% to 56% of the labour force involved in agriculture for the same period, while it recorded an increase from 5 to 8% for industrial employment and 19 to 27% for that in services.

The question that arises is why has this been so? The contention of this chapter is that the advent of an alternative source of capital accumulation and the inevitable confrontation between capitalist and peasant modes of production are largely responsible. In fact, the Nigerian "power elite" has since independence had the perception that "rural small farmers have failed the nation, and that they have failed the nation because they are illiterate, ignorant, use primitive tools and methods of farm management and do not have muscles that are strong enough to create plantations" (Oculli, 1979:64). This unfortunate colonial-type notion not only ignores the impact of past regimes but also the fact that these farmers produced the crops whose revenue was siphoned away by the colonial authorities. After independence, the rural areas were conceived as providers of resources, capital, cheap food and labour for the cities as well as markets for imported and locally produced goods. Oil changed all this: the rural areas are now perceived just as markets, an area in which to display affluence and a reservoir for cheap labour.

The displacement of the rural people from the land was the precipitate of two major factors among others. The first was the direct involvement of the new Nigerian state and the World Bank in agriculture, usually large-scale and capital-intensive (Andrae & Beckman, 1986). And a consequence of massive state patronage was the erection of state and private infrastructures which not only encroached on available land but also drew unskilled labour away from the rural areas. These two factors will be treated separately in order to show how they have been encouraged by the state and have enhanced the migration of rural people to the urban centres.

State involvement will be examined on three levels: (a) deliberate neglect of agriculture in the rural areas and involvement only in a few large-scale capital intensive agricultural projects; (b) dependent food policy in which urban food consumption came to depend on food imports; and (c) support for World Bank projects that do not appear to be helping the peasants. We must add here that these measures have furthered the penetration of capitalist relations into the countryside but have done little thus far to shake the new footholds of international finance capital in the country.

The most glaring evidence of an anti-rural policy lies in budgetary allocations by federal and state governments to agriculture. Between 1972-1976 there was a steady decrease in federal allocations and between 1977-1979 almost all states (except Niger and Ondo) experienced substantial decreases even after the Second Plan had recognised agriculture as providing employment for over 70 per cent of the 80 million Nigerians. That Plan also noted that about 80 per cent of these people were rural dwellers; between 1970 and 1974 they got only 17.9 per cent of total expenditure. And over the same period government spending on rural industries totalled f5.9m out of a total industrial expenditure of f42.5.

The response of the Nigerian government to the related agricultural and urban problems has not been to initiate progressive policies that would facilitate mass mobilisation and the provision of services and opportunities for rural dwellers in order to retain them in the countryside; the state has not tried to strike a balance in economic, social and political power relations between the rural and urban areas. Rather, it has engaged in fund-wasting propaganda and poorly articulated projects like the OFN and has gone <u>directly</u> into large-scale agriculture itself. This latter <u>activity</u> has led to the establishment of farm projects, plantations, river basins and state farms. Some of these were simply dropped into villages along with huge machines and clerks with minimal inputs from the rural society.

The problem here is not with state participation in agriculture. But in a peripheral capitalist economy like Nigeria, taking the place of the peasants means displacing them from the land. The consequence is reinforcement of the drift to urban centres with the long-term consequence being the creation of a large army of frustrated, unemployed or underemployed lumpen proletariat (Williams 1976a). The pressure from this growing urban mass continues to force the government to concentrate services in the urban centres which further increases the drift. The proletarianisation of the peasants with very limited opportunities is, over time, tantamount to the creation of a time bomb by the bourgeoisie themselves. Because the alienation of the peasants by the state directly militates against the peasants' commitment to the state farms, most of the new centres have failed woefully. And as deproletarianisation has proceeded with the process of

deindustrialisation in the 1980s so alienation has increased.
The failure of farm and other projects forced the state to adopt a dependent food policy on a large scale. But food imports did not begin with the oil boom; they only took a dramatic upward turn in 1973. While food production increased in Nigeria between 1960 and 1975 by roughly 1.8 per cent per annum, from 1974 food imports began to take up to 10 per cent of the total budget reaching 15 per cent in 1977. Much of this imported food consisted of basic foodstuffs needed by the urban working class and their dependents – meat, rice, fish, stockfish, flour and wheat (Andrae & Beckman, 1986). As Bill Freund (1978) noted, fish imports reached a value of N30m in 1976 and N67m in 1977, sugar imports went from N76m to N129m in the same years, maize imports worth N1.4m in 1976 rose to N3.5m in the first eight months of 1977, while wheat was imported to the tune of N98m in 1976 and N129m in 1977. However, the most spectacular increases were in rice. In 1975, Nigeria imported 15m kilos of rice. In 1976, imports tripled to 45m and in the first nine months of 1977, attained 246m kilos. American rice undersold the grain and root staples produced by Nigerians to such an extent that it found a ready market even in rural areas.
Most of the food imports came from the United States, growing from $40m in 1972 to $144m in 1975. Instead of stimulating internal food production, and having failed to do so through state farms, the government turned to imports to make up for the deficiency (Oculli, 1979).
Grain production declined so badly that the marketing boards began to lose revenue. The boards bought 454,000 tonnes of groundnuts in 1972, 270,000 tonnes in 1973, 114,000 in 1974, 178,000 tonnes in 1975, 42,000 tonnes in 1976, 12,000 tonnes in 1977 and just 50 tonnes in 1978! Peasants continued to produce, but either withheld from the market or smuggled their produce across the borders to areas where prices and currencies were more attractive. Others simply used their land to produce food while some were displaced through state policy of land acquisition. There is no doubt that the Nigerian state was able to import food exclusively because it benefitted from the world energy crisis as an oil exporter. But given continued increases in urban populations and declining revenues from oil it was always doubtful whether this policy could be sustained without crisis.
This brings us to the third and final level: the involvement of the World Bank. Historically, the Bank has been distrusted in many Third World countries as an agent of Western "imperialism". Writing on Tanzania for instance, Gavin Williams (1976a:139) argues that "under the label of ujamaa the World Bank extended schemes of supervised production of tobacco and tea so as to meet the requirements of capitalist companies rather than to ensure the best return to the farmer

for his (sic) labour." Writing in a similar vein of distrust on Nigeria, the editors of the <u>Review of African Political Economy</u> (<u>ROAPE</u>) viewed with suspicion the twelve World Bank projects aimed at increasing cash crop production for export. Accusing the Bank of trying to re-establish the agricultural economy of the colonial period with a difference - ie. the neglect of small holders who expanded production in that era - they argued that

> Contrary to the World Bank's hypocritical rhetoric about concentrating resources on small farmers and aiding the rural poor, their projects are designed to subsidize rich farmers and have created a class of absentee "overnight" farmers to take advantage of their assistance. Small farmers are specifically discriminated against in the allocation of resources or are unable to meet the cash costs of participation (13, September-December 1978, p. 4).

Irrespective of opinions about the World Bank, the fact remains that its involvement in Nigerian agriculture has encouraged the displacement and alienation of peasants from the land. This has further promoted the drift to urban centres. The World Bank, it should be remembered, works in collaboration with the Nigerian bourgeois state; thus its activities are manifestations of the interests of the dominant ruling class. One direct impact of Bank-state cooperation is the alteration of land-use patterns and consequently the relationship of farmers to their land.

The World Bank agricultural projects in Nigeria are usually large-scale and capital-intensive, involving extensive use of imported machinery, large loans and expertise usually superior to those available to the peasants. In Northern Nigeria, the Bank's projects have led to displacement and sometimes resettlement, usually in less suitable areas, of thousands of peasants. Compensation for displaced farmers is meagre. This not only leads to pauperization but also encourages the drift to urban centres. In some cases the farmers are pushed to less large and fertile isolated farmlands. These conditions pressure established peasant farmers to sell their land to "absentee farmers", usually bureaucrats and businessmen resident in the cities.

Evidence of peasant resistance in reaction to state violence is abundant. They have resisted state attempts to break the "peasant way of life" and incorporate them into the capitalist system as waged agricultural labourers. The state in turn has responded with all the brutality it could muster. One infamous example involved the 23,000 hectare irrigation project at Bakolori where hundreds of resisting farmers were murdered (Oculli, 1979a). The experience of one of us at the World

Bank Oil Palm Smallholder Project at Umuduke-Umuahia was of a project which started out as labour-intensive thus providing employment for people in the area. Without warning, however, the project suddenly turned capital-intensive with the introduction of sprinkler machines. This is one example of a common pattern of agricultural projects sponsored by the World Bank. The Bank's rural development projects, irrespective of propaganda, are aimed at "the application of advanced farming techniques which are particularly adapted to larger farming units either group or individually operated" (ROAPE Editorial, 13, September-December 1980:4). This has led to the massive acquisition of land, encouragement of capitalist agriculture and the creation of a reservoir of unemployed people.

This rapid displacement of rural people has further encouraged the penetration of the rural areas by the Nigerian bourgeoisie who have within a short period accumulated substantial sums from the "contract mania" of the federal and state governments and ubiquitous corruption within the dominant classes. The youths and farmers who drift from the rural areas need accommodation and transportation. Thus the construction of roads, bridges and expressways with little regard for the spatial consequences has also contributed to the displacement of farmers. So also did the laying of a South-North oil pipeline. What was worse, however, was the oil-induced real estate boom!

Paul Lubeck (1980:39) writing on Kano, a situation which has been repeated for all other cities in Nigeria, noted that:

> not only has the construction of infrastructure drawn unskilled rural labour out of agriculture but the spatial expansion of the city has encroached upon peasant areas in the close settled zone (CSZ).

Thus capital rapidly accumulated through the oil boom by state and bourgeoisie has aided the expansion of urban and peri-urban areas as money was spent on the establishment of schools, hospitals, airports, army barracks, hotels, offices, commercial buildings and office malls. Lubeck (1980:39) notes that these activities and the practice of enclosing land in the peri-urban areas with barbed wire expands the urban land market, devouring the peasantry, who migrate to the city. The migrants in turn are forced to pay high rents for overcrowded and hastily erected buildings with few or no facilities.

However, where farmers are able to remain in the rural areas, the neocolonial content of Nigerian education directly classifies agriculture as the profession for the illiterate. The petty-bourgeois aspirations imbibed by students, coupled with the "get-rich-quick" mentality of peripheral "booty-capitalism", means constant migration from the countryside. The discrimination practiced against poor farmers by bureaucrats and planners creates a situation where peasants encourage their children to migrate to the cities, experience the "good life" and send the surplus home. Commenting on groundnut production, the Financial Times (29 September 1980, p. xx) noted that the "drift of the young towards the cities to find work has left the groundnut farmers unable to find labour for what used to be a labour intensive crop. What labour there is has become increasingly expensive because of the competition from the urban centres".

So, the drift is likely to continue as opportunities are simply not available in the neglected rural areas. The peasants are seen as obstacles to capitalist agriculture and accumulation and therefore dispensible. Services continue to be concentrated in state capitals and major cities. As Diejomaoh (1972:103) noted:

> On the basis of seasoned observation, it can be concluded with a high degree of confidence that the benefits of government expenditures on education, health, water supplies, transportation, housing, administration and industries are concentrated almost exclusively in urban areas. In sum, substantially less than 40 per cent of total government expenditure is designed for the benefit of rural communities who make up more than 70 per cent of the population.

Under these circumstances there is no reason why the rural people should not migrate to the centres of attraction. But it must be understood that the concentration of services in such centres is a function of the bourgeois character of public policy and planning in Nigeria. Even in the urban centres, a majority of the people have little or no access to services. In a society where the bourgeoisie appears to have located the seeds of their future dynamism and capacity for self-reproduction in commerce, real estate and joint ventures with foreign capital, one can only look elsewhere for a solution to rural-urban migration and the exploitation of the majority by a privileged minority.

g) Conclusions

It is not possible to give immediate solutions to a process that has been created through long-term planning and manipulations, though current consequences appear not to have been anticipated. For instance, the World Bank, Nigerian state, and indigenous bourgeoisie apparently expected displaced peasants to accept low compensation and possibly take up wage employment on large projects or farm centres. However, the majority refused to do so; rather, they resisted while others drifted to the urban centres to swell the ranks of the proletariat. Within a liberal framework, it is possible to propose solutions that will "cool issues" but only temporarily. Nigeria does not have a comprehensive rural development policy worth the name, but rather haphazard ad hoc and unco-ordinated intrusions into the rural areas. Yet with the current alliance between the Nigerian state and international finance capital and the open attacks on the peasant mode of production we expect a continued attempt to develop capitalist agriculture. This will not stop the rural-urban drift, but will rather increase it. The crucial factor, however, is whether Nigerian bourgeois fractions are yet interested in capital accumulation through agriculture. With the continuing desire to make "instant profit" and the belief that with the oil boom money can be made through commerce and real estate, it appears the World Bank and the Nigerian state will have to bear the burden of breaking the peasant mode of production.

No amount of propaganda or bourgeois reform can absorb the contradictions inherent in peripheral, Nigerian capitalism. The crisis generated by the clash of the forces involved in this struggle will in the final analysis determine what social relations of production operate in Nigeria. This will in turn determine whether the rural people will find contentment in the rural areas and so remain there or if they will continue to migrate to the cities in search of opportunities.

4 Towards a political economy of ideology: planning the mixed economy

Though the incidence of planning in developing countries underscores the central role of the state and its bureaucracy, the literature on development planning in Nigeria has tended to ignore the social dimensions of plan initiation and implementation. Hence, the roles of social classes, the peripheral state, the bureaucracy and its specialised institutions and the country's location and role in the world system have largely been neglected. Instead, the majority of works have concentrated on expenditures, capital programmes, specific projects and an analysis of the "problems and prospects" of development planning. Even at this level, the dynamics of capital accumulation, the historical origins of planning procedures and institutions, the circulation of struggles and internal/external forces influencing budgetary allocation have been largely ignored. Planning at this level of analysis is not conceived as a social activity but rather as a technical affair involving economists, bureaucrats and foreign "experts".

The net result of this elitist and limited "technocratic" approach to planning is the continued reproduction of the peripheral capitalist system along with all its attendant social contradictions and struggles. The efforts by the dominant social classes to employ planning as a tool for containing class opposition, isolating or incorporating workers, peasants and communities, as well as creating a viable environment for foreign capital have been constantly challenged by the exploited classes who do not appear to have benefitted from successive planning exercises since 1945. The effects of conflicts within the ranks of the dominant classes and, specifically, how fractions or factions of the bourgeoisie have conditioned such planning in Nigeria, have not been given serious attention until very recently.

This chapter does not intend to address all the issues raised above. However, by adopting a class-based mode of analysis, it hopes to contribute to the growing body of literature which has challenged bourgeois/liberal approaches to development planning in Nigeria, recognising that current IBRD and IMF strictures - reform and structural adjustment, respectively - make the future of such exercises problematic.

a) Alternative approaches to planning

Underlying the issue of development planning is the question of what constitutes i) planning, ii) development, and iii) ideology. In most Third World countries, economic development (as against "development" per se) has been promoted through the design and implementation of plans. These are deliberately aimed at expanding some or most specific sectors of the economy. Though one can hardly identify a grand or integrated "theory" of development planning, several partial theories of decision-making that influence or determine development planning do exist. We can identify three of these in the orthodox mold - "incremental", "synoptic" and "mixed scanning" - and point to a fourth more radical variant.

Any alternative approach to development planning that is aimed at meeting the basic needs of the majority must include policies aimed at popular mobilisation and education. Emphasis must be placed on sectoral integration, the involvement of local people in the initiation and implementation stages, and the promotion of self-reliance. The use of state power to initiate policies which promote private capital accumulation and the further integration of the social formation into the world capitalist system is antithetical to popular comprehensive planning. Thus, to use planning as a unique tool for liquidating underdevelopment in peripheral states, the "democratisation" or "socialisation" of institutions must be a priority objective; ie. politics as well as economics as an enterprise. Alongside, an attack must be made on the peripheral role and location of the economy in the world system, the patterns of capitalist accumulation and the dominant role of foreign capital to mention a few. The ability to realise these will of course be dependent not only on the class nature of dominant forces but also on the intensity and direction of class struggles. The case of Nigeria is both illustrative and informative.

b) Planning for (Under) Development in Nigeria: contradictions of a "mixed economy"

Planning in Nigeria since 1945 as indicated in the previous chapter has been directed at rationalising private capital accumulation while using state power to subsidise the private sector. Planning has not been employed as a weapon of social change, through the elimination of socio-economic and political inequalities. Instead, these inequalities have been consolidated or heightened through the country's structured incorporation into the world capitalist system.

In terms of initiation, institutions and procedures, planning has remained in Nigeria, as almost everywhere else, elitist, distorted and biased in favour of factions or fractions of the dominant classes and foreign capital. Not only have the plans been hastily prepared by bourgeois intellectuals randomly selected to aid established bureaucrats, they have been treated as "war secrets", kept hidden from most Nigerians but not from international capitalist institutions and agencies. Irrespective of the fact that the "top down" or "trickle down" approach to planning has been severely criticised and proven ineffectual in most parts of the world, the Nigerian state has continued to believe in it.

Thus, as indicated in the previous chapter, planning does not involve most people. Because of the bankruptcy of the national social system, rabid corruption within the ranks of the bourgeois classes, unregulated competition for power and spheres of control, as well as an inability to create a viable hegemony, the state has been unable to introduce a clear-cut and viable national ideology to guide its policies. So the success of the plans have been evaluated according to expenditures rather than achievements, prestige projects have been introduced half-way and plan-indiscipline have characterised efforts to date.

Though the official description of the ideological values underpinning the management of the Nigerian economy is that of "mixed economy" - the economic analogy of purported "political neutrality" between the East and West - the reality has been that Nigeria has never been economically (or politically) "neutral". The country through the world view of its leadership and the nature and accumulative base of its dominant classes has always been pro-West. Nigeria is a peripheral <u>capitalist</u> society. The inability (refusal?) of the "power elite" to restructure the distorted system inherited at independence, has meant the continued reproduction of the country's peripheralisation in the international division of labour. Akin Fadahunsi (1979:117) has argued that "the institutions, values and procedures of the mixed-economy ideology have been responsible for the mismanagement, confusion and corruption in the nation's economic life - private or public". In a similar vein, Bade Onimode (1977:297) has argued that, despite the propaganda about being neutral ideologically,

> ...the intellectual philosophy of Nigerian planning and plan implementation has essentially been capitalist empiricism marked by its pragmatism and piecemeal approach to economic problems. As a direct result of this, comprehensive planning has given way to the so-called planning of the mixed economy, which in effect means planning for public programmes only, being pragmatic about the private sector with plan execution being staccato and uncoordinated.

Neo-colonial capitalist planning in Nigeria, initiated and implemented by a techno-comprador bourgeoisie, has traditionally been against the interests (short- and long-term) of the weak and nascent national bourgeoisie and the masses of workers, peasants, women, professionals and the unemployed. On the contrary, the primary beneficiaries have been international finance capital and the techno-compradors themselves. The extent of the former's strength is demonstrated in the observation by a federal Permanent Secretary, Allison Ayida:

> As a matter of historical interest, both the World Bank in Washington and the United States Agency for International Development, through an appraisal mission led by the late Arnold Rivkin, were given facilities and the confidential information which enabled them to finalize their assessment of the New National Plan (1970-1974) <u>before the data were made available to the public in Nigeria</u> (Nzimiro, 1975:237. Emphasis added).

The ubiquity of foreign influence is further demonstrated in the observation by another scholar that:

> Neither the planning process nor the resultant plan shows evidence of any serious attempt to make the economic targets and policies represent national goals in more than the vaguest sense. For all practical purposes, the Federal Plan was drawn up by a limited number of expatriate economists working virtually in a vacuum...The social and political preferences of the plan, as was inevitable given this method of preparation, represent what the planners preferred or felt Nigerians ought to prefer rather than any expressed Nigerian preferences (Nzimiro, 1975:237).

The elitist nature of the planning process is underscored by James O'Connell's (1971) observation on the <u>Second National Plan</u> that it was an "exercise that took place with little consultation" and "does not bear out the concept of a mobilization and allocation of 'total developmental resources'. Moreover, it does not demand 'sacrifice' of all sections of the community – not least because most sections of the community have never even <u>heard</u> of the plan, and hardly any of those who have, know what is in it." Onimode (1977:301) makes a related point that:

> ...the collective impact of elitist conception of planning with bureaucrats and bourgeois economists alone and the grossly unequal distribution of the gains of development have been the inability of Nigeria to mobilize a mass base for planning. In spite of vitriolic and suffocating propaganda about planning from the grass roots, the truth is that the masses of Nigerian peasants, workers, market women, artisans, youths and patriotic professional people have not been participating actively in our national planning at any level.

This is essentially what differentiates a neo-colonial capitalist "plan" from a socialist or collective one.

Planning in Nigeria has, then, always had a class character. The unproductive (dependent) nature of the dominant classes as well as the country's peripheralisation in the world division of labour have combined to block all attempts (even at a nationalist or defensive radical level) at restructuring the spatial, political, economic and social unequalities that have characterised post-colonial Nigeria.

c) **Colonial and Post-colonial Development Plans, 1945-1980**

As part of the politics of decolonisation, which was aimed at consolidating the metropolitan stronghold on Nigeria, "planning" was introduced in 1945. As indicated in chapter three, this was embodied in the <u>Ten Year Plan of Development and Welfare for Nigeria</u> which envisaged a total expenditure of £110 million of which the colonial government was to contribute £46 million. As Dupe Olatunbosun (1975:51) has argued, this "was actually not a plan but a collection of projects which the colonial government felt would help it achieve its twin objectives in Nigeria, mainly to provide markets and raw materials for industries in the mother country." Not only did this initial so-called <u>Plan</u> lay the path which subsequent ones have followed ever since, it was characterised by dependence on foreign aid and external funding, development of a limited range of export (as against food) crops, the development and location of infrastructure and services without regard for spatial consequences, and an emphasis on import-reproduction industrialisation. The <u>Plan</u> did not pay any attention to the creation of linkages between sectors of the economy and the initiation and implementation were elitist.

In this initial post-war period there was also an intensification in the process of creating a dependent bourgeois class that could be relied upon to preserve the status quo after political independence. Bade Onimode notes that the role of the colonial government "was merely the classical one of providing physical and social infrastructure or overhead capital as the foundation of the economy. Private enterprise was entrusted with the major job of developing the economy. The government(s) role was merely to create favourable conditions for this through loans, subsidies, and technical assistance. As this private enterprise was essentially British, this meant mobilising Nigerian resources for British capital accumulation (Nnoli (ed), 1981:138).

The constitutional changes which granted some level of autonomy to the regions - North, East, West and Southern Cameroons as well as the Federal Territory of Lagos in 1951 - did not help matters as the regional governments introduced divergent, competitive and conflicting plans. The weak centre was unable to co-ordinate the activities of the regions particularly in light of the inter- and intra-elite class struggles which emerged following the granting of regional autonomy. So the development plans introduced between 1955-1960 were distinguished for their underfulfillment, distortions in project implementation, substantial waste, administrative inefficiency, and continued revision and extension. Colonial planning, according to Onimode, "was highly undisciplined, uncoordinated and largely irrelevant to the priority requirements of the country. Though designed for strict accountability, some planned expenditures were not increased. Some development expenditures were not planned, while some expenditures were neither developmental nor planned" (Nnoli (ed), 1981:139).

The first post-independence development plan, 1962-1968, inherited all the distortions, inequities and contradictions which the colonial state had generated. This <u>Plan</u> envisaged a total expenditure of N2.4 billion and foreign assistance was expected to contribute half of this amount. Planned total public investment was about N1.6 billion; ie. an annual average of N265 million for the 6-year life span of the <u>Plan</u>. In addition, the <u>Plan</u> aimed at achieving an average growth rate of 4 percent in the Gross Domestic Product. Transportation and communication received 26% of the total budget with electricity coming next with 15%.

While some major projects such as the establishment of a petroleum refinery, the Niger Dam, the Nigerian Security and Minting Plant, a paper mill, the sugar mill, the Niger Bridge and several trunk roads were completed in this <u>Plan</u> period, the overall design was a total failure, at least in terms of its being a "development" plan.

This failure of the first attempt at "independent" comprehensive planning was due to several factors. First, planning was conceived as a technical affair which required the "brains" of foreign experts. Thus planning offices were all centralised in the regions and in Lagos and were stacked with foreign bourgeois economists who lacked any sense of Nigeria's history and pretended not to notice glaring social contradictions. Second, planning was employed by the bourgeoisies in the regions and centre as an instrument for sustaining and advancing so-called "economic growth" and creating suitable conditions for capital accumulation through the subjugation of pre-capitalist structures to the alliance between dominant indigenous forces and foreign capital. Third, the failure of post-independence regimes, in spite of their nationalist popularity, to undertake radical changes, contributed to the exclusion of vast numbers of Nigerian people from the developmental process. Rather, planning was used as a mechanism for imposing the domination of the local elites on the masses and for "appropriating" all the privileges, arrogance, and institutions which the colonial state had introduced and enjoyed. A typical example was the marketing boards which, according to Gavin Williams (1976:133) "have never been used to protect farmers who have had to bear the full brunt of fluctuations in world prices and the additional costs of government marketing and deductions, usually between 25-70% of the price realised in the world market."

The weak federal government was unable to mediate the intense inter- and intra-class struggles within the regions. The National Economic Council, which was created in 1955 to "discuss development policies and common economic problems", consisted of the Prime Minister and the regional premiers, along with some federal and regional ministers. This Council was a consultative body. It could not meet regularly and neither could it come up with a coherent alternative to the confusion and competition which characterised regional policies. Thus:

> From its inception, it did not constitute a unified planning institution. Rather, it was no more than a congery of separate, diverse and independent regional planning units with the tacit role of rubber stamping the individual plans of the separate regional units (Odetola, 1975:140).

The Joint Planning Committee (JPC) and the Economic Planning Unit, which were established to aid the planning process, did not either eliminate the irreconcilable objectives of the regions or attempt to broaden participation in plan formulation and execution.

d) Planning in a Post-War, Post-OPEC Context

The <u>First Plan</u> was disrupted by the outbreak of the Civil War in 1966. This event forced a <u>Plan</u> "holiday" on the country until the end of hostilities in 1970. The war itself, among other things, demonstrated very clearly the elusiveness of hegemony within the social formation, the intensity of intra-class struggles, the interests of imperialist countries in ensuring the break up of Nigeria and, finally, the hollowness of the institutions, structures and processes which the British had left behind.

The end of the war witnessed a dramatic change in power relations between the federal government and the twelve states which had been created out of the four regions in 1967. The size of the federally controlled army had increased to 250,000. The defeat of "Biafra" had demonstrated the might of the centre, the break up of the regions created antagonisms and competition between the states, and most regional "power elites" now focused their attention on the centre. Another very important change that followed at the end of the war was the growing dependence of the states on the federal government for revenues. As agriculture began to contribute less to national revenues and exports (see Chapter Two), oil began to emerge as almost the sole export and source of foreign exchange earnings. In addition, the command-top-down-character of the military streamlined decision-making and eliminated regional competition over fundamental issues already decided by the Federal government. By 1974, with increasing revenues from oil, all the states had become dependent on the Federal government for revenues to finance projects and to mediate class contradictions and struggles. While oil wealth made the central state relatively financially autonomous internally and less dependent on foreign aid, it also generated severe contradictions and heightened existing conflicts and corruption which pre-empted all efforts at imposing bourgeois hegemony on the society at large (see next chapter).

During the war, General Yakabu 'Jack' Gowon had declared to the capitalist West, which had abandoned Nigeria, that the country's future depended on its ability to remain within the capitalist world. After the war, developmental policies and programmes were initiated to ensure that capital accumulation in the private sector and the presence of foreign capital in the commanding heights of the economy were revived, rationalised, formalised and legalised. In terms of planning institutions and structures, while there were physical changes which reflected the nature of military rule, the capitalistic ideological underpinnings of planning methodology remained intact.

Bourgeois ideology expressed in the <u>Second National</u>

Development Plan was hinged upon so-called "five principles", none of which were really achieved:

  i) united, strong and self-reliant nation;
 ii) great and dynamic economy;
iii) just and egalitarian society;
 iv) land of bright and full opportunities; and
  v) free and democratic society.

Though the Plan had a commencement date of 1 April 1970, General Gowon on 1 October (Independence Day) 1970 had declared a nine-point programme which was to pave the way for a return to civilian rule. These points were i) the reorganisation of the Armed Forces; ii) the implementation of the national plan; iii) the eradication of corruption in the national life; iv) the settlement of the question of the creation of more states; v) the preparation and adoption of a new constitution; vi) the introduction of a new revenue allocation formula; vii) the conducting of a national population census; viii) the organisation of genuinely national political parties, and ix) the organisation of elections and installation of popularly elected governments in the states and at the centre.

As is obvious, the Second Plan (1970-74) served only to complement this nine-point programme. By 1975, when Gowon was overthrown, Nigeria was far from achieving the objectives of either the Plan or the programme. National reconstruction and integration had not been achieved and in spite of the oil boom the majority of Nigerians were significantly worse off than before the Plan.

This Second Plan proposed public investment spending of N2 billion over four years with external assistance to be less than twenty per cent. The total was later raised to N3.27 billion or N818 million per annum. But the actual amount spent in the Plan period amounted to N5.5 billion. Once again, transportation took the lead in allocations with 24% of the total public sector programme and 30% of the federal government's programme. For the twelve states, education was the largest single sector - 19% - and the second largest for the public sector all together - 14%. This was followed by agriculture 11%; defence and security 9%; industry 8%; and administration 5%. The Plan witnessed huge underspendings. Funds were divested to 'white elephant' and wasteful projects. The actual expenditure turned out as follows: transportation 23%; education 11%; agriculture 8%; defence and security witnessed an increase 10%; industry 4%; and administration, which also witnessed an increase, 11% (Kirk-Greene & Rimmer, 1981:142).

As mentioned earlier the structure of planning and decision-making changed under the military in the 1970s. The main politico-economic bodies were: The Supreme Military Council (SMC), Federal Executive Council (FEC), Joint Planning Board (JPB), National Economic Advisory Committee (NEAC), Central Planning Office (CPO) in the Federal Ministry of Economic Development and Reconstruction (the 'Reconstruction' was removed after the Second Plan presumably because the power elites assumed that the task of post-civil war reconstruction had been accomplished!); and the State Planning Offices.

The Second Plan claimed in its ideological preamble to be comprehensive and integrated:

> The Plan sets out clearly the national objectives and priorities of post-war Nigeria. It also outlines the general policy measures and programmes of action which flow from the objectives as well as the agreed national scale of priorities...The Second National Development Plan has to be implemented by the governments as well as the people of this country, all public sector institutions as well as the private sector and individual initiatives will be involved in the execution of the Plan in one way or the other. Much sacrifice will be demanded of all sections of the community. The reward lies in the noble national economy which is expected to emerge half-way through the Plan period and from the years to the civil war. All Nigerians must be made to feel part of, and share from the resultant bouyant economy...National planning should be aimed at the transformation of the whole society, and must be directed at the power centres of economic and power decisions. The Plan views the whole economy as one interdependent unit, growing through time in response to a set of mutually consistent policies and programmes (pp. 5, 31 and 39).

Though the above statement appears to be comprehensive and to create room for popular participation, the majority of those being called upon to aid in plan implementation had nothing to do with its formulation. The contradictions inherent in the neo-colonial economy which have heightened corruption, institutional inefficiency and decay, the neglect of rural areas, misuse of state power, and so on, have been responsible for the wide gap between well-worded development plans and characteristic confusion evident on implementation.

While the establishment of i) the Sapele and Ijore salt refineries, ii) the Peugeot assembly plant in Kaduna, iii) the Volkswagen assembly plant in Lagos, iv) the super-phosphate fertilizer plant in Kaduna, v) the construction of trunk roads, vi) increase in school enrollment – primary enrollment increased from 35 million in 1970 to 45 million in 1973, secondary, from 343,000 in 1971 to 649,000 in 1974 and university from 14,500 in 1971 to 25,000 in 1974 – and so on have been identified as major achievements, once again as far as "Reconstruction" and "Development" go, the <u>Plan</u> was a failure.

The excessive concentration of power at the centre did not encourage mass mobilisation. The emphasis on GDP led to "growth without development". The over-dependence on oil wealth, joint ventures with foreign partners, and foreign technical advice led to the creation of a "mono-culture" economy, dependence on foreign capital and Western markets, and crisis in the rural agricultural sectors of the economy (see previous chapter). Attempts at income distribution and indigenisation failed woefully due to corruption within the ranks of the bourgeoisie and the strength of foreign capital in the economy.

In a very effective critique of the institutions and structures of planning in this period, T.O. Odetola (1975:145) notes contradictions between the Central and State Planning Offices and the supremacy of the centre:

> Such planners or state governments cannot even be sure that these projects will go through the different processes towards final approval. Since not only do they depend on the Federal government for capital funding, the new process of planning must ensure that these state projects are capable of being integrated into a final national plan. Thus, while decision at state level represents a source of plan projects, it is a low level of decision since it can be thrown out or modified or completely altered. The power of the regions during civilian democratic era to initiate, follow through, control and execute their own plans almost independently of and sometimes in spite of Federal government plans, stands in bold relief to the palid and almost ingratiating dependence of the states on the present Federal government.

James O'Connell (1971:52) equally addressed some of the weaknesses of the <u>Plan</u> when he argued that "There is a good deal of insensitivity, laziness, bullying and corruption which alienate people from the state generally. It would take a more popular as well as a more competent public service to devise and implement a more comprehensive form of planning than Nigeria has enjoyed in the last decade."

To demonstrate its elitist nature and the hypocrisy involved in the numerous calls for popular involvement in <u>Plan</u> implementation, the Federal government declared in 1974 that "the planning exercise had become increasingly technical and could no longer be left to general administrators who are more concerned with broad matters of policy" (Odetola, 1975:52). In spite of this claim, the <u>Second Plan</u>, like those before and after it, was more of a "list of all things that everyone would like to have done or that everyone believes ought to be done. Specification of the things of strategic importance is lost" in the process (O'Connell, 1971:52).

The policies implemented in the name of planning were, directly or otherwise, aimed at stabilising the process of economic growth in order to encourage the private sector. Limited attacks on foreign domination such as in the indigenisation decrees only extended the integration of Nigeria into world capitalism. Increasing state participation in the oil industry on which the state was absolutely dependent for revenues did not challenge the domination of foreign capital in terms of technology, manpower, capital, information, and the world oil market. However, in "the growth process, wealth and economic power get concentrated in the hands of the powerful interests in the private sector. The state becomes a pipe drawing resources from the masses and passing them to capitalist interests" (Oni, 1975:89). This is made easier by the academic mysticism which has accompanied planning and the narrow base of plan initiation. In a critique of the CPO, Odetola (1975:146) wrote:

> How broad is the base of participation at this crucial state? The CPO (Central Planning Office) seeks only professional advice from which it prepares a draft for the plan. The CPO, after identifying areas that need attention and emphasis, requests papers from non-governmental actors (for instance, intellectuals) on such areas. <u>These non-governmental actors are not told what the framework, goal or rubric within which they will be writing is.</u> They do know in what other areas advisory papers have been requested and consequently do not have a coherent picture of the development. Thus, input from non-governmental actors are fed in only in an advisory capacity and piecemeal in the form of commissioned papers, and only at a secondary not primary level of decision making. However, since this draft plan is the working basis for the decision-making of all other units in the structure, it can be concluded that the decision-making does not have a broad enough base.

e) The Military's Legacy of Mixed Economy: Third Plan

The <u>Third Plan, 1975-80</u>, was the last initiated during the first military period. At the time it was also the most ambitious development plan ever initiated in Nigeria, all of which had claimed to be "comprehensive". The <u>Third Plan</u> involved an expenditure programme of N30 billion, later increased to N42 billion of which the Federal and state governments were to account for N20 billion, while the private sector was to account for N10 billion. The plan broadly claimed that its goal was the acceleration of economic growth and the improvement of living standards for all; specifically, a growth rate in real terms of 9.5% per annum was envisaged, per capita income in real terms was anticipated to increase by 30% between 1975 and 1980 from N205 to N274, private consumption was expected to rise in real terms by 10.5% per annum, and oil exports on which the plan was dependent were expected to increase in value from N6,458 million in 1974-5 to N10,633 million in 1979-80; revenue from non-oil sources was expected to increase from just N304 million to N396 million within the same period. The planners also anticipated a significant change in the structure of imports as capital and intermediate goods were expected to account for 70% of the total and consumer goods just 20%. Imports were projected to increase in value from N1,637m in 1974/75 to N7,085m in 1979/80. Education was expected to grow at a 22% rate per annum, electricity and water supply — 21%, building and construction — 20%, health — 20%, manufacturing — 18%, mining and quarrying — 15%, distribution 11.3% and agriculture — 5%.

While the five basic principles of the Second Plan noted in the previous section were retained, the Third Plan specifically geared itself to the attainment of i) an increase in GNP per capita, ii) improved income distribution, iii) more employment, iv) diversification of the economy, v) increase in the supply of intermediate and high level manpower, vi) balanced development and vii) indigenisation of economic programmes (Nnoli (ed), 1981).

Under this Third Plan, the Federal government initiated Universal Free Primary Education (UPE) (the "Free" was subsequently dropped when the programme ran into technical, administrative and financial problems) in 1976; enrollment was expected to rise to 11.5 million by the end of the plan period. The universities of Jos, Calabar, Maiduguri and Sokoto were founded, hundreds of secondary schools established, the iron and steel project was pursued with vigor, the Warri and Kaduna petroleum refineries were constructed, and teaching hospitals, liquified natural gas projects and new berths at Warri, Calabar an Port Harcourt were also built.

By the time the Fourth National Development Plan, 1980-85, was launched by the new civilian regime, the bureaucrats and planners had pronounced the Third Plan as "successful". Certainly some specific achievements were made. But it is essential to weigh these against the conditions — political and economic — and the opportunities which the government had wasted. Shehu Shagari in introducing the Fourth Plan to the National Assembly in January 1981 eulogised the achievements of the Third Plan:

The Third National Development Plan was launched against a background of rapidly rising price and production of crude oil. Our oil production was projected to rise from 2.3M barrels per day at the beginning of the Plan to about 3.0 M barrels per day by the end of the plan period. This projection under the circumstances then prevailing justified optimism in the potentiality of public sector investment. This was what was responsible for the upward revision of the public sector side of the Third Plan. As it turned out the <u>dream</u> did not come true. It was probably a case of over-optimistic optimism.

The retiring military regime had at its disposal billions of Naira from oil exports. Over-dependence on an oil industry and market over which it had no control meant that minor fluctuations in the oil market created far-reaching problems within the economy. The contradictions generated by the capitalist orientation of the <u>Plan,</u> the expenditure on ostentatious and prestige projects and the waste in plan implementation, intensified class struggles in Nigeria. Attempts to bribe workers through the 1975 Udoji Awards failed woefully. As Anthony Kirk-Green and Douglas Rimmer (1981:146) noted:

> It is perhaps now part of folk-memory that the inflation of 1975 resulted from the Udoji wage awards, but the fundamental cause was rather the attempts of the Nigerian governments to buy more than the economy was capable of supplying, given its inflexible productive structure, shortages of technical skills and executive capacity, and limited physical ability to import and distribute foreign products.

With increasing dependence on oil wealth, the country was gradually converted into a consumerist import economy. The cliché at the time was that Nigeria could "import all importables". With inflation reaching 45% by 1977, increasing unemployment and the rural areas subjected to a heavy capitalist onslaught from the state and international capital, the <u>Plan</u> only attempted to lubricate the process of instituting bourgeois hegemony through oil wealth. Projects were removed from or added to it with little or no regard for the consequences or for consistency as Onimode (Nnoli (ed) 1981:145) has lamented:

> The patent lack of plan discipline is one of the greatest similarities between colonial and neo-colonial capitalist planning. Though plan projects acquired priorities since 1962, these are invariably ignored by the bureaucratic bourgeoisie in a blatant demonstration of the superiority

of its selfish class interests over avowed national objectives and in constant reflection of the mounting contradictions of class struggles and neo-colonial underdevelopment in the country. To take most recent examples, FESTAC, which cost hundreds of millions of Naira, is nowhere in any plan document. The Universal Primary Education (UPE) programme, which is the most expensive educational programme in the entire history of the country, was not in the Second Plan, its implementation started during that Plan though its critical phase commenced during the Third Plan.

Under the Third Plan, agriculture witnessed a significant set-back. All the states as well as the Federal government significantly reduced allocations to a sector which still provided employment for over 70% of the population. Yet while the mismanagement of the oil economy and the over-extension of the country's external responsibilities were generating problems internally, foreign firms flowed into the country to assemble or distribute foreign produced goods. They all reported huge profits.

Like other plans before it, the Third Plan was initiated and formulated in great secrecy, at least to Nigerians. The style of the Second Plan was that as far as procedure was concerned, "no general public discussions preceded the planning stage. No study groups were set up to investigate any aspect of the country's life and advise planners accordingly. The only known form of discussion that took place was the highly restricted Ibadan Conference," (Nwannene, 1973:121). This exclusivism equally applied to the Third Plan. The allocation and spending of the billions of Naira involved were left in the hands of a few bureaucrats and members of the bourgeois class. Omougbe Nwanwene (1973:123) draws some crucial conclusions from his critique of the Second Plan which apply equally to the Third:

> Having failed completely to democratise the method and machinery of producing the development plan, the Nigerian governments have gone on to list the plan's principal objectives which they think will make the people accept the plan as their own...Since the plan is essentially an economic document, it is impossible to see how it can produce a democratic society. Since Nigeria is studded with thousands of natural and spiritual rulers whose control over their subjects and flocks is still more meaningful than that of a distant Federal and state governments and since the Nigerian society is made up of an amazing variety of classes and sub-classes, it is unimaginable to see how, short of a total revolution in which to use the delicate and graphic phrase of a French

philosopher, the entrails of the last priest are used to strangle the last nobleman, the plan or even a series of plans can produce an egalitarian society.

The <u>Third Plan</u>, like those before and after it, avoided the real issues. Instead of a national ideology aimed at mobilising and educating the masses, the document and the bureaucrats emphasised "attitude to work". Instead of addressing Nigeria's peripheral role and location in the international division of labour and the domination of the economy by foreign capital, the <u>Plan</u> emphasised the "indigenisation" of unequal exchange, exploitation and mis-used state power. Rather than lay a popular basis for "cultural liberation" firmly rooted in the economic, political and social independence of Nigeria, the Nigerian bourgeoisie sponsored international cultural jamborees like FESTAC. And instead of promoting unity and self-reliance, the bourgeoisie i) exploited religious, ethnic and regional differences and ii) emphasised joint ventures with vertically-integrated transnational corporations which in turn cashed in on the oil bonanza.

Other than the failure of the indigenization decrees (subsequently revised by new civilian and military regimes), through the use of Nigerians as fronts and the dispersal of shares among many indigenes so that foreign capital could retain control (Biersteker, 1978), the state continued to emphasise that the goal was not nationalisation. Rather, it claimed, its intention was to encourage foreign capital to move into the strategic or commanding heights of the economy such as mining. In addition, as Ankie Hoogvelt (1980:269) points out, since indigenisation, "there has been a negative effect on the industrial labour absorption rate...(and) negligible increase of job availability in industry as compared with its capital expansion since indigenisation."

In addition to the fact that foreign enterprises took advantage of simplified naturalisation laws and automated production processes in order to qualify for exemption under the indigenisation decrees, the latter expanded the ranks of the bourgeoisie in Nigeria; expansion, not in the sense that the bourgeoisie moved into productive sectors, but rather, that it entered into joint ventures, won rights to distributorships and realised other minor roles in the economy. These dynamics did not alter the neo-colonial and dependent nature of the economy, with its urban bias.

While it is true that the <u>Third Plan</u> encouraged increased school enrollment, one can <u>raise</u> several points against the context and content of educational policies and programmes in the country. At a time when its technological programme was in total confusion and students in polytechnics were boycotting classes, Nigeria installed a multi-million Naira project of airlifting Nigerian youths to virtually every country in the world to acquire "technical expertise" of a middle-level range. No attempts were made to restructure the neo-colonial "top-down" decision-making structures of schools and universities; research and development beyond concern for the few poorly-staffed research institutes did not feature in the Plan; and the established content of school curriculum remained intact. The net result was that education in Nigeria since the colonial period has been for domination and exploitation not for liberation, mobilisation and service. School children spend years studying North American and West European history and geography while only a few months are devoted to Nigeria's political economy.

Finally, the Third Plan hardly lived up to general expectations. As far as the masses of Nigeria were concerned, it was a complete failure. The economy received numerous Western trade missions, experienced a heavy oil binge, strengthened its defence and voice in external affairs, and contracted out virtually every economic and social activity. In the light of widespread corruption, inefficiency, apathy and decay, efforts to rationalise and mediate contradictions through the long-abandoned Operation Feed the Nation (OFN), the National Youth Service Corps (NYSC), sending soldiers to schools to maintain discipline, introducing a new national anthem and national honours and creating of a new federal capital to mention a few, only increased tensions, contradictions and social violence.

To take one example: in 1977, General Olusegun Obasanjo was so enraged by the clear evidence of confusion, drift and violence in the country that he lamented in his popular Jaji speech, entitled "Our Nation Lacks Discipline", that the countrywas being run by "trading outpost agents" who dominated the intellectual, technical, commercial and professional sectors of the economy. Though, Obasanjo did not provide an alternative to this bankrupt system, it was evident to all that the confusion and drift were the precipitates of a mismanaged economy, of the influence of profit- and hegemony-seeking transnational corporations, and of intra-class struggles within the ranks of the bourgeoisie.

Nowhere was the indiscipline more evident than within the army. Other than the detention of opposition forces, the raids on newspaper houses, the massacre of defenceless students, the expulsion of progressive lecturers from universities and its rabid corruption, the military often went on open rampages during which they destroyed civilian lives and property.

Under the Third Plan, then, the economy as well as the policy reached a crisis point, if not a conjuncture. The decline in oil revenues due to the world market situation forced a cutback in public spending. Projects were abandoned or left floating and fees were reintroduced into the universities indirectly through a 300% increase in boarding fees. Loans were raised internally and externally by the government and propaganda on the impending crisis was initiated to prepare the public for the crash. Inspite of all this, the bourgeoisie continued to sign massive contracts with foreign firms, while those indigenes who had succeeded in cornering some "oil naira" hurriedly siphoned their loot into foreign banks. Thus, in 1975, G. Prono an Italian firm, got a N185 million agreement to build an annex to the Federal Palace Hotel in Lagos. 1977 was the "Year of Contracts". Dumez, a French construction company won federal contracts of N107 million for the construction of the Okene-Kaduna road and N96 million for the Shagamu-Benin road. A N10 million pact for transformers was signed in December 1977; the Ondo State government awarded a N5.8 million contract to Aihaji W.O. Lawal, and N3.1 million to Metal-Wood Engineering; a N400 million contract was signed between the Federal government and a German company for supplies to the second iron and steel complex; a N734.3 million contract was signed for telephone switching; N810.9 million for transmission; N742.5 million on external lines plant; N91.4 million on subscribers instruments; and N30 million on power plants.

This is just a tip of the contract "iceberg" which all the governments (state and Federal) embarked upon to enable the technocrats, compradors and petty-bourgeoisie to collect their 10-25% commissions. The simple fact that most of these contracts went to foreign firms whose final products were of doubtful quality or ability, demonstrates the inability of the state to employ planning as a tool for creating a <u>productive</u> and dynamic bourgeoisie. The unproductiveness and inefficiency of the bourgeoisie is demonstrated in the shamelessness with which it handed national parastatals and institutions to foreign firms and managers, even in the pre-privatisation era.

In light of these facts and crises, one tends to understand why Usman Zahradeen, in frustration, advocated the following verse in place of the Nigerian anthem:

> Nigeria we hail thee,
> Where no tap flows,
> Where no light burns,
> No telephone rings,
> No traffic light works,
> No train leaves on time,
> No airplane arrives on schedule,
> Where no student stays in class,
> No official stays on seat,
> Where no drinks are available,
> No tea, no coffee on the
> shelves (Nnoli (ed), 1981:72).

The <u>Third Plan</u> had boasted that emphasis would be placed on "Those sectors which directly affect the welfare of the ordinary citizen, these include housing, health facilities, water supplies, rural electrification and community development. The aim is that by the end of the plan period every Nigerian should experience a definite improvement in overall welfare" (p. 10). By the end of the <u>Plan</u> period, however, 95% of Nigerians had not experienced any improvement. In fact as the 1981 ILO study argued, most Nigerians were poorer by the end of the <u>Plan</u> period. Worsening conditions in the rural areas due to the neglect of agriculture, and in the urban areas due to the concentration of amenities (e.g. the bourgeoisie's "government reservation areas" – (GRAs) – combined to depress the mental and psychological condition of most Nigerians. As Chinwezu notes:

> The state of the nation's physical and mental health is simply bad. Life expectancy is 37 years. One doctor announced long ago that 800,000 Nigerians are mentally sick and 8 million need one form of mental check up or other. Other published estimates put the figures much higher. If a conservative estimate is anywhere near right, that means that 10 per cent of Nigerians need to have their heads examined, and 1 per cent are outright mad (<u>South</u>, February 1982:65).

f) Post-Military and Post-Boom Planning: the fourth period

The <u>Fourth Plan, 1981-85</u> came a year late in order to allow the new civilian administration time to prepare. According to Shehu Shagari in his National Assembly address, it was "geared towards strengthening the foundations already laid by the earlier Plans. It was geared towards removing known constraints to the growth and modernisation of our nation and our national economy." However, the specific objectives of the <u>Plan</u> included i) the achievement of increased real income for all Nigerians, ii) a more even and equitable distribution of income; iii) increase in the supply of skilled manpower, iv) priority to agricultural production and processing, v) provision of food for the large and growing population, vi) production of adequate raw materials for industries, vii) national self-reliance, viii) priority status to housing, education and manpower development, and ix) priority status to power generation and supply, water supply and telecommunication, health care, industrial development, transportation – rail, land and water. According to G.P.O. Chikelu (1985), this <u>Plan</u> sought to relate the self-reliance goals of the <u>Lagos Plan of Action</u> to the specificities of the Nigerian situation.

It thus appeared that the civilian regime was determined to grant "priority status" to all sectors of the economy simultaneously! This determination was anchored on the huge rents being collected from the oil sector when the Plan was being conceived, which the regime had hoped would not only lubricate expenditure but also enable it to paper-over the growing discontent and contradictions in the society. As the new President noted in his January 1981 introduction:

> The Fourth Plan is being launched at a time when the country's production of crude oil, which is the main source of government revenue and foreign exchange earnings, has virtually stabilised. A basic strategy of the Fourth Plan would therefore be the promotion of optimal utilisation of resources. Oil is a wasting asset. The resources generated from this sector must therefore be used to promote all-round expansion in the productive capacity of the economy so as to ensure self-sustaining growth in the shortest possible time. This calls for a high degree of cost-consciousness by all government functionaries involved in the conception, design and in the execution of projects. For the avoidance of doubt, there will be no room in the Plan for grandiose or prestige projects such as we have witnessed in our recent past. Rather, emphasis will be placed on simple, functional designs especially with respect to standard amenities such as schools, hosptials, and residential building. Government agencies will be encouraged, where appropriate, to develop internal machinery for the execution of projects.

The Plan itself envisaged a total investment expenditure of N82 billion. Of this total, N70.5 billion was to be accounted for by the various governments and their agencies, with the private sector responsible for the N11.5 billion balance. The governments involved were all expected to generate budget surpluses totalling N54 billion over the 1981-85 Plan period. The federal government expected planned investment to generate an overall growth rate of 7% per annum in real terms and, with this, it concluded that the average citizen (whatever this means) over the Plan period should experience "a significant increase in the standard of living."

In terms of specific allocations, agriculture, which was expected to grow at an annual rate of 4%, received 13 per cent of the total capital investment of all governments. The emphases were to be on food production and on "direct assistance to small farmers in the form of extension services, improved seeds, fertilisers, credits, tractors and implements, grains stores and land clearance...provision of access needs to the farms to improve distribution of farm output and the provision of irrigation facilities through the eleven existing River Basin Development Authorities". In addition to these, the government hoped to go into direct production in the agricultural sector, to encourage foreign partners and Nigerians to invest in agriculture.

Manufacturing was expected to grow at an annual rate of 15 per cent over the period, while specific programmes to be executed included: iron and steel, liquified natural gas, integrated sugar, cement, nitrogenous fertiliser, petrochemicals, and pulp and paper. Education received N20 billion and seven new universities of technology were to be established. An open university system was to be introduced and expansion of existing Federal Government Colleges was to be undertaken. Housing was allocated N2.7 billion; 400,000 units of accommodation were expected to be provided and the Federal Capital Territory received N2.5 billion with 13,000 housing units to be completed.

Without doubt this was a very ambitious programme at a time when the new civilian governments at all levels were attempting to get established, reduce the powers of incumbent bureaucrats particularly of permanent secretaries, dismantle the "top-down" or "command" pattern of administration and decision-making employed by the military, reconcile political party differences, compensate party supporters and candidates who lost their bid for offices, and attempt to implement the diverse and often conflicting programmes of the five political parties.

Other than the continuing problems of implementation and infrastructure, which always hamper the success of development plans through such gigantic spending programmes this one was basically flawed because it tied Nigeria's prosperity almost completely to the vagaries of the international oil market. This contrasts sharply with Shagari's "optimistic optimism" that oil production and revenues had virtually stabilised. Thus, the subsequent glut on the world oil market generated a severe liquidity crisis for the very naive and ambitious <u>Plan</u>. It would be wrong however, to attribute the crisis of the <u>Fourth Plan</u> to the decline in oil revenues alone. Yet the decline did mean that while crude oil production was about 2.1 million barrels per day in January 1981, by July it had declined to 770,000 bpd; a drop of over 63 per cent. Exports declined accordingly as did revenues which fell by N4,350 million in 1981 or 30 per cent of the expected total. Rather, the failure of this latest <u>Plan</u> to rectify the myriad mistakes of the three previous ones intensified the crisis.

While the Joint Planning Board (consisting of Permanent Secretaries of Ministries of Economic Development in all states, and the Ministers and State Commissioners responsible for Economic Planning), the National Economic Council chaired by the Vice-President, the Nigerian Association of Chambers of

Commerce, Industries, Mines and Agriculture, and the Manufacturers Association of Nigeria were all involved in the initiation and formulation of the Fourth Plan, 90 per cent of the working people of Nigeria were effectively barred from making inputs. The Nigeria Labour Congress, which consists of 43 industrial unions, professional market women's associations, peasant organisations and co-operatives, student union organisations and so on as not consulted. In fact, no part of the Plan was subjected to public debate. Thus, the established elitist and bourgeois content of the planning process remained intact. While education received only N2.0 billion and housing for all Nigerians received just N2.7 billion, the Federal Capital Territory alone received N2.5 billion. The relative concern for projects that would directly satisfy the tastes and political aspirations of the bourgeoisie influenced the pattern of allocation. Meanwhile, BHN were still neglected.

Under the Fourth Plan, the Nigerian economy deteriorated to its worst post-civil war situation. Rising levels of unemployment, rural-urban migration, inflation, armed robbery, waste, social violence, corruption, and intra- and inter-class struggles, all accompanied by the arrogance of power, drift and carelessness of the ruling class, combined to disrupt the strategies initiated to consolidate the private accumulative base of the bourgeoisie.

As Karin Barber (1980:437) has noted: "The theme of petro-naira millionaires has become more prominent since the return to civil rule in October 1979, for obvious reasons. Politicians running for office have 'to buy' the electorate; having got in, they have to recoup their losses from public funds – by one method or another – and they have also to continue to spend to ensure that they will stay in office after the next election. Thus oil fortunes are much more publicly in evidence." Barber listed some allegations and counter-allegations published by local newspapers, some of them with overt party affiliations. The evidence of corruption which circulated within the ranks of the bourgeoisie at the time included: officials of the Federal government involved in hemp-smuggling using diplomatic bags; 13 members of the ruling party – the NPN – donating N5 million to party political funds in a one-hour ceremony, an act denounced by other state governors (not from NPN states) as a "shameless display of illgotten wealth"; a high-ranking Nigerian leaving f500,000 in a London taxi, another giving f3 million to an English lady and so on; the list is endless and was extended during the Buhari/Babangida enquiries. And such monies were either public funds diverted into private pockets or "commissions" from inflated contracts.

Under the lacklustre NPN government which initiated the Fourth Plan, the country and the Plan moved in opposite directions. Food imports increased tremendously bringing Nigeria into an even more dependent position on Western, especially American, farmers. At the time the civilian government came to power in 1979, food imports alone were N818 million; by 1981, they had increased to N1.86 billion (January-September). External reserves showed that Nigeria often spent more than it received. Several "austerity measures" as well as "scapegoatism" were introduced to deal with this crisis, which culminated with the coup on new year's eve, 1984.

While the <u>Fourth Plan</u> has yet to run its course, the current trend does not demonstrate that its achievements would in fact mean a better life for the majority. As usual the government can mention expressways, universities, airports and offices constructed and billions spent on each sector. It cannot, however, claim that these expenditures affect the common person positively in either the short- or long-term.

g) Conclusions: continuity and change in Nigeria's planning policies and practices

Planning exercises in Nigeria since 1945 have failed woefully in terms of meeting the Basic Human Needs of the majority. Though, with time, the decision-making processes have become more elaborate, the institutions more sophisticated and the wording of documents more elegant, the fundamental neo-colonial, capitalist and elitist underpinnings have remained constant. The whole question of conceiving planning as a holistic activity within a social context has been completely ignored. Rather, the Nigerian bourgeoisie has employed planning as a process for allocating public funds to its fractions/factions in the states, parastatals and other official institutions; sponsoring accumulation in the private sector through contracts, joint ventures and all forms of assistance; trying to rationalise the presence and participation of foreign capital in the economy; and, finally, attempting to introduce values and ideologies which it hopes would stabilise capitalist accumulation and exploitation processes.

The bourgeoisie has not been too successful in this bid. While class divisions appear to be becoming more crystalised, in other respects they are becoming more confusing. The continued ability of bureaucrats to collect commissions which they re-invest in other sectors of the economy creates problems for clear analysis. The fractional struggle between the technocratic compradors and the rapidly gorwing <u>national</u> bourgeoisie is yet to take critical dimensions. Increasingly some members of the dominant class are no longer interested in distributorships and commissions. Even if the dynamics of accumulation and struggles are to be deepened or altered, the current process of "planning for underdevelopment" which only reproduces Nigeria's peripheralisation in world capitalism must be altered. There is no reason to expect this to occur in the near future in spite of the oil crisis and the cash flow problems it has created for the state.

On the contrary, we can see a possible march towards corporatism (Shaw & Ihonvbere, 1987) even fascism in order to convince the capitalist powers and finance capital that Nigeria can "do it" i.e. keep order, guarantee "stability", protect foreign investment and keep the country "safe for democracy". Evidence of detention without trial, proscription of trade unions, the prevention of certain persons from trade union activities, the non-registration of "militant" political parties, the legislation of numerous anti-labour acts, the use of the police and army on behalf of capital, the massacre of students, peasants and the unemployed, the expulsion of "illegal aliens", and the deportation of Nigerians are just a few examples of concrete steps taken in the march towards corporatism and fascism. They are also manifestations of the inability to mediate effectively class contradictions, rationalise capitalist accumulation and initiate an acceptable ideology.

Segun Osoba (1980:18) commenting on the conceptual and ideological aspects of development planning in Nigeria has argued that:

> The first colonial development plan in Nigeria (1946-56) was predicated on a number of mythical notions which have become part and parcel of the conventional wisdom in development planning in contemporary Nigeria. The first of these notions was that of 'philanthropic imperialism' which was subtly suggested by the formula prescribed for the capital financing of the plan...The logical conclusion intended by the British colonial authorities from the stated 'financial implications of the ten-year plan' was that the development of Nigeria was bound to depend, critically, not so much on indigenous Nigerian enterprise or resources as on the initiative of, and generous donations by, British and other foreign philanthropists.

Furthermore, Osoba (1980:18) notes:

> ...the most dangerous notion of development planning inaugurated by the British in 1946 and which has persisted most stubbornly in the thinking and policy actions of planners in Nigeria is that planning as an exercise in spending large sums of money on a number of separate and unrelated projects. This notion of development planning was predicated on the naive optimism that this kind of spending spree would generate growth and development in

the various sectors of the Nigerian society as "to evaluate the conditions of life of its people so that their output might be greater and their economy correspondingly improved.

Since political independence in 1960, there has not been a single recorded instance where an official or department has been publicly censured or drastically reorganised due to misuse of allocations. The only basis on which efficiency and effectiveness have been measured is the ability to spend allocations completely. This point is underscored in an observation by Osoba (1980:19)

> ...all the subsequent development plans...are only different from the 1946-56 plan in degree and scale rather than kind. They were all conceived and formulated in the intellectual and ideological tradition of confusing development planning with merely spending increasingly huge sums of money, both locally raised and borrowed from abroad, on big projects which are neither conceptually or functionally related and which, in spite of advertised official rhetoric, cannot perceptibly improve the quality of life of the Nigerian masses.

Unfortunately, Nigerian social science like successive political regimes has historically done a lot of injustice to the cause of planning and consciousness-raising. This can be deduced from the fact that the majority of the intellectuals, having gotten their education from Western bourgeois institutions have only come back to "join the rat race" (see Chapter Seven). However, the continued use of long-discarded concepts and methodologies, the continued refusal to acknowledge the growing class divisions and contradictions in society, the continued mystification of planning processes and inability to present education as a liberating force, have combined to contribute to the backwardness of the country. Most of the planners, bureaucrats and so on are products of the neo-colonial educational system.

Despite its resources, Nigeria does not have a reliable census figure or data on rural-urban migration, inflation, cost of living, unemployment and other basic indicators. Its borders are virtually unprotected, and migrants regularly flock in from neighbouring countries unregulated. Under such circumstances, the planners can only plan "without facts" as Wolfgang Stopler the originator of early Plans has put it. This creates room for manipulations, guesswork and generalisations, as no concrete or definitive plans can be made for any sector of society. Osoba (1980:20) in relation to this point notes:

Saddled with this baggage of colonially derived concepts and values on development, successive governments and their advisers among professional economists and other social scientists have come to find themselves in a most vulnerable situation whereby their ideas and projects on national development have yielded no palpable results and yet they are totally incapable of forging new ones...
This lack of creativity is rooted in the academic tradition of bourgeois western science which is dominant in our university institutions, acculturates our social scientists to explain and deal with social reality, including the issue of development, with the theoretical and value of equipment of those who are responsible for our underdevelopment.

It is clear, therefore, that what has been going on in Nigeria since 1945 can hardly be called either <u>planning</u> or <u>development</u>. The net result of the efforts at building capitalism and establishing a workable relationship between international and domestic capital has been the formulation of vague and bogus objectives which no one takes seriously. This lack of seriousness is evident in how far the formulators of the various plans move away from original objectives and how each new plan laments the failure of the preceeding one.
Experiences from all over the Third World have demonstrated the impracticality of any attempt to plan a neo-colonial capitalist economy effectively. No power-elite, no matter how broad its formal power may be, can really plan what it does not control. Oni and Onimode (1975:88) have noted that "a neo-colonial capitalist plan expresses and advances the interests of foreign monopoly capital and their domestic agents among the ruling class at the expense of the masses. This is why planning of this type typically lends itself to manipulation by the privileged classes for selfish capital accumulation. Arising from the above feature is that neo-colonial capitalist planning means planning what the planner and the people do not control." Thus the starting point, even for a bourgeoisie interested in securing its own future through a reliable basis for class reproduction and political power, would have been the nationalisation of the commanding heights of the economy, an intensive programme of technological innovation, the encouragement of inter-sectoral linkages, and massive investment and re-investment internally. The Nigerian bourgeoisie has realised the exact opposite of all these characteristics. It has discouraged science and technology through the politicisation of technologically-innovative processes, failure to encourage scientists, and misguided belief that the future of Nigeria's technology would ultimately be determined by the generosity of Western countries and corporations. Of course, the indigenous bourgeoisie has

carted off all its profits and loot to foreign banks in the West where metropolitan bourgeoises use them to strengthen their productive capacities.

On nationalisation, the dominant faction has historically been hostile to the idea and to the nationalist faction which had some level of sympathy for it. This became clear from parliamentary debates immediately after independence.

This antagonistic perception has not changed since these debates took place in the 1960s. Though some members of the bourgeoisie recognised the peripheral and dependent nature of the economy even then, they, like their conservative counterparts, were incapable of suggesting alternatives beyond nationalisation which, in reality, would have changed nothing. The whole issue of mass mobilisation, education and popular struggle to control the exploitation and consumption of the nation's resources were never raised.

The bourgeoisie still holds firmly to the views it held in the 1960s. Thus, the Second Plan, in its efforts to reassure foreign capital stated that:

> Indigenisation is therefore not inimical to foreign investment. Foreign investment is still welcome and will for a long time be welcome as an important component of Nigeria's economic development. In fact, many business incentives operating in this country today are aimed at encouraging private foreign investment in Nigeria. (p. 35)

It is clear, therefore, that an alternative route must be sought if the problems of underdevelopment are to be addressed. Over two decades of "independence" and experimentation with "planning" have shown that the interests of the dominant classes are distinct from and indeed opposed to those of the masses. Nnoli (1981:29-30), in a critique of the established capitalist path has argued:

> Theoretically, the Western model for Nigerian development is clearly bankrupt. First, bourgeois theory of development is based on a method characterised by a checklist of factors whose connecting links are at best tenuous. Development is dissected into the economic, social and political aspects...
> The obvious question regarding the relationship between these various aspects of development remains unanswered. It becomes obscured by the concepts of modernisation and nation-building which profess to integrate them but which end up by merely giving us another checklist of characteristics.

Nnoli (1981:30-31) also notes that the bourgeois theory of

development i) divorces philosophy from socio-economic and political action and is not guided by the notion of what ought to be; ii) history is divorced from social analysis; iii) has a single-minded devotion to quantification and the statistically manipulable which obscure and mystify rather than clarify the process of development; and iv) suffers from the worst form of economic determinism, which is a consequence of the emphasis on quantification.

Commenting generally on the planning processes and claims to success by the various governments in Nigeria, Oni (1975:91) raised

> The question which the ordinary man continues to ask is: Why is this high achievement (sic high growth rate of 12% pa), not being reflected in his living and working conditions? Why is it that a peasant farmer finds it difficult to secure one meal a day or many like him have to desert farming for urban exploration? Why is it that the majority of the petty-traders and artisans languish in under-employment? Why is it that the majority of office and factory workers hoard in urban slums?

The need to eliminate totally all the vestiges of colonialism and neo-colonialism if the true mobilisation and development are to take place cannot be over-emphasised. This has not happened yet in Nigeria. It is exactly the existence of colonial institutions, which determined initially and have since continued to reproduce Nigeria's peripheral role in the international division of labour, that must be eliminated through popular struggle. Immanuel Wallerstein (1975:16) strikes this important chord when he contends that "to understand the internal class contradictions and political struggles of a particular state, we must first situate it in the world economy. We can then understand the ways in which various political and cultural thrusts may be efforts to alter or preserve a position within this world economy which is to the advantage or disadvantage of particular groups located within a particular state."

It is indisputable that there are powerful social forces within Nigeria who benefit from extant socio-economic and political arrangements. It is also indisputable that Nigeria, as a dependent class society, has been i) dominated by foreign capital and ii) with class contradictions and struggles that have generated severe constraints and fractures within the social formation to such an extent that considerable social-engineering would be needed beyond development plans and annual budgets to arrest the politics of idiosyncracy, corruption and drift (see next chapter). Meanwhile, after a quarter-century of independence, the forces of socialism can no longer be wished away or taken for granted in spite of the fact that they still lack a common front. The left in Nigeria must aim at a mobilisation/development strategy that will promote the elimination of "micro economic irrationalities" which would create a "disalienated Nigerian who is no longer materialistic, status obsessed, obsequiously subordinate to authority, uncreative and unspiritual" (Onimode, 1977:305). The democratic reorganisation of society is the historical task of all progressive Nigerians. As Oni (1975:93) notes:

> The task of promoting economic development in Nigeria today is the advancement of the Peoples Democratic Revolution. This revolution demands that Nigeria should break off immediately from the path of the exploiting capitalist mode of development and embark on democratic re-organisation of the society so that the masses of the people, the producers, can govern themselves and solve their problems by themselves and for themselves.

Such a transformation would require a profound redefinition of the national poliical economy including, in particular, a reformulation of the ideology and practice of planning. Thus far, no regime, civilian or military, has been prepared to either undertake or permit such radical change.

5 Materialist insights into coups: the crisis of hegemony in the Nigerian state

The primary aim of this chapter is to use Antonio Gramsci's concept of hegemony as a basis for comprehending the nature and crisis of the Nigerian state since political independence in 1960. We can only understand the crisis of this state and its vulnerability to military coups, like so many Third World states, if we locate these in the inability of the Nigerian bourgeoisie to create a viable hegemony in the social formation. Our position, reflected in earlier chapters, is that this bourgeoisie has been unable to constitute itself into a hegemonic class because of its peripheralisation in the world capitalist system, its tenuous relation to production, the domination of the national economy by international capital and the consistent challenges it has faced from other social classes in the country.

Military coups as part of this crisis - the first in 1966 and the most recent in 1985 - can be understood not from the various theories or motives that dominate the established literature but rather as part of the strategy of the dominant social classes to retain control of the social formation in times of crisis which result from challenges to their weak or pseudo hegemony. Coups are also the precipitates of contradictions between the dominant classes and international capital. These result, then, either from the internal reproduction of the crisis of capitalism at the centre of the world system or from efforts by a faction or fraction of internal dominant forces to extend control over the accumulation processes in the economy.

In this chapter, we begin with a brief discussion of the concept of hegemony as advanced by Gramsci (1980) in <u>Prison Notebooks</u>. We then look at the hegemonic crisis of the Nigerian state and conclude by looking at military coups as a specific instance of hegemonic crisis in peripheral capitalist societies using the Nigerian example.

a) The Concept of Hegemony in Gramsci

In <u>Prison Notebooks</u>, Gramsci notes that a social group can be supreme at two levels, which are linked. The first, is the level of control over the coercive instruments of the state; this is the level of class "domination". And the second is the level of moral and intellectual leadership exercised by the dominant class through which it imposes its will on society without the use of force; this form of domination or supremacy is exercised through state institutions in "civil society". Civil society encompasses the educational, religious, social and cultural institutions through which the dominant class "releases" ideas and beliefs into the social formation which, in actuality, reflect and encompass their interests but are presented as the interests of the society at large. It is this latter form of manifestation of class supremacy that constitutes "hegemony". The use of state power and coercion does not constitute hegemony because it is only resorted to when a dominant social class cannot impose its will and values on society in other ways. When a hegemonic order prevails in a social formation, the supremacy or domination of the hegemonic class is established, maintained and reproduced through consent over other social classes. The concept of hegemony does not preclude control over the institutions of the state, particularly the means of coercion by the hegemonic class. Rather, control over these areas is concretised and rationalised through the use of subtle and "normal" forms of control. The masses are made to believe in a so-called "national interest" without raising questions about it. They come to believe in the "neutrality" of the judicial system, the protective powers of the police and army, the existence of freedom in the society for all and the fact that eventually every one would "make it".

In short, the masses become victims of an all-pervasive notion of "false consciousness", false in the sense that in reality the consciousness employed in the reproduction of the social formation is the consciousness of the ruling class. In peripheral capitalist societies, attempts are made to rationalise the peripheralisation of the economy and to promote capital accumulation. Peasants can be made apathetic, workers can become very conservative or made to direct their energies into effective collective bargaining for bread and butter issues. "Socialist" parties, trade unions and "radical" intellectuals can begin to believe in the possibilities of capturing political power through <u>democratic</u> means; i.e. by participating in general elections or serving in bourgeois cabinets. At this level, class struggle is domesticated perhaps with occasional ruptures and a particular form of emotional acceptance of the status quo reigns.

The acceptance of an effective hegemonic class is demonstrated in one of two ways. First, it could involve an active participation in the process of reproducing the domination of the hegemonic class. And second, acceptance could be "passive": a form of acceptance often manifested in failure to challenge the institutions and ideas of the hegemonic class.

It is our position, however, that at no point in the history of societies can hegemony, no matter how well entrenched, be permanent and free from challenges. This implies that hegemony cannot be imposed on all citizens at any point in time — there will always be challenges from various sectors of the society — and it will not prevent crisis within the ranks of the hegemonic class itself. Yet it is only when the hegemony of the dominant class at the level of material production and at the level of the superstructure is effectively challenged through the creation of an alternative world view which permeates society and overtakes that of the "hegemonic" class that we can talk of <u>challenge</u> or the development of a <u>counter hegemony</u>.

At this point the intellectuals of the dominant group begin to lose their grip on the minds of the public, institutions lose their sanctity, conflicts within the ranks of the dominant social class get out of control, the agents of the state especially the police and the army become unreliable, and the spontaneous consent hitherto enjoyed by the dominant class withers away. Thus the historical "bloc" imposed on the society begins to give way to a new bloc.

Where a state is unable to use force on a consistent basis and the dominant class is incapable of imposing its will on society, it experiences a permanent crisis leading to the seizure of political power by factions or fractions of the dominant class. In peripheral capitalist societies, with underdeveloped structures and institutions in which the state is controlled by a techno-comprador class, the military is usually the fraction that seizes political power for itself or on behalf of the bourgeoisie. The reason why the military succeeds in this effort has little or nothing to do with its level of organisation or its modernising role in the society. Rather, it succeeds because of its historical development: an institution that was created and nurtured to use violence on behalf of imperialism.

b) **The Hegemonic Crisis of the Nigerian State**

The now-extensive literature on the post-colonial state emphasises the role which the state assumes not only in the mediation of class struggles but, more importantly, in the overall reproduction of the social system. In the course of the debate regarding its nature, efforts have been made to identify and present the corollary of the advanced capitalist state by presenting it as "overdeveloped" or "relatively autonomous". In this regard, the extended bureaucracy of the post-colonial state, its decisive role in the economy and the influences of metropolitan bourgeoisies on it have been highlighted. The central roles of the military and of the state in the protection of the interests of the dominant classes have also received attention; in the words of Hamza Alavi (1972:59), who set the tone of this debate:

> the historical specificities of the post-colonial societies, a historical specificity which arises from structural changes brought about by the colonial experience and alignment of classes and by the super-structures of political and administrative institutions which were established in that context, and secondly from the radical realignment of class forces which have been brought about in the post-colonial situation.

Thus, the bottom line of the argument was that the colonial state set the power basis of the post-colonial state. The structures and institutions inherited on the attainment of political independence, though overdeveloped for the post-colonial state, had their roots in the colonial period. Finally, the relatively autonomous role of the post-colonial state, coupled with the domination of an over-extended apparatus, facilitated the super-imposition of state power over the allocation of scarce resources in the name of economic development. This control over society's resources has made the post-colonial state the focus of capital accumulation and class competition and struggles.

Unfortunately, to a large extent the debate on the nature of the post-colonial state has been escapist and time-wasting. The use of given categories has failed to capture the peculiarities of underdeveloped social formations in the Third World. In addition, the state in post-colonial societies has been treated as given with attempts made to understand its nature through the attitudes of state functionaries. However, relative autonomy and centrality as well as interventionism are not peculiar to the post-colonial state. If "overdevelopment" of this type of state is the product of the extensive institutions inherited from colonialism, one could argue that indigenous elites have been involved in its initiation, operation and reproduction before political independence. In fact, it is difficult to accept the whole idea of "overdevelopment" since it suggests that a "normal" size exists. Because colonialism is employed as the starting point, without using processes of decolonisation or interplays of class forces in this period as dynamic points for understanding continuities in the state's class role, the literature has remained incapable of presenting the post-colonial state for what it is.

For the post-colonial is essentially an underdeveloped and dominated crisis-ridden state type. While it inherited the institutions of colonialism, it did not inherit the ability of the colonial state to use force and manipulation without any moral censure. It also did not assume the role of the colonial state in the international division of labour, neither did it inherit the finances, metropolitan support (military or otherwise) or ideological backing of metropolitan bourgeoisies. Rather, in the programmed transition to political independence, its peripheralisation in the world capitalist system and domination by foreign capital were concretised. The tenuous relation of the dominant classes that captures state power to productive activities, meant not only a reliance on the productive activities of the metropolitan bourgeoisie but also the "indigenisation" of the unequal exchange system implanted by imperialism. The failure of colonialism to revolutionise the forces of production in the colony meant that various powerful forces were left ununified by capital and, therefore, outside the sphere of control inherited at independence.

Finally, dependence by the post-colonial state on foreign aid, political protection and assistance in all respects, coupled with the domination of the social formation by a world-view which was not initiated by the internal bourgeoisie but originated from the metropole, meant an inability either to impose effectively a hegemonic view on other social forces or to mediate effectively class contradictions and struggles. This explains the frequent resort to the use of force unlike in the advanced capitalist state and the perpetual instability resulting in military coups or civil disorder. As Gramsci (1980:261) put it

> 'State' should be understood not only (as) the apparatus of government, but also (as) the 'private' apparatus of 'hegemony' or civil society.

And as Lenin (1971:267) conceived it, "The state is the product and manifestation of the irreconciliability of class antagonism. The state arises where, when and insofar as class antagonisms objectively <u>cannot</u> be reconciled. And conversely, the existence of the state proves that the class antagonisms objectively cannot be reconciled. And conversely, the existence of the state proves that the class antagonisms are irreconciliable."

Thus in order to capture the nature, power and crisis of the state in post-colonial societies, it is essential to return to an historical understanding of the role of imperialism and colonialism in restructuring social formations, class forces, class alignments and re-alignments, content and direction of class struggles; i.e. to provide a clear analysis of the class forces in the specific society. We shall attempt to highlight aspects of these factors and the way they aid understanding of the crisis of hegemony faced by the Nigerian state following political independence in 1960.

c) The Nigerian State and its Post-Colonial Version

Colonialism as a logical extension of imperialism imposed the colonial state to protect and reproduce the interests of the metropolitan bourgeoisie. In the Nigerian case, the British ruling class was directly responsible for fashioning the structure and power of the colonial state which was supreme within the colony. It controlled the use of force, had the support of the metropole and, unlike the period of informal empire during which imperial capital secured its interests indirectly and through nonformal means, the colonial state was very interventionist. By 1900, the Royal Niger Company had laid the foundations which, in conjunction with the introduction of formal institutions, were to contribute to the systematic exploitation of the geopolitical entity which was named Nigeria in 1914. The starting point was the subjugation of the pre-capitalist social formation to foreign capitalist interests, the programmed effort to deny and distort the history of the peoples of Nigeria and the imposition of an alternative world view which reflected the interests of the imperial bourgeois class. Following this, the colonial state endeavoured to reorganise the economy towards a capitalist mode of production. Since colonialism did not need to create a capitalist state in Nigeria in order either to obtain raw materials for British industries or to control the market for the metropole, it introduced elements of capitalism but not capitalism per se.

The colonial period distorted the Nigerian economy, introduced new relations of production and accumulation, introduced a new world view and integrated the peripheral economy of Nigeria into the emerging international division of labour. However, it is also important to highlight three aspects of colonial society which throw some light on post-colonial hegemony or lack thereof. The first is the educational policies of the colonial state; second, the underdevelopment of Nigerian entrepreneurship or, rather, the confinement of the emerging bourgeois class to commercial activities; and third, the creation and role of the military in this period. First, missionary groups were in the forefront of the colonial educational system. The colonial state assumed a largely supervisory role and ensured that the establishment of institutions and content of the curriculum did not contravene policies. Education in Nigeria as in other colonies was an important ideological weapon because it served as an avenue for disseminating the values of the metropolitan bourgeoisie. Essentially, the system was structured to provide the colonial system not only with scientists, entrepreneurs or administrators but interpreters, clerks, dispensers and house-boys. The limited goals of the educational system are evident in the fact of the isolation of the Northern part of the country from missionary influences. In addition, when the colonial state became directly involved in the school system in the 1920s, it ensured that the content of the curriculum effectively denied the existence of Nigeria's history while the glory and virtues of Queen and Empire lay at its core.

The point to emphasize is that the system was aimed at and succeeded in creating so-called "educated gentlemen" or elite. This served to ease the incorporation of the Nigerian social formation into the world capitalist system. It also ensured that those who were to become the "intellectuals" in the dependent capitalist system would be products of this educational process. In addition, colonial education served to reconcile the world views of colonial bourgeoisies and those of the emerging bureaucratic and commercial class in Nigeria.

Second, the colonial state did not need to create a viable capitalist system in the colony in order to promote capital accumulation. In fact, if the colony was to serve as a source of raw materials and as a market for British products, it was necessary to ensure that it never achieved self-sustaining production. The educational system laid a foundation for diverting the attention of the emerging educated class to the service sector. The imposition of a state monopoly on the purchase of agricultural commodities ensured that the peasants received much less than the world price of their products, thus leaving them with no funds to invest in rural industries. The use of licensed agents by the state enabled internal elites to accumulate capital by short-paying the peasants. Yet they could not invest in production because the colonial state initiated measures to ensure that production did not take place in the colonies, linkages were not created between industry and agriculture, and indigenes were not allowed into areas that would fundamentally challenge the domination of the economy by foreign capital.

The colonial consolidation of its domination over the Nigerian economy was possible because of the weak role of the indigenous classes and the dominant role of international capital which had the support of the colonial state. As Segun Osoba (1977: 369) has put it:

> ...several of the unsophisticated indigenous industries had to close down or continue to run at a loss because their crude products could not compete effectively with the cheaper and finer articles being imported into the country by the foreign firms...(a) disastrous fate..befell most of the Nigerian-owned banks, described by a top Federal Government official as "mushroom institutions with signboards across derelict windows."

Consequences of colonial policies in relation to industrial production included the dependence of the Nigerian bourgeois class on the state for capital accumulation through the granting of sinecure posts in government and public corporations, the award of inflated contracts and the granting of loans for existing and inexistent projects. In addition, foreign capital, beginning with the granting of internal self-government in 1952, voluntarily initiated a programme of incorporation. Through this, indigenous power elites were incorporated as advisers, legal representatives, counsellors, shareholders, sole distributors and major representatives by foreign firms both as a means of rationalising their participation in the economy and as a form of 'political insurance'.

The post-colonial relations of production and accumulation imposed on the Nigerian social formation in 1960 were such as to convert the Nigerian state into a regulator of the interests of foreign capital and indigenous elites.

The Nigerian economy at independence did not change much even though the civil service was 'Nigerianized' and the post-colonial state acquired a problematic capacity to mediate class conflicts through the use of patronage, violence and other means. The tenuous relation of the Nigerian bourgeoisie to production meant that the state itself was controlled by a techno-comprador class which was in turn dominated by foreign capital in the form of an international bourgeoisie.

The problems which faced the post-colonial state went beyond the socio-economic and political fragmentation and distortion which the colonial state had caused to include the release of hitherto suppressed intra-class conflicts primarily within the ranks of the dominant class. The challenges posed to the state by other social classes, the manipulations of international finance capital, the inability of the dominant social classes to either create a new world view or maintain the world view of the colonial state, and the scarcity of resources with which to buy time all combined to galvanise the initial seizure of political power by a fraction of the bourgeois class in 1966; i.e. the army.

The third aspect that must be examined, which is an integral part of the Nigerian state, then, is the army. Colonialism was established in Nigeria through the use of force. The subjugation of the indigenous peoples and the imposition of the world view of the metropolitan bourgeoisie as well as the operation of the colonial superstructure - collection of taxes, conscription of forced labour, seizure of land or the conversion of farmers into cash crop producers - were all achieved through the use of force by the colonial state. Though the British government prided itself as practicing indirect rule, the system was in actuality quite direct.

To make its rule effective as well as direct, in the first instance the colonial state relied on the aura of the metropole as well as the latter's armed might. In the second instance, partly to save costs and partly because of the need to institute an indigenous military, the colonial state created an internal military machine. Recruitment for it initially focused on minority elements and outcasts and was later extended to include other social groups especially royal or feudal and new middle class elements. Generally, these were groups who had specific interests to gain in new relations of accumulation, interests to protect or grudges to settle. It can therefore be understood why the colonial police and army were brutal on their own people and why they took the sides of the dominant classes after political independence. The role played by the military in the colonial period largely laid the basis for its post-colonial role. Many first generation officers could not understand why they should not continue to play exactly the same role after the government had been Africanised.

Finally, in this section, it is important to underline the crisis of hegemony which faced the post-colonial state arose from the distortion of the social formation in the colonial period, the peripheralisation of the economy in the international division of labour, the domination of the economy by foreign capital, the relegation of the indigenous power elites to commercial and exchange activities, the relative power of other social classes, the inability of the post-colonial state to create and impose an alternative world view on the other social classes, and the intra-class conflict that characterised the politics played by the power elites following independence. The crisis of hegemony also had its roots in the exclusion of the majority from plan initiation and implementation, the attempts to preserve the colonial relations of production and accumulation (e.g. by the continued use of Marketing Boards), the increasing levels of organisation, militancy and consciousness among the working class, the frequent use of force by the post-colonial state in the face of popular protests, the massive rate of corruption, ethnic chauvinism, religious bigotry, opportunism, political brigandage, and the use of state power and institutions to divert public funds into private pockets and accounts.

Together these and other factors combined to throw the Nigerian social formation into perpetual crisis. The use of vague and shallow ideological tools, the preservation of the neo-colonial educational system and the intensification and expansion of the system of patronages did not reduce the challenges to the state. At this level the military could intervene to protect the interests of the dominant class especially when it becomes clear that opposition from other social classes has reached a level where they have created a counter hegemonic force due to the inability of the dominant class to maintain control over capital accumulation and the distribution of patronage. Second, the military could intervene to advance and consolidate its own interests. In this regard, it acts not as an opposition to the ruling class but as its replacement within the established mode of accumulation. This could occur because the ruling class has neglected the military or over-extended its functions; or because the military wishes to instil new vigor into state institutions, strengthen the alliance between it and international capital or contribute to the emergence of a more corporatist or fascist state. And the final reason why the military might intervene arises from the desire by progressive forces to use it either as part of a larger social movement or in isolation.

In peripheral capitalist societies, the ability of the military to capture political power has been demonstrated again and again, even within the same country and at short intervals. The possibility of outside forces, internal or external, using it to capture political power has also been demonstrated. Thus it is possible for revolutionary forces to infiltrate the army and use it in the overthrow of the social order. Such an intervention is more likely to succeed when the hegemony of the dominant class is under attack, even if no counter-hegemony has been developed.

We shall now turn in the final part of this chapter to military interventions in Nigeria and argue that the coups which have taken place in the 1960s and 1980s are precipitates of the first type rather than the last two; i.e., intervention of behalf of rather than against the dominant classes as a result of challenges to the state.

d) Military Interventions in Nigeria
Before we discuss military interventions in Nigeria, it is

essential to make some comments on existing attempts to analyse the causes of coups in the Third World. Attempts to do this have sometimes strayed into the area of "grand theorizing", providing cosmetic and escapist explanations and therefore inadequate solutions. There are, in fact, two major schools of thought: the "Janowitz" and "Huntington" schools. While their theories are not essentially wrong, they do not capture the fundamental basis of military intervention in peripheral capitalist social formations. They have relied on attitudinal, institutional or cultural approaches to the comprehension of motives behind coups rather than on historical or social structures.

First, the "Janowitz school" argues that there are certain characteristics inherent in modern military organisations which dispose them to intervene in politics. (Janowitz, 1977) This school argues that African armies as outgrowths of colonial European armies, with officer corps trained by ex-colonial powers, are ipso facto "modern" institutions. This school's position is unhistorical and can be criticised on several methodological and conceptual grounds. The nature of military interventions in the African continent as well as the performances of the military in office have disproved every idea it has advanced in its attempt to explain military intervention. The analysis of the military and its role in society is undertaken without regard to its social environment, its history and its role and location in the international division of labour.

By contrast, the second "Huntington school", emphasises the nautre of society in general in an attempt to explain military coups and interventions in politics. (Huntington, 1968) According to Samuel Decalo (1976:7), this school streses "societal and structural weaknesses - institutional fragility, systemic flaws and low levels of political culture - which act as a sort of magnet to pull the armed forces into the power and legitimacy vacuum". Samuel Huntington (1968:237), a powerful proponent of this position has argued that:

> the most important causes of military intervention in
> politics are not military but political and reflect not
> the social and organisational characteristics of the
> military establishment but the political and institutional
> structure of society.

The bottom line in the argument of this school is that political institutions as instruments for mediating societal conflict or resolving societal contradictions are weak and ineffective. This ineffectiveness allows other social forces to begin to make crucial demands which imported institutions and corrupt politicians cannot satisfy. In such a situation of institutional fragility and inability to operate society effectively, the only institution capable of saving the country and resolving its contradictions is the army.

The position of the "Huntington school" certainly represents an improvement over the ideas advanced by the "Janowitz school" in terms of recognising the activities of the army as an integral aspect of the structures and contradictions of society. However, it is still defective as an explanation of the dynamics that prompt military intervention in politics, especially in Africa. In the first place, there appears to be a problem of tautology in that society is praetorian because political institutions are ineffective and political institutions are ineffective because society is praetorian. And second, this school appears to neglect the fact that political institutions are determined by more fundamental structures and processes. In short, their nature is conditioned by the mode of production and the use to which societal institutions are put and so cannot be divorced from the accumulative <u>base</u> of the dominant social classes. The notions that the military in Africa is a modern elite capable of leading societies and that the problems of Africa are such that only militarism can resolve them appears to be well-entrenched in this school. But Decalo (1976:13) provides an accurate critique of it when he argues that:

> It is both simplistic and empirically erroneous to relegate coups in Africa to the status of a dependent variable, a function of the political weaknesses and structural fragility of African states and the failings of African civilian elites.

Thus once again we are left with the explanation of military intervention in terms of either of the first two of the three conditions identified at the end of the previous section of this chapter.

Aside from the "Janowitz" and "Huntington" schools, other specific motives identified by various commentators can be fitted into them. For example, Decalo (1976:21) emphasises a host of issues which include "corporate, ethnic and personal grievances". In fact, he states explicitly that:

> detailed examination of motivations for coups reveals that the main weakness of attempts to explain them by pinpointing major areas of systemic stress is that insufficient weight is placed on the personal motives of ambitious or discontented officers who have a great deal of freedom and scope for action in fragmented, unstructured and unstable political systems.

The problem with Decalo's position is that he fails to explain why the political systems are "fragmented, unstructured and unstable". The failure to do this diverts analysis into areas of personal motivations and ambitions without explaining the fact that such motivations are rooted in the materialist foundations of society.

The inadequacy of established explanations advanced demands that we return to the Marxist notion of historical materialism for a more comprehensive understanding of the causes of military coups in underdeveloped social formations. Historical materialism asserts that legal relations, forms of state, social consciousness, power relations and so on cannot be comprehended in isolation but only by tracing them to their roots in the material conditions of life; i.e. to the system of material production in society. Historical materialism also asserts that in all existing societies, the process of production, exchange and consumption determines the social and class structure as well as their specific juridical, political and ideological forms. Finally, it asserts that the history of all hitherto existing societies is the history of class struggles.

To comprehend the basis of political instability, dependent accumulation and military intervention in Africa, therefore, we must begin any analysis from the time when the continent was incorporated into the world capitalist system, the restructuring of the political economy of the continent to meet the needs of the metropole, the arrest of the natural process of state formation, the creation of "alien" social structures and institutions, and the introduction of new relations of production. It is also important to note the underdeveloped social classes as well as the partial transformation of the pre-capitalist mode of production, the grouping of different ethnic groups into single units without regard to cultural and historical differences and the structuring of economies into one-crop exporters. In light of these transformations and developments, political independence in Africa witnessed the inheritance of a very fluid state of affairs: a weak state, institutions with low legitimacy, absence of an autonomous dynamic for development and thus an inability to meet the promises of the nationalist period or the demands generated by the euphoria of self-rule. Political instability resulting in military intervention in this period can be seen then as manifestations of inherent contradictions in the struggle by dominant power elites to consolidate their position, put down challenges to their power, and expand their accumulative base.

Part of the struggle within the ranks of this dominant class arises from its desire to emerge as a strong national bourgeoisie and the struggle to create a strong state from the heterogenous super-structure left behind after colonialism. But in a society where at least two modes of production co-exist, where foreign capital is fully-entrenched, where no strong state emerges to resolve contradictions and where no dominant ideology exists, military intervention can be regarded as almost inevitable. It is indeed inevitable to the extent that the monopolisation of tanks, guns, and bullets by the soldiers puts them ahead in their bid for power among other social classes. It is only this fact that enables them to "hijack" the struggles by trade unionists, students, peasants and other oppressed groups for power.

The Nigerian experience validates our argument so far. When self-government was granted to the regions in 1952, the geopolitical entity called Nigeria operated as three separate countries - the East, West and North. Even at independence the regions were more powerful than the federal centre: in fact, the top political figures were regionally- and ethnically-based. The struggle to consolidate and expand acquired spheres of influence gradually generated a state of insecurity and confusion. Politics became a zero-sum game: a kind of primitive accumulation was introduced and competition within the ranks of the dominant classes assumed proportions which the weak state structure, inherited at independence, could not support. The struggle at this time related more to efforts by regional elites to carve out for themselves economic and political spheres of influence than with an attempt to challenge the dominant role of foreign capital. In the process, ethnic and religious differences were manipulated and where they did not exist, differences were artificially generated and magnified. The institutionalised means for overcoming or mediating these strains were inadequate. As Billy Dudley (1973: 100) has noted, "so inadequate were these means that stress and strain had led, by November 1965, to conditions best described as near anarchy".

In addition to this institutional deficiency, the military had been heavily politicised especially by the competition between the Prime Minister and President to control the army. Rumours about the intention of particular ethnically-based political parties to use the army against other ethnic groups were rampant. The issue of corruption was an open one: bribes were given and received in the open, political offices were sold, and ministers were heard to boast in public about the fat size of their foreign bank accounts. In the midst of mass poverty, illiteracy, unemployment and hunger, they rode in long luxurious American cars protected by thugs. Elections were rigged especially in the Western region in 1965, intra-party conflicts assumed a proportion leading to disarray in the ranks of the regional bourgeois classes, and the trial, conviction and imprisonments of the petty-bourgeois leader of the Action Group did not help matters.

Given this unsteady state of affairs, the wanton destruction of lives and property by the agents of politicians and parties, the inability to keep public services functioning, the indiscriminate use of state power by politicians and the free use of force on civilian populations by the police, it became clear that the politicians did not have any hegemonic influence left, that they were incapable of mediating contradictions and, finally, that they were incapable of creating a suitable climate for capital accumulation by either foreign or internal capital. To drive this home, the workers staged numerous strike actions, workings to rule, demonstrations and riots, the market women and students joined in and so did the peasants who became very insecure as the political thugs ravaged the countryside.

It was at this point that the Nigerian army "hijacked" the struggles of the workers against the ineffective civilian regime in January 1966. The army was able to do this not because it was more modern, educated or sophisticated, but because it controlled the means of violence. Thus the first coup led by Major Chukwuma Kaduna Nzeogwu was expected.

No one doubts Nzeogwu's sincerity, though he did not stay in power long enough to put his ideas into practice. In his broadcast statement he declared: "Our enemies are the political profiteers, swindlers, the men in high and low places who seek bribes and demand ten percent, those that seek to keep the country divided permanently so that they can remain in office as ministers and V.I.P.'s of waste, the tribalists, the nepotists".

In an interview, Nzeogwu also revealed that "we had a short list of people who were either undesirable for the future progress of the country or, by their position at that time, had to be sacraficed for peace and stability". (Dudley, 1973: 103) He called his coup a "revolution" and stated that it was carried out in the name of "Nigerianism": the officers had wanted to "gun down all the big wigs". (Dudley, 1973:107)

This was a classic instance of the military intervening directly in politics to protect itself and its own interests using populist slogans and efforts. "Nigerianism" is no ideology, though it could buy a regime some breathing space. Second, Nzeogwu came to power without any clear-cut programme that would ensure that other "big wigs" did not replace the ones the officers had planned "to gun down". By July 1966, rightist forces within the army had taken full control and put an end to Nzeogwu's disturbing populist rhetoric. Similarly, in 1984 and 1985, officers' coups were preemptive of more radical elements within and outside the military.

Even under the military, in both the mid-1960s and -1980s, inherent contradictions in the peripheral capitalist social formation remained. The state did not become stronger irrespective of the numerous decrees passed in both periods and its several attempts to reconcile warring factions of the bourgeoisie. Unstable states of affairs resulted in the civil war which lasted until 1970 and reactions against "austerity" in the second half of the 1980s. Neither the civil war nor the devaluation/privatisation exercise solved the problems of the Nigerian bourgeoisie or demonstrated the supposed "modernity", "sophistication" and "abhorrence of corruption" among the military. By the time Gowon and Buhari were overthrown in reactive coups in 1975 and 1985, respectively, the same reasons of tribalism, corruption, lack of direction, wastefulness and arrogance which had been leveled against the politicians in 1966 and 1984 were made again. Similar objective conditions under which the military intervened in 1966 existed in 1975 as well as between 1984 and 1985 when factions of the military intervened.

Mismanagement and instability of oil revenues created a cycle of inflation and recession, wage reviews, a series of internal and external prestige projects, journalists, lecturers, students and trade unionists were detained or molested by the soldiers, and the government lacked an effective rural development programme. In addition, bureaucratic inefficiency and institutional decay reached their highest points in the nation's history.

In 1975 and again a decade later the response of the workers, peasants and students, despite the emergency powers of the police, the numerous decrees of the army and the ban on industrial action by workers, followed the pre-1966 pattern. It became clear to the factions of the military that intervened that the Gowon and Buhari administrations had lost their legitimacy and power. The world view which they represented had broken down and the workers, peasants and junior ranks were beginning to constitute an alternative power bloc which had to be nipped in the bud. This galvanized the military into action. Brigadier Murtala Mohammed who emerged as the leader of the 1975 coup (he was also involved in the coup of July 1966), justified it (as did Ibrahim Babangida in mid-1985) by declaring that, "the affairs of state, hitherto a collective responsibility became characterised by lack of consultation, indecision, indiscipline and even neglect". (Daily Times, 31 July 1975) Other reasons advanced by the new Mohammed regime in the mid-1970s included the failure of Yakubu Gowon to remove state governors from office as he had promised to do, widespread allegations of graft, misuse of public funds, complaints of ostentatious living, flagrant abuse of office and deprivation of people's rights and property, perversion of time-honoured procedures and norms, desecration of traditional institutions, humiliation of highly respected traditional rulers and so on. (Williams(ed) 1976: 185) These allegations like similar ones in the mid-1980s were all true. In fact, by the time Gowon and Buhari were overthrown, they had lost the support of virtually every class. In the case of the former, the politicians had withdrawn support because Gowon reneged on his promise to return the country to civilian rule in 1976: the military governors, realising that they still had some time to stay in office, began to loot the public treasury as fast as possible; and this led to the emergence of anti-corruption crusaders all over the country while students, market women and peasants resented the limited attention paid to their problems and complaints. Likewise by mid-1985, Buhari had come to alienate all his regime's support.

Mohammed was assasinated by Buka Suka Dimka, who led an unsuccessful counter-coup in 1976. Dimka accused the Mohammed regime of going "communist" even when it had made no structural changes in relations of production and accumulation and had not taken any steps to redefine Nigeria's role and location in the international division of labour. Olusegun Obasanjo, who came to power following the assassination of Mohammed, virtually returned the country to the Gowon era but managed to prevent other coups until a new civilian regime came to office in 1979. Likewise, the 1985 Vatsa coup against Babangida failed.

One variant of the dependency argument is that Western powers cause coups in Africa. In the Nigerian situation, it is difficult to ascertain the direct role of the West in the several coups beyond its domination of the economy as a fundamental factor responsible for continued underdevelopment and hence for the continued reproduction of social contradictions and struggles. However, the roles of the British High Commissioner and American Ambassador in providing advice to Yakubu Gowon after the July 1966 coup and their efforts to ensure that Murtala Mohammed did not become head of state because of his secessionist ideas are known. The unresolved nature of the contact between Dimka and the British High Commission following the assassination of Mohammed has continued to intrigue analysts. The ambivalent attitude of the British government to the initial overthrow of Gowon and the consequent assassination of Mohammed has convinced a lot of Nigerians that Britain was interested in assisting Gowon to regain power. But the situation in Nigeria prior to each coup (except the unsuccessful coups of 1976 and 1985) were such that no outside government was required to encourage a well-armed group to seize power.

Finally, from the actions of the military in office it is evident that intervention took place when the unstable world view of the dominant social classes (military or civilian) was subjected to fundamental and persistent challenges from below. Thus, the series of interventions can be interpreted as an aspect of on-going class struggles in Nigeria. The coups were planned and executed by military elites who, in terms of status and income, were part of the Nigerian bourgeoisie. On coming to power they did not alter the social relations of production and accumulation neither did they attempt in any serious way to wage a fundamental struggle against foreign domination. On the contrary they proceeded to rationalise the participation of foreign capital in the economy by defining spheres of interest and balances of power through indigenisation decrees and numerous partnerships with foreign capital. The army was converted into an avenue for rapid capital accumulation just as the civilians had done with political office in the pre-military period. Efforts were also made to initiate and impose an alternative world view on society, one which, while using Nigerian symbols like a new political arrangement and foreign policy (see next part), was in reality a reflection of the world view of the international bourgeoisie. (See Ake (ed) 1986, Onimode 1977, Nnoli (ed) 1981 and Oni 1975)

e) Conclusions

Military organisations are part of the political forms in any society. Each stage of social progress produces military organisations that fundamentally reflect its needs, ideas, classes and culture. The nature and structure of the military and the points of intersection between its interests and those of factions or fractions of the dominant class are also dependent on the modes of production and accumulation. These points of intersection of interests ultimately condition and determine the role which the military ascribes to itself, the specific interests it is expected to play in society and the frequency with which it intervenes in politics.

Military intervention in Nigeria has been part of the struggles to establish a strong bourgeois state, an element in its corporatist inclinations (Shaw and Ihonvbere, 1987). Thirteen, and now another four, years of military rule have certainly led to the emergence of a stronger centre (this was also greatly aided by the civil war and the oil boom which followed) and a more organised techno-comprador fraction. The bottom line remains, however, that the domination of the economy by foreign capital has never really been challenged. What successive military regimes have done in Nigeria include attempts to establish Nigeria in West Africa as the "sub-imperial power", initiate a dependent food policy, create conditions for near-total dependence on oil revenues and re-structure the labour movement in the hope of imposing a pro-establishment leadership on it.

Finally, there is no reason not to expect a series of returns to military rule in Nigeria - a cycle including 1966 and 1983 - given the extent to which the Nigerian state has been integrated into the world capitalist system. The net impact of this integration has been the internal reproduction of the crisis of capitalism at the centre of world accumulation. The situation has not been helped by near-total dependence on an oil sector dominated internally by the international oil majors. This dependence on oil revenues has meant the generation of major contradictions in the economy whenever the price of oil fluctuates at the world level: from boom in the early-1970s to glut in the early-1980s. In addition, patterns of state expenditure, massive levels of corruption, gross inefficiency in the civil service and parastatals, frequent resort to violence and the arrogance of power which followed the initial oil boom, have all characterised politics and political competition in contemporary Nigeria. Hence the prospect of recurrent coups as well as economic cycles, periods of political conflict as well as of control.

6 Resource availability and foreign policy change: affluence and influence

The primary aim of this chapter is to analyse the nature of the first 20 years of Nigeria's foreign policy, between political independence in 1960 and 1980 and demonstrate the chain of continuity through the various regimes and crises. Therefore, rather than examine the country's external relations in isolation, this chapter intends to locate foreign policy initiatives and action in the socio-economic and political dynamics of Nigeria both as an oil exporting country and as an aspiring "sub-imperial" power.

Traditionally, attempts to study the foreign policy of underdeveloped countries have been fraught with problems. These problems arise apparently from the domination of external relations by single individuals, the constantly changing nature of regimes and ideological orientation, the lack of consistency and the general constraints imposed by the peripheral location of underdeveloped countries in the international division of labour. But if the study is approached from the perspective of political economy, the task becomes less of a problem.

For our purposes, the political economy approach will enable us to examine, in the case of Nigeria, at what point the availability of revenue yielding resource(s) began to change, extend or deepen the nature and pattern of external relations as evidenced in foreign policy declarations, initiatives and operations. Our major contention in this case is that despite the size and resources of the country, Nigeria's foreign policy has not changed since 1960 when it became politically independent. The foreign policy has no doubt witnessed a lot of actions, declarations, conferences and monetary expenditures. The latter were facilitated by the increased oil revenues following the 1973 OPEC oil price increases with their precipitous decline a decade later, but what has actually taken place can be described as "motion in a barber's chair".

a) Resource Availability and Putative Power

It is important to examine the place of resource availability in Nigeria's foreign policy. Prior to 1973, other than in population terms Nigeria had practically no other advantage over other African states. Its huge population of 63 million at independence certainly attracted foreign investment but the very conservative nature of the political leadership at that time did not serve to generate the need for special attention from the great powers. However, following the 1973 and subsequent oil price increases, the question of the role of resource availability and foreign policy change became important in analysing Nigerian foreign policy.

The dependency and underdevelopment literature unfortunately provides few insights into the international relations of underdeveloped and dependent states. However, implicit in the position of this approach is the contention that the underdeveloped institutions and structures, the backward mode(s) of production and thus the peripheral location of these societies in the world system makes them junior participants in the international system, the pawns of the developed countries, incapable of making significant moves in their own interests.

This position appears rather simplistic, however, because it neglects the crucial part of the equation. It completely neglects the internal social structure that maintains and reproduces this so-called dependence, the internal class that benefits from it and the nature of internal support the policy enjoys. More importantly, it neglects the room for independent action which the dependent state might enjoy even among other dependent states and efforts explicitly or otherwise being made to alter or consolidate the system. However, the real issue we wish to clarify is that resource availability is only a basis for putative power. It only contributes to the power potential of the state but not its absolute power. Were this not the case perhaps Saudi Arabia, considering its vast oil resources would have been a great power in the 1970s. Available resources must be identified, tapped, refined, marketed and the revenues or gains used to create the basis for more wealth. Moreover, there are several ways of increasing the power of a state even without resource availability in the immediate instance. Through alliances, external aid in return for strategic location beneficial to a larger power, rapid economic development and so on, a country can increase its influence and power. But above all these factors is the emergence of a dominant class interested in creating a relatively powerful and independent basis of existence and participation in the world system. It is in fact this situation that will condition the nature, direction and content of foreign policy initiative and action, pattern of economic development and world view. In relation to Nigeria the resource issue has been the source of several myths concerning the power of the country. The incorporation of the area today called Nigeria into the capitalist world economy in the late eighteenth century marked the beginning of a peripheral capitalist society. British colonialism arrested the natural process of state formation and development while it imposed new structures and institutions. It further undertook, directly and indirectly, the creation of a class configuration which was not only out of tune with the objective level of economic development but more importantly, was under the domination of Western European capital, after political independence.

Thus, at independence in 1960, the Nigerian power elite perceived its country as the greatest in Africa. Analysts of the Nigerian scene also neglected the historically determined location of the country in the international system and the origins of this elite. Such analysts failed to examine the role of Nigeria as a "semi-industrial" power in the periphery and as a "sub-imperial" power in the sub-region. They also neglected or at least paid limited attention to the continued dependence of the Nigerian state on external trade, imported technology, food and expertise, the process of class formation and class struggle in the country and how these factors among others have influenced the content and direction of the country's foreign policy leading to over-extension of interests; a lot of motion but very limited action (Shaw & Fasehun, 1980).

At independence in 1960, Nigeria was essentially an exporter of agricultural raw materials. It relied exclusively on the West for technological, financial and political support to maintain internal stability and keep development projects afloat. In turn, the country undertook to support Western policies in the African continent and on other international issues. The power elite, created through the activities of European finance capital and the Western press on the other hand, undertook to convince the leadership and public that the country was destined to lead Africa and the black world. The country was hailed as the cradle of democracy in Africa. The first Prime Minister was called "the golden voice of Africa"

Table Seven Exports of Major Commodities

Commodities	Quantity ('000 tones)			Value (Nm)		
	1983	1984	1985	1983	1984	1985
Cocoa beans................	108.3	125.3	137.8	381.2	220.0	208.5
Other cocoa products.......	18.1	16.2	16.4	19.1	22.2	24.1
Palm kernels...............	80.0	13.5	11.9	16.8	5.4	4.8
Other palm kernel products.	18.0	2.0	8.4	8.6	1.0	4.2
Rubber.....................	28.8	28.8	25.2	23.0	23.9	20.0
Other non-agricultural commodities.......	–	–	–	87.5	17.2	37.5
Total non-oil exports	–	–	–	536.2	290.6	300.0
Crude oil exports (m barrels)	335.8	394.6	430.7	7,201.2	8,840.6	10,449.6
Total	–	–	–	7,737.4	9,131.2	10,749.6

Source: Government statistics.

and in their pronouncements and writings the power elite developed this belief which in reality lacked a credible basis. For instance, the first Minister for Foreign Affairs declared that, "our country is the largest single unit in Africa...we are not going to abdicate the position in which God Almighty has placed us...The whole black continent is looking up to this country to liberate it from thralldom". (House of Representatives Debates, January 1960).

The basis of this belief has changed over time – population, size, wealth, largest army in Africa, democracy and now oil – but analysts of Nigerian foreign policy have continued to stress the leadership role of the country in Africa. For example, Olajide Aluko (1973:162) declared that "Nigeria cannot readily give up the bid to play a leading role in the OAU". The Nigerian Government also lent support to such interpretations when in the Second Plan it argued, "The country is fortunate in having the resource potential in men and material and money to lay a solid foundation for a socio-economic revolution in Africa. The uncomprising objective of rising economic prosperity in Nigeria is the economic independence of the nation and the defeat of neo-colonialist forces in Africa" (p. 32). Furthermore, in a speech to the nation on October 1974, General Gowon emphasised the country's continental responsibility thus:

> Our policy has been one of upholding the dignity of the African, safeguarding his interest and promoting his wellbeing and protecting him from all forms of oppression and exploitation...The support which Nigeria gives for the struggle for human dignity and eradication of all racialism and colonialism in Africa and our determination to pursue these goals will continue to be intensified until the whole of Africa is free from the stain of degradation (New Nigerian, 3 October 1974, 12).

The curious aspect of this over-extended responsibility which the Nigerian power elite has imposed on itself becomes clear when it is realised that the country has remained under-developed in all respects. For the Nigerian state, this pre-occupation with external issues provides a breathing space and diverts attention from pressing internal issues.

This belief that Nigeria was destined to lead Africa became stronger with the oil boom. Combined with a population of about 100 million, a standing army of about 200,000 and oil production (prior to the glut) of over two million barrels per day, there was very little one could do to convince the Nigerian power elite that the country was still poor, under-developed and peripheral in the world economy. With the oil boom providing the Nigerian state with huge revenues, the power elite was able to buy its way into several activities

Table Eight　　　　Nigeria's External Trade by Commodity
Values in million Naira

	1981 Imports (cif)	1981 Exports (fob)	1985 Imports (cif)	1985 Exports (fob)
Food and live animals............	1,820.2	214.8	999.7	232.6
Beverage and tobacco............	16.5	2.6	13.1	—
Crude Materials except fuels....	218.9	35.4	387.1	2.4
Minerals, fuel, etc.............	151.1	10,687.8	74.5	10,449.6
Animal & vegetable oil, fats....	128.7	6.6	76.6	4.7
Chemicals.......................	1,220.4	2.8	2,110.4	—
Manufactured goods..............	2,540.7	23.6	1,255.5	10.0
Machinery and transport.........	5,548.1	—	2,640.0	1.1
Miscellaneous manufactured articles..	947.7	0.3	283.3	0.4
Commodities and transactions....	10.2	39.6	7.6	48.6
Total.........................	12,602.5	11,013.5	7,852.8	10,749.6

Source: Federal Office of Statistics

in the international arena thus creating the impression that some dynamism existed in foreign policy.

But the nature of oil production and marketing on which the state became absolutely dependent for revenues introduced a new and often neglected dimension into the relative power and independence of Nigeria. Though at independence, Nigeria was an exporter of primary products by 1975 oil had become almost the sole source of foreign exchange earnings (see table three). Agriculture was neglected and military expenditure increased tremendously. But the oil sector in Nigeria is dominated by foreign oil companies especially in terms of technology, marketing information, prospecting capacity and ability to withstand the crises of the new international oil market. The danger inherent in this dependence on oil is evidenced in the fact that the Nigerian state is now dependent on the continued cooperation of a handful of workers and oil companies. Yet this situation was very beneficial to the power elites: the oil companies handled all the risks and the state through the Nigerian National Oil Corporation (NNPC) collected the rent.

b) Nigeria in West Africa: a sub-imperial power?

Four major principles guided Nigeria's policy towards its neighbours at independence in 1960. These were, the respect for the territorial integrity, sovereignty and independence of every African state, equality of all states, non-interference in the internal affairs of other states and, finally, commitment to functional co-operation as a means of enhancing continental unity. It was in line with these principles that Nigeria joined the OAU and embraced non-alignment. However, until the outbreak of the civil war in 1967 Nigeria remained aloof from political and economic activities in the West African sub-region.

Several reasons have been advanced in an attempt to explain this situation of aloofness by the most populous nation in the region. The argument that the relative economic and military weakness of the other states in the region called for limited attention appears rather unacceptable in face of the reality of socio-economic conditions in Nigeria. Rather, the problems of unity and stability coupled with a preoccupation with economic growth were so enormous as to leave little time for the pro-Western and conservative government that replaced the colonial authority to have time for extensive external affairs. Moreover, unlike post-1973 regimes, resources available to the immediate post-independence government were severely limited in all respects. The limited breathing space available to the government of Tafawa Balewa was spent on dealing with Ghana – preventing the spread of Nkrumahism and socialism.

Table Nine

Imports by End-Use
Values at current prices in million Naira

Item	1981 Nm	1981 %	1985 Nm	1985 %
Consumer goods:				
Non-durable consumer goods				
Food..................................	1,991.2	15.80	1,076.3	13.71
Textiles...............................	201.6	1.60	79.1	1.00
Others................................	806.6	6.40	237.6	3.03
Durable consumer goods.............	655.3	5.20	558.1	7.11
Sub-total.............................	3,654.7	29.00	1,951.1	24.85
Capital goods:				
Capital equipment....................	2,596.1	20.60	2,253.8	28.70
Transport equipment..................	1,928.1	15.30	1,988.8	25.32
Raw materials........................	2,961.6	23.50	1,516.4	19.31
Fuels................................	151.1	1.20	74.6	0.95
Sub-total............................	7,636.9	60.60	5,833.6	74.28
Passenger cars.......................	1,310.9	10.40	68.1	0.87
Grand total..........................	12,602.5	100.00	7,852.8	100.00

Source: Government statistics.

In the light of this situation, Nigeria had very limited bi- or multi-lateral relations with other states in the region, particularly the francophone states. It was not until the civil war broke out and the realisation of the fact that Nigeria's security could not be totally divorced from those of other regional states that a more active interest began to be taken in West African affairs. This realisation came primarily from the support given to the secessionist forces by the francophone states.

We shall now take a brief look at one of the most "successful" manifestations of the country's foreign policy action in the region - the initiation and creation of the Economic Community of West African States (ECOWAS). Nigeria was able to see this scheme through because of its renewed interest in the affairs of other states in this sub-region after the civil war in 1970. The military government was able to win the support or co-operation of other states because it was willing to use oil as a foreign policy weapon and was prepared to spend oil revenues to achieve its foreign policy objectives. These actions were also made possible by the socio-economic crises which the rise in oil prices had created in other regional economies coupled with the desires of other states to take advantage of the benefits which Nigeria was likely to provide as the "core state" in the integration scheme.

Thus, it is incorrect to perceive the formation of ECOWAS as an exclusively Nigerian affair and therefore a major success in the country's foreign policy goals as the government has repeated again and again. Moreover, it will be an oversight not to recognise the fact that, apart from possible diplomatic pride in Nigeria, other regional states are likely to benefit more from the integration scheme because it meets their perceptions and expected benefits more than it does those of Nigeria. In relation to the first point, the major role of foreign capital, which is any case is the only sector sufficiently organised and integrated to take full advantage of the removal of trade barriers, cannot be overlooked. This major role is evidenced in the complete silence of the ECOWAS Treaty on the fate of extant and future foreign investment in the region and the influence of the Nigerian Chambers of Commerce in the whole affair. In relation to the second point, the continued membership of the francophone states in their own West African Economic Community (CEAO), their marginal support for ECOWAS Protocols, their failure to meet financial obligations and the continued promulgation of nationalist economic policies all go to demonstrate the fact that they still lack confidence in Nigeria and ECOWAS. One could also note the continued fear by the smaller states that Nigeria could end up dominating the regional economy and thus emerge as a "regional imperialist power".

It is therefore interesting to note that though the dominant power elite that controlled the Nigerian state prior to the civil war had been opposed to integration on the grounds that the country had nothing to gain from the other relatively smaller and poorer states, this perception changed completely after 1970. The impact of the civil war, the realisation that the country was not as secure as it had been assumed, the role of France on the side of the secessionist forces and its initiative immediately after the civil war in Nigeria to create in the sub-region an exclusively francophone economic community, pushed Nigeria to take immediate action. The general perception was that France was planning to create conditions for the isolation of Nigeria in the sub-region.

Thus, beginning in 1972 Nigeria began making moves to Togo in relation to the formation of an economic community that would embrace all the states in the region for the first time. By May 1973, Nigeria had virtually succeeded in achieving this objective and ECOWAS was born in 1975 embracing all the sixteen states in the sub-region. This established for the first time a regional community that cut across colonial, linguistic and cultural barriers, making provision for the harmonization of all economic, social, cultural and ultimately political spheres of activity. Most important was the fact that the Treaty was completely silent on the participation of foreign capital in the regional economy despite the outright domination of the economies by international finance capital. The only reference to foreign capital in the Treaty relates to the desire to employ the ECOWAS Fund for Co-operation, Compensation and Development to guarantee foreign investments in the region.

The reason for this is very simple. Except for Guinea Bissau and Cape Verde Islands in a very limited sense, ECOWAS is nothing more than an agglomeration of neo-colonial branch plant economies inspired by a country with a very weak national bourgeoisie. The principal and immediate beneficiary of labour mobility, elimination of tariff barriers, mobility of production factors and so on, will be international finance capital. Perhaps in terms of prestige Nigeria might make some gains, but without a credible productive base, these can at best be tenuous. Moreover if we take a look at the mechanisms employed by Nigeria to win the support of other states in the region to join ECOWAS, we find a mixture of bribery and indirect blackmail: bribery in the sense that Nigeria suddenly became very generous to the francophone states in terms of financial aid and unsolicited donations; and indirect blackmail in the sense that by bribing and winning the support of some major states in the sub-region, the relatively smaller, landlocked and poorer states had little choice but to join. Even some relatively developed states like Senegal, despite its opposition to ECOWAS and fear of possible domination by Nigeria, had little choice but to join the Community. How did Nigeria bribe these states into joining ECOWAS?

Nigeria virtually purchased its dominant position in the subregion. Admittedly, countries like the Ivory Coast now see Nigeria as a market for their manufactures while the landlocked states in the region saw ECOWAS as a way of avoiding stultifying tariff barriers. The drought-stricken Sahelian states also expected some financial assistance from Nigeria which had joined OPEC in 1971. The inability to translate available resources into a credible base that could serve long-term interests meant that Nigeria had no choice but to take the route constantly taken by capital-surplus economies − financial contributions. Thus Nigeria took this wasteful path to establishing its influence in the region and continent through the hosting of all kinds of meetings. The country also employed soft loans, joint investments and donations. A few examples of this will suffice.

In pursuit of its aims, Nigeria constructed a highway linking Idi-Iroko in Nigeria to Porto-Novo in the Republic of Benin at a cost of N1.8 million to Nigeria. A N2 million, 25 year interest free loan was also granted to Benin, while Nigeria agreed to take over 30% of the equity and invest 7.2 million in a joint cement project in the Republic of Benin. It also undertook to participate to the tune of 20 million in a joint sugar project in Benin. This flagrant display of wealth between 1972 and 1975 when ECOWAS was formed did not stop there. Nigeria donated printing machines worth N42,000 to Benin and on foreign trips in the region, Nigerian leaders virtually wrote out cheques at every stop. In 1972, on a visit to Guinea, the Nigerian leader donated N50,000 to the ruling party, N20,000 was donated for cultural development in the Republic of Benin and N5,000 was given to a horticultural and nutritional centre also in Benin. While electricity was scarce in Nigeria, a situation in which the National Electric Power Authority (NEPA) experienced a drastic reduction in power and industries reported that over 30% of productive capacity was immobilised due to constant power cuts, the Nigerian government undertook to supply Niger with electricity from its Kainji Dam at a maximum rate of 30,000 kilowatts.

The benefits Nigeria hoped to gain from ECOWAS did not materialise, however. The francophone states are still very close to France and CEAO. More important, perhaps, is the fact that it has become very clear to the francophone states that Nigeria cannot replace France as an aid donor and military ally. The ECOWAS scheme to which Nigeria committed lots of time and funds was also unpopular at home, as the Nigerian public came to blame most of their ills − unemployment, crime, lack of housing, prostitution and inflation − on the influx of "ECOWAS citizens" following the agreement on labour mobility. In the light of this general perception, it becomes difficult to see the initiation and formation of ECOWAS as a major foreign policy achievement as Nigerian governments felt. More important is the fact that ECOWAS in the long run, even if it benefits the Nigerian state, is currently under the firm grip of international capital. The alliance between the agents of the Nigerian state, represented by the Federal Commissioner for Economic Development and Reconstruction and international capital represented by the Nigerian Chambers of Commerce, Trade and Industry, was clearly demonstrated in the nature of the activities, negotiations and trade-offs that culminated in the formation of the economic community (Ojo, 1980).

The foreign capital dominated Chambers of Commerce cashed in on government support for its location and role in the Nigerian political economy to move outside the national boundaries. In the words of the Chambers' president, Chief Henry Fajemirokun, the Federation of West African Chambers of Commerce which was created on the instigation of the Nigerian Chambers "went a long way towards preparing other West African governments to commit themselves to ECOWAS...The Federation, its corporate members and officials served as advisers in the negotiations which produced the ECOWAS Treaty" (New Nigerian, 22 November 1976). Thus, it would be right to argue that the comprador role of the Nigerian power elite prevented it from using ECOWAS as a base to advance its fundamental interests without making it secondary to a process of using its oil revenues to advance the interests of international capital. The comments of the Nigerian Head of State in relation to the formation of the Federation of West African Chambers of Commerce lends support to such a position. General Obasanjo declared in March 1975:

> May I express our great satisfaction with the bold initiative taken by the businessmen in our West African sub-region who have given practical demonstration of our hopes and aspirations by forming the Association of West African Chambers of Commerce. They deserve our fullest support.

The group that was to receive this support was foreign capital, a sector which in fact deserves serious and extensive control and regulation if the region is to reap gains from the scheme.

The availability of oil resources has also enabled the Nigerian government to move out of West African affairs while counting the formation of ECOWAS as a successful instance of foreign policy initiative and action. We shall next examine Nigeria's foreign policy towards Southern Africa and the world.

c) Nigerian Foreign Policy Towards Southern Africa

In his address to the 35th session of the UN General Assemby in 1980, President Shagari, just like the military leaders before him, declared:

> Nigeria will no longer tolerate the provocations by South Africa or the dilatory tactics of her allies in the Western block with regard to self-determination and majority rule for Namibia. We deeply deplore the collusion between South Africa and its Western allies which continue to deny the people of that territory of their inalienable rights (<u>New Times</u>, October 1980:13).

This declaration was in fact only a restatement of successive governments' declared commitment to the total liberation of the African continent from colonialism. This desire to liberate Africa and Africans also included a wider objective of contributing to the upliftment of the living standards of black people the world over.

Without doubt this foreign policy position, which was formulated and made very explicit in the seventies, cannot be divorced from the oil boom and the declining reliance on foreign aid. But there were several constraints which clearly prevented the Nigerian power elite from pushing its objectives to the logical conclusion. The government was dependent on a very shaky basis for the revenues with which it wished to liberate the African continent. The sector producing this revenue is still dominated by foreign oil companies and since the elite in charge of state policy is a technico-comprador bourgeois class, the necessity of good relations with Western countries was and remains of primary importance. In the light of these constraints, Nigerian foreign policy towards Southern Africa has witnessed a lot of activities and financial contributions to liberation movements but limited or no change. If one removes oil as a source of revenue, one finds very little to stand on in understanding the force behind the selfimposed leadership of Nigeria in the struggles to liberate Southern Africa. It is also very doubtful if a country which is so fully integrated into the world capitalist economy can speak of the "total liberation" of other territories beyond its narrow understanding of the concept.

Given the underdeveloped nature of the Nigerian economy in comparison to South Africa, its acclaimed principal enemy in the continent, it is easy to understand why the liberation of Southern Africa has come to be interpreted as primarily a financial responsibility; i.e. making generous donations to liberation movements and liberated territories. Nigeria cannot therefore afford to organise and execute a major assault militarily or economically against South Africa or the Western world on which it is heavily dependent. This is not to discount the various efforts by Nigerian governments to impose sanctions against South Africa both unilaterally or otherwise. The crucial question, however, is to what extent did oil contribute to invigorating the country's foreign policy towards Southern Africa?

Prior to the civil war in 1967, Nigeria's opposition to the minority regimes in Southern Africa was based on moral grounds. In fact, South Africa was invited to Nigeria's independence celebrations and trade sanctions against Rhodesia were not imposed until 1963. However, the civil war gave Nigeria a new basis for opposition - security. The material support which South Africa and Rhodesia provided for the secessionist forces forced Nigeria's leaders to come to the realisation that the existence of hostile regimes in the continent also posed a threat to its national security. The Federal Commissioner for External Affairs in the period of the civil war along with the Federal Cabinet strongly believed that the first bomb dropped on the Federal capital by the rebel forces came from Rhodesia. Thus, after the war, the government decided to change its policy towards South Africa and other minority regimes by giving full support to the liberation movements. This new commitment has involved virtually every diplomatic and economic move short of direct military support for the liberation movement even though the idea has been floated around from time to time. The crucial obstacle to such an action arises not only from the relative weakness of Nigeria compared to South Africa but also from the fact that in the event of a military confrontation between Nigeria and South Africa, the latter can count on the direct support of its Western allies. Whatever the obstacles to effective action in Southern Africa, it cannot be disputed that Nigeria's self-imposed leadership role in the region, its search for security in the sub-region and continent and so on were made possible by the oil boom.

Since the civil war, South Africans have been declared prohibited immigrants in Nigeria and a total trade embargo/boycott has been imposed. This has been extended over time to cover all areas of sports, culture and education. Direct bilateral aid mainly in the form of materials has also been extended to the liberation movements in Southern Africa. In 1972, for instance, the Nigerian government contributed £126,000 to the OAU Liberation Committee's fund, in 1973, it contributed $ 180,000. The traditional harassment of the leaders of liberation movements which was very common in the pre-military era has been stopped and the government has used all possible opportunities to denounce the minority regimes in Southern Africa.

An interesting aspect of Nigeria's foreign policy towards Southern Africa has to do with the somewhat contradictory support for armed struggle and peace initiatives at the same time. This position is evident in its support for the peace proposals of the OAU and the UN while at the same time providing moral, financial and material support to the liberation movements. In President Shagari's UN statement he declared:

> I...find it intolerable that the independence of Namibia continues to be bedevilled by the intransigence of South Africa...I sincerely hope that the international Conference on sanctions against South Africa, which the United Nations in co-operation with the OAU plans to hold next year in Paris, will succeed in addressing this important matter as an effective alternative to the use of force by the United Nations to bring about the birth of a new society in South Africa (New Times, October 1980:13).

In the same speech, the civilian leader went on to declare:

> But sanctions alone will not destroy apartheid and racism in South Africa. They can however be used to support the armed struggle. That armed struggle is now gathering momentum. If South Africa persists in its defiance of international will for fundamental changes in its policies, none of us has the right to deny the struggle of the South African nationalists full support. Certainly not Nigeria. We shall continue to assist, encourage and support that struggle with all our might and resources.

This rather contradictory posture has constituted the direction of Nigeria's foreign policy towards South Africa. It has enabled Nigeria to remain friends with both camps involved in that struggle. While Nigeria has found it pertinent to pull some diplomatic strings in support of its initiatives in Southern Africa, it has been careful to select its policies in such a way as not to hurt its fundamental mutual interests with the Western powers. Practical actions like the 1978 and 1986 withdrawal from the Commonwealth games, withdrawal from the Davis Cup in protest against Israel which also has links with South Africa and refusal to participate in the World Amateur Squash Championships and the junior Tennis Championships at Wimbledon all in protest against South Africa's participation, though significant, have not made serious demands on the Nigerian government.

Finally, though the government has declared that the country was compiling information on enterprises which operated simultaneously in South Africa and Nigeria, nothing concrete has come out of that declaration (West Africa 3158, 29 August 1977: 1754). Such tough talk characterised the military era and has been adopted by the civilian regime. As we have pointed out above, Nigeria has no alternative but to see the conflict in Southern Africa in racial terms, while neglecting the fundamental problems posed by international capital. It cannot present a fundamental challenge to South Africa because not only does it lack the military power to do so but also because its location in the international division of labour as a (semi)-periphery dominated by international capital inhibits it from doing so. Thus, at best Nigeria can continue to increase its financial contributions in so far as oil maintains a good price in the international market. It is at this level and in this ambitious manner that Nigeria confronts the major powers.

d) Nigeria in the Global Arena: continuity or change?

At independence in 1960, the conservative government that captured political power in Nigeria was, without inhibitions, pro-Western and anti-communist. Though the country claimed to be non-aligned, it was difficult to define the ways in which non-alignment applied to Nigeria. Indeed, the pre-1966 Balewa government had a distaste for non-alignment. It was prepared to sign a defence pact with Britain, its economic, cultural and political relations were pro-West and it took concrete attempts to restrict the activities of Eastern block countries in Nigeria while at the same time discouraging Nigerians from travelling to communist countries.

In order to comprehend the ideological basis for this pro-Western outlook of the Balewa government, we look at the nature of the transition from colonialism to neo-colonial dependence on Britain and the West. Arising from the latter was the capture of political power by a conservative and aristocratic power elite which interpreted international politics in moralistic and legitimist terms. The colonial state, relations of production and accumulation, patterns of decision-making, institutions and values, were either fully preserved or slightly modified in the process of Nigerianisation. The domination of the economy by colonial capital later joined by either Euro-American interests remained intact. A grand strategy of incorporation was employed by international capital prior to and immediately after independence, through limited Nigerianisation, partnerships, and joint ventures with the state to rationalise the free existence and participation of foreign capital in the economy. This trend became so alarming following independence that a Nigerian Senator made the bitter observation that: "The trend now is to call every company a Nigerian company. That is, somebody is appointed from the outside, a Nigerian, one foolish man, who is usually given a big salary so that they can call the company Nigerian. He has nothing to do with the company" (Osoba, 1977:374). It is against this background that one must attempt to understand the pro-Western foreign policy prior to the military take-over in 1966.

There are several examples to support the view that the pre-1966 policy was pro-West. The Anglo-Nigerian Defence Pact of 1960 was seen as an anti-communist weapon. It was abrogated in 1963 due to widespread protest against it in the country. While no limit was placed on the Western diplomatic staff in Lagos or on their freedom of action and movement, the staff of the Soviet Embassy was limited to ten and constantly checked to ensure conformity. The Balewa government never considered the recognition of Mainland China or Mongolia. Communist literature was banned and no financial or technical aid was sought or accepted from Eastern bloc countries. While Western diplomatic bodies were granted a hundred diplomatic car plates each, the Soviet embassy got five.

However, this situation was slightly altered during and after the civil war. The lukewarm support that the Federal government received from the Western Powers and the direct support given to "Biafra" by France "showed Nigeria the way to the East". The government realised that it was dangerous to rely solely on the West for all economic and military transactions. In fact Britain, which was then Nigeria's largest trading partner, initially refused to aid the Federal government until the Soviet Union agreed to supply urgently needed military materials. The anger that Soviet assistance generated in the West further convinced the military leaders that economic interests were foremost in the calculations of the Western powers. Thus, the general agreement among Nigerian leaders was that the pro-Western policies of the Balewa government must be reviewed.

Unfortunately, diversification of the country's foreign policy could only be executed to a limited extent. It was not as if a marxist government took power. The Nigerian power elite was still essentially comprador in nature. But the big difference which was to make diversification possible was oil and the revenues it brought. This enabled the military rulers to rely more on their own resources, buy from whichever market they wished and upgrade themselves to the status of a "sub-regional" and "continental super" power. The fact that Nigeria had the largest population in Africa meant that it had a market which the West needed and so could afford to diversity its policies without much fear of alienating the Western powers. What are therefore the indicators of change in Nigeria's foreign policy? How fundamental has the change been?

Perhaps the best way to demonstrate some of the changes in policies would be to contrast them where possible to the first pre-military period. The most obvious indication has been the attempt to make the internal and external relations and decision-making in the country independent of foreign manipulation. For instance, when in 1969 the US Ambassador to Nigeria pointed out to the military leaders that the Soviet Embassy had increased the number of its staff from 10 to 13 and demanded an explanation, the government replied that the number of diplomats it allowed into the country was entirely its own responsibility. Had this occured under Balewa, the government would have thanked the Ambassador. In terms of making its policies independent of foreign manipulation, however, very little was achieved. Internally, the Nigerian bourgeoisie has a very tenuous relation to productive activities. This bourgeoisie has been content with its role as a commercial class, which opened the way for foreign capital to dominate productive activities in the country. On the external front, foreign policy was characterised by a lot of action but few concrete achievements. The Western powers have never been against the expenditure of huge sums of money by oil-producing economies. Thus, it is difficult to see the extent to which the country's foreign policy has become independent of the international oil market and the maintenance of productive activities by foreign companies internally. The country's trade is still almost exclusively with the West and the United States of America has remained the largest market for Nigeria's oil still its sole source of revenue. (See table seven).

Unlike in the pre-1966 period, when only Eastern bloc activities received condemnation from the Nigerian government, the post-66 period witnesed the condemnation of whichever power was deemed to have violated international law. U.S. activity in Vietnam and Cambodia received condemnation; the 1968 Soviet invasion of Czechoslovakia was roundly condemned also. The tone of language employed in condemning the minority regimes in Southern Africa and their Western allies became more radical while restrictions on contact between Nigerians and Eastern block citizens were abolished. In the military sphere, serious diversification took place. Prior to the civil war, the training and equipping of the Nigerian Armed Forces was exclusively a Western affair. But with the attitude of the West to the civil war, Nigeria entered into several bilateral economic, cultural and military aid agreements with Eastern bloc countries. The influence of the Soviet Union on the Nigerian airforce after the civil war increased substantially. While the Nigerian government still obtains military supplies from the West, it realises that with its oil wealth and the interest of the Soviet Union in gaining more influence in the country, it could purchase its requirements from the Eastern bloc in times of crisis. With the evident reluctance of the West, particularly Britain and the United States, to help with the building of an iron and steel complex, once again it was easy for Nigeria to turn to the

Soviet Union. As Aluko (1971:186) has observed, "in spite of all this, Nigeria's trade, economic and cultural links remain firmly with the West". In terms of diversifying Nigeria's foreign policy, the post-66 period witnessed efforts in this direction, however.

This diversification coupled with the oil wealth provided Nigeria with the required leverage with which to pull some diplomatic strings in support of its foreign policy initiatives. It also allowed Nigerian leaders to undertake certain measures internally without much fear of sanctions from the Western powers. The constant threat to nationalise Western investments in Nigeria cannot be divorced from this perception. This threat was made very clear in Obasanjo's address to an Anti-Apartheid Conference in Lagos when he declared that Nigeria was:

> ...compiling information on all enterprises who depend on our raw materials and markets but continue to help our enemies. Such enterprises must decide now to choose between us and our enemies and all that goes with that choice. We have a festering sore on which these flies have landed and are feeding in full glare of the world. And when we move to destroy these flies, no one should complain. Foreign contractors who are known to have links with South Africa are already barred from taking part in tenders of any kind...An economic intelligence unit has been set up to ensure successful implementation of this policy (West Africa, 3138, 29 August 1977:1754).

In spite of such tough talk, Nigerian leaders know full well that any economic action is likely to hurt Nigeria more than any Western economy. Its economic sanctions against South Africa have had little effect because the latter was never dependent on the former for anything. But Nigeria has been able to take some concrete actions against Britain over Southern Africa especially on Zimbabwe. Instances of this include the Federal Government's action against Barclays Bank because of the latter's links with South Africa, the nationalisation of British Petroleum as a means of forcing the hands of Britain and the refusal to award some government contracts to British firms. These actions have not affected Nigeria's official relations with Britain in any significant respect. But what should concern any observer is: Why did Nigeria pick on Britain alone, over South Africa?

The answer to this question is not that difficult if we note the pattern of the so-called nationalisations. The Nigerian government, in the first place realised that only Britain could force the hands of the minority regime in South Africa. However, while the actions were being taken, the government was careful to pay full compensation in order not to jeopardise its trade relations with Britain. For instance, it agreed to pay N71 million in oil to the British government for the nationalisation of British Petroleum. That government, other than being satisfied with the compensation, was also careful not to take actions that would lead to the loss of its most lucrative market in the African continent. British investments in Nigeria in 1971, totalled N3,000 million and its exports to Nigeria in 1980 alone stood at N2.2 billion against Nigeria's exports to Britain a paltry N300 million. The United States has increased its investments in the oil sector and, other than being Nigeria's largest market for oil, in 1971, it had $ 1.500 million invested in Nigeria. The Soviet Union which had increased its influence in the country following the civil war, also won a major contract for the construction of Nigeria's iron and steel industry. Countries such as Japan, Brazil, France and Italy have also won major contracts in the construction sector, in agriculture or the services. They have also cornered various sections of the vast Nigerian market. These relations among others, coupled with the fact that Nigeria now had enough money to spend on imports, allowed for accommodation of pronouncements which would never have come from Nigeria in the First Republic.

The new Nigerian foreign policy became characterized by radical pronouncements on major issues and a desire to contribute generously to liberation movements all over the continent. More importantly, in contrast to the pre-military era, the policy exhibited an open desire to intensify relations with Eastern bloc countries. On the issue of external intervention in Africa when a cry was raised by the West over the presence of Cuban troops in Angola, Mozambique, Ethiopia and other areas, Obasanjo had this to say:

> Unless we wish to indulge in self-deception by avoiding unpalatable truths, we should recognise the recent intervention by certain ex-colonial European powers in Central Africa for what it really was. Simply put, it is a most naked and unshamed attempt to determine what Africa's true and collective interests should be. We reject the notion that Africa's interests or collective security needs can be discussed or determined by Western nations...To the extent that any African country can be considered by the West to have "gone communist", it was as a direct result of the failure of Western policies. The fact of the matter is that Africa was colonised by Western powers and not the Soviets. In the struggle for independence and freedom, the only source of effective support was the Eastern bloc countries. The Soviets were therefore invited into Africa for a purpose and that purpose was to liberate the countries to which they were invited from centuries of cruelty, degradation, oppression and

exploitation (<u>African Currents</u> 12/13, Autumn/Winter 1978/79:9).

Commenting specifically on the issue of Cuban presence in Africa, the Nigerian leader took his audience at the OAU by surprise when he declared:

> In every case where Cuba's intervention was established they intervened as a consequence of the failure of Western policies and on behalf of legitimate African interests. We have no right to condemn the Cubans, nor the countries which felt they needed Cuban assistance to consolidate their sovereignty or territorial integrity. (<u>African Currents</u> 12/13, Autumn/Winter 1978/79:9).

As we have pointed out earlier, this increasing radicalism on the part of Nigerian leaders was made possible only by two bargaining advantages which brought them some accommodation from the Western nations – oil revenues and large market. These leaders were, however, very careful not to overdo these advantages so as not to attract sanctions which might lay bare the fragile foundations of the new foreign policy.

The same tough talk was addressed to France by the military leaders who had served as field officers during the Nigerian civil war and were quite familiar with French support for the "Biafran" forces. While receiving the outgoing French Ambassador in 1977, Obasanjo told him that:

> ...the time had come when France should lay more emphasis on her foreign policy formulation and executing the political aspirations of Africans over French economic interests...the activities of the French government in Africa since 1960, through the Nigerian civil war and up to now, showed sharp conflicts between the economic interests of France and the political aspirations of Black Africa. The time has come for France to reduce her pre-occupation with economic considerations which run counter to the interests of Africa by ensuring that events like those of the past do not occur again (<u>African Currents</u> 9, Summer 1977:28).

The rather strong position towards Western powers was not moderated when the External Affairs Commissioner declared in 1976 that "Nigeria would not be deterred from assuming its historical responsibility because of the interests of foreign powers". The Commissioner went on to assert that "Nigeria's new foreign policy abhors any form of confrontation with any super powers, big or small, but if challenged by any foreign power on matters of interest to the nation, Nigeria would stand its ground and would not flinch". The civilian president reinforced this assertion in 1980 when he visited the United States and declared that:

> ...oil has become a weapon in international politics. I am on record as saying that we shall use all weapons at our disposal, including oil if it becomes unavoidable, to pursue and fight for the interests of Nigeria (West Africa 3270, 24 March 1980:516).

While it is true that increasing agitation by intellectuals, public opinion, changes in the international system and personality factors have all contributed to the initiation of this new policy, there is no doubt that the ability to talk tough with limited consequences and back up such tough talk with financial contributions to the OAU and liberation movements has been made possible by oil wealth. It was this oil wealth that enabled Nigeria to initiate and orchestrate the formation of ECOWAS; it has also enabled Nigeria to write off a large chunk of the Community's expenses other than contributing 32% of the annual Community budget. Oil wealth and the direction and content of the new foreign policy, has increased Nigeria's influence in the OAU. Thus, following Britain's entry into the EEC, Nigeria was able to convince the OAU that it must negotiate with the EEC as a collective unit. The new policy also witnessed a diversification or widening of relations with countries in the "Third World" (Carlsson & Shaw (eds), 1987).

This widening is evident in the military's relations with the Western and Eastern bloc countries, the exchange of visits with leaders all over the world and the accommodation of countries ideologically opposed to that professed by the Nigerian power elite. But since the country is heavily reliant on international investment, it has to create a suitable climate attractive to those who wish to invest. It is in this regard that Nigeria, despite its oil wealth and huge population finds it difficult to transcend the tough talk and financial contributions to liberation movements in Southern Africa. Thus, while the Nigerian leaderships have been able to widen the area of economic partnership, they have in fact not adopted any newer revolutionary approach to foreign policy. Leaders have been careful to realise that any drastic action could scare off foreign investors and hurt the country more than the enemy. This could spell danger for a country heavily dependent on imports like Nigeria. In his twentieth independence anniversary speech, President Shagari declared to that nation that, "Our *monthly* import bill which stood at a level of about six hundred million Naira at the beginning of this administration (October 1979) now stands at an average of *one billion Naira per month*. With our policy of liberalising restrictions on import, this figure is likely to rise in months ahead (News from Nigeria, September 1980:3).

With such a policy in mind, it can be seen that Nigeria cannot be expected in the near future to take concrete actions whether military or economic, in support of its foreign policy actions beyond withdrawal from sporting competitions and tough talk at international conferences. The Director of the NIIA has observed that "there is a limit to the retaliatory acts Nigeria can take against industrialised countries for violating her national interest because she needs the transfer of technology" (Akinyemi (ed), 1978:xi). More important that the transfer of technology which can be purchased from within the "Third World" is the fragile degree of internal cohesion which cannot withstand any external crisis. This lack of internal unity is made worse by the peripheral location of Nigeria in the international division of labour which is reproduced by the internal elites who are content to serve as agents to international capital. This means that they cannot be expected to move beyond peripheral attacks on major issues at least to the extent that they do not have to make major military commitments. Oil wealth provides a very good cover for as well as limits to this illusory radicalism.

e) Conclusion

What we have tried to do in this chapter is to draw attention to some apparent directions in Nigeria's foreign policy and to identify the extent to which oil has influenced the "new" policy. The attempt to play the sub-regional or continental superpower role has been identified and it has been argued that this desire to be concerned with the issues affecting other countries in the continent emerged from two sources. The desire to rectify the problems of security which arose during the civil war and the new oil wealth which allowed Nigeria to translate its desires into concrete actions resulted in the diversification of external relations, the initiation and formation of ECOWAS and increasing support to liberation movements. We have also argued that oil wealth and huge population have had to be employed cautiously due to dependence on Western markets for the sale of oil, the domination of this singular revenue source by foreign oil companies, the lack of internal unity and the desire not to create a situation that would demand concrete military commitments. Irrespective of these, the new "radicalism" evidenced in the foreign policy pronouncements of the Nigerian leaders, demonstrates a major shift from the first pre-military period.

The "major shift" referred to above does not suggest a major change in the content and direction of Nigeria's foreign policy, however. Though the leaderships have been consistent in their support for the liberation movements and commitment to schemes such as ECOWAS, the fundamental ideological content of their actions has not changed with regimes. Nigerian leaders have seized every opportunity to re-state their foreign policy objectives and while limited attention has been paid to pressing internal problems, the continental and global responsibilities of the country have been emphasised over and over again. For instance, in his 1979 New Year Broadcast. Obasanjo found time to address the following:

> Our foreign policy of focusing on Africa without ignoring our interests in other parts of the world has yielded dividends in the past year. In concert with other African brothers, we have played our modest part in restoring peace between some warring neighbours in Africa and in encouraging others who might have gone to war to adopt reconciliatory postures...(W)e have not relented our efforts towards hastening the pace of liberation in Southern Africa. While we continue to give full support and co-operation to any fresh initiatives which seek to achieve our purpose in Southern Africa without further bloodshed, we shall continue also to strengthen the hands of the lberation movements and the Frontline states in every way we can (Federal Ministry of Information: 8).

While no one doubts the commitments of Nigerian governments, the position above has been formulated in such a way as not to hurt any one involved in the conflict.

The government has also pursued its global commitments with vigour. During his visit to the United States in 1980, President Shagari declared that Nigeria believed that "so long as one inch of African territory is occupied territory, we remain in bondage, and wherever a black or African is oppressed, we share the indignity...Nigeria shall work relentlessly to uphold the dignity of the black race anywhere in the world". And in the President's address to the Black Caucus in the United States he stressed that "it is honourable, imperative and within the real self interest for United States Black entrepreneurs to invest in Nigeria" (New Times, October 1980:27 and 4).

Finally, the possibility for a deepening of the content and direction of Nigeria's foreign policy still exists. Perhaps as the oil dries up or as Western markets discover new energy sources among other possibilities, Nigeria will begin to experience regional and continental challenges to its power. It might then be forced to employ its military capabilities in order to restore its prestige and safeguard its interests. As the conflict in Southern Africa heightens, the pressures to involve Nigerian forces in it could develop and if this happens, Nigeria cannot refuse considering the fact that it has flirted with the idea openly in the past. Increasing economic prosperity could intensify the desire to consolidate Nigeria's involvement in external issues, but the level of internal unity and the strength and readiness of the army for such external engagements will determine the extent to which the government would push such involvement. Defence expenditures have increased considerably in the 70s (see chapter five). But whatever Nigeria's foreign policy will look like in the next decade will depend not only on perceptions of the leaderships in the country but also on the level of internal mobilisation and stability. Considering the fact that the prospects for oil in the international market over the medium term are not encouraging, the time is running out for Nigeria to utilise its oil wealth in creating a solid internal basis for its foreign policy actions. On the whole, although there have been new developments and issues in the content and directions of Nigeria's foreign policy since the fall of the First Republic in 1966, no fundamental change has occurred.

7 The state of Nigeria: oil crises, power bases and foreign policy

a) **Introduction**

Current events as well as continuing debates have generated a "crisis" in studies of Nigerian foreign policy in particular and of African foreign policy in general (Shaw 1983b) as well as in comparative or development studies (see first half of this volume). The immediate issue is whether regime changes or oil shocks affect policy more; but the underlying tension is about whether "politics" or "economics" (or both) determine direction. In the Nigerian case, the transition from innovative military rule to introverted civilian government (through 1983) led to comparative reviews of regime types in foreign affairs while the roller-coaster of oil price and demand produced dramatic swings in estimates of national "power." With a unstable regime and resource base, can Nigeria in the 1990s still aspire to be a Newly Influential or Industrialising Country (NIC)? Mode of analysis, as well of prescription, for Africa in the world system is being reconsidered as the continent's condition deteriorates and as the continent's relations mature with the approach of the twenty-first century (Shaw, 1980). This chapter treats the controversy about Nigeria's international position and potential in the context of changing global situations, economic, strategic, and analytic.

The intensity of the current economic and academic crisis has led at least to a serious questioning of established assumptions, conclusions, and prescriptions in this case as in others; the comfortable and optimistic perspectives of development and power "theories" have been undermined as underdevelopment and decline have become widespread. The orthodox focus on diplomacy has been superceded by a concern with dependence; idealistic assertions of "African personality" and sovereignty have been replaced by realistic evaluations of peripheralisation and "intervention" (Shaw 1983c). And the optimistic era of nationalist movements and economic "modernisation" has yielded to a reluctant realism about the limits to independence and growth. Even now, hard choices about diplomatic and developmental priorities are avoided as ruling classes pass on the costs to internal subordinates and external financiers. However, critical decision-makers as well as scholars are beginning to look beyond the superficial and towards the structural for the roots of the crisis as well as for insights into dramatic shifts in foreign policy perception and potential.

b) Nigeria in the World System: powerful and/or peripheral?

In the Nigerian case, the orthodox "superstructuralist" position is that transitions to and from military or civilian rule have been crucial, hence the positive evaluations of the soldiers' legacy of "radical" external actions (Akinyemi 1979; Ogunbadejo 1980). By contrast, the critical "sub-structuralist" explanation of Nigeria's Afrocentric activism lies in the dialectics of the national political economy; hence the concentration on the contradictions of capitalism at the semi-periphery. This chapter provides an overview of this debate, reflective as it is of wider issues of analysis and *praxis*. It seeks to situate the contemporary "palavers" about oil, dependence, debt, migration, and conservatism (Schatz 1981 & 1982) in the context of (i) the structures of the Nigerian state and system, (ii) the history of its incorporation and marginalisation in the world system, and (iii) broader disputes about mode of analysis and type of prescription.
 In addition to being generaliseable as well as salient in Africa, Nigeria's possibilities and problems can be taken as typical of a group of emerging "middle powers" in the world system: a minority of new states with significant potential based on oil, industry, population, and/or geostrategic location. Clearly, Nigeria has always been *primus inter pares* in Africa; yet its distinctiveness was enhanced considerably in the 1970s not so much because of the planned return to civilian rule but rather because of the dramatic reorientation and expansion of its economic base − from palm oil to fuel oil. However, perceptions about and attributes

of "power" have been almost as changeable as the price of and demand for "black gold." This was especially so at the start of the new decade of the eighties when production varied from 0.5 to 2.0 million barrels per day with the price peaking at US$35 a barrel in mid-1982 and declining to around $30 a year later and below $15 by 1986. With the oil industry determining 95 percent of Nigeria's export earnings and contributing 45 percent of government revenue, the future of the "rentier" state has clearly become closely tied to one commodity (see chapter one) and so to the position of OPEC in the global economy (Caccia 1983). In turn, rates of industrialisation, let alone the satisfaction of "Basic Human Needs" (Diejomaoh 1982) and the modernisation programme of the armed forces, are now largely a function of the value of oil, or at least of international bankers' estimates of credit-worthiness based on anticipated oil revenues. This "new dependence," reminiscent of pre-colonial reliance on the palm oil trade, also from "eastern" Nigeria, has created power potential but not necessarily actual power or influence. And awareness of the fragility of any imputed "power" coincided with the revival of civil rule - with all its controversies and divisions - and the soldiers' return to the barracks (or the generals' return to their ranches). The glorious days of leading Africa were seemingly short and transitory, even if Babangida aspires to revive Mohammed's heady achievements (see next chapter).

The new modesty or maturity displayed by Nigeria's foreign policy as the boom fades is matched at the analytic level by a trend away from "realism" and towards revisionism or radicalism. How can one explain the apparent rise and fall in Nigeria's power? In reality, the contemporary crisis of oil glut (Aluko 1982; Wright 1981) merely reinforced or accelerated a debate which had already been joined about the character of Nigeria's political economy. So, while the immediate catalysts of the re-examination were cycles in the oil market and return to civilian rule, the beginnings of the debate were already present. Is Nigeria a dependent or national capitalist state? Can elements within the indigenous bourgeoisie transcend their inheritance and advance a more autonomous class or corporate base for accumulation and reproduction?

And these fundamental questions can be translated for the prupose of foreign affairs into issues of national resources and leadership. What has been the balance between continuity and change in foreign policy? Have African and extra-African issues been primary? Can Nigeria redefine its conception of nonalignment and patterns of exchange to moderate its vulnerabilities? In short, given the vagaries of world politics and trade as well as its own class contradictions and coalitions, can the Nigerian state reorient its development policy and potential to maximise its autonomy and capability?

The impetus for this new scepticism about the bases of political economy and so foreign policy lay not only in the return to civilian rule or in the suddenness of the reverse "oil shocks" but also in a series of apparent setbacks to Nigeria's external goals. Has Nigeria become weaker in resources and resolution? By contrast to the apparent "golden age" of foreign policy under Mohammed and Obasanjo, the Shagari administration, operating in an immensely complex domestic system, suffered "setbacks" in regional, continental, and global affairs: disarray in Chad and border clashes with Cameroon, stalemate over Namibia, and less respect in Europe and the United States. During the soldiers' halcyon era they had created ECOWAS, recognising the MPLA and nationalised BP, respectively. And the very conjuncture of changing regime (internal), fortune (external) and situation (global) makes the debate about explanations and implications so intriguing and intense. This debate throws some light on (i) Nigeria's distinctive political economy in particular, (ii) African foreign policies in general, and (iii) prospects for national capitalism and industrialisation in the late twentieth-century, a period of economic contraction and strategic confrontation, especially among the NICs.

To date, for both Nigerian and other African cases, the most prevalent framework for "explaining" changes in policy orientations and results has been chronology. Given the frequency of recourse to such an approach and its considerable limitations, we do not intend to linger on it. Suffice it to say that characteristic of the prevailing superstructural perspective on Nigeria's foreign relations is such a periodisation of its degree of assertiveness and Afrocentricity according to regime changes. Billy Dudley (1982,278) reflects a widespread view by suggesting that such a chronological framework - "1960-65;1966-69;1970-75; and post 1975 (at least till 1979 when the second republic came into being on 1 October and then 1983 when on 31 December the generals returned) - does offer a useful starting point within which Nigeria's external relations may be examined." This chapter attempts to go beyond such superficial and simplistic description-cum-categorisation, while recognising that policies do indeed change in design, intention, and impact, seeing any shifts as reflective of underlying evolutions and contradictions - "conjunctures" at the level of production as well as of politics.

c) **Levels and Roles**

The new scepticism apparent in Nigerian foreign policy circles has generated a debate about alternative explanations for the constraints on national effectiveness and influence. Given

Table Ten

Oil Refineries

* Existing oil refineries:

	Operating capacity b/d	Technical capacity b/d
Port Harcourt.	60,000	60,000
Warri.	85,000	100,000
Kaduna.	73,000	100,000

Refineries' output (maximum production of refined products from existing facilities and planned output from fourth refinery, tonnes/year):

	Existing refineries	Fourth refinery
Liquified petroleum gas.	280,000	123,000
Gasoline.	2,830,000	2,780,000
Kerosene.	1,550,000	930,000
Diesel.	2,960,000	820,000
Fuel oil.	1,430,000	2,350,000
Total	9,050,000	7,003,000

Source: NNPC

the several spatial levels at which Nigeria operates, distinctions among them and about the country's relative power capabilities at each constitute one form of understanding. The other major source of explanation, the one advanced by more radical scholars, is the character of Nigeria's political economy; this is treated in the next section. These two very different types or modes of analysis are advanced by *realist* and *radical* advocates, respectively; the ideal response (discussed latter) is essentially prescriptive rather than evaluative.

Distinctions about levels of interactions and types of role conception are most compatible with a realist viewpoint: where does Nigeria exert "power" and under which conditions and guises? In the Nigerian case, one characteristic of a middle power is the tension between "dominance" at the continental or regional levels and "dependence" at the global level. Nigeria's intermediate status does not guarantee influence in world forums (e.g. "global negotiations" for a New International Economic Order), although it may do so in African arenas (e.g., recognition of MPLA or involvement in the Chadian and Saharan situations). Nevertheless, because of its middle power position, Nigeria may attempt to mediate between Africa and the world (thus its leadership role in EEC-ACP negotiations for Lome I). Likewise, extra-African actors may encourage it to represent them towards other African interests (between the Front Line States and the five-nation Western "contact group" over Namibia). In almost all instances, however, Nigerian mediation serves to exacerbate its own tensions with Western countries and corporations, particularly with the United Kingdom and the United States over Southern Africa.

Like most states, Nigeria's global and regional relations are interrelated. Its efforts at (i) conflict resolution within the OAU system, (ii) political liberation in Southern Africa, and (iii) regional integration in West Africa cannot be separated from either its national political economy on the one hand or its global associations of the other hand. African activity and advocacy are interrelated with continuing issues at the national as well as global levels. Given the increasing Afrocentricity of Nigeria's foreign policy, Kal Holsti's (1972, 121-127) typology of national role conceptions can be usefully applied to official policies and self-perceptions despite the constraint of global positions and connections.

At the continental level Nigeria has continued to be a *status quo* "mediator;" in Southern Africa it has become something of a "liberation supporter," whereas in West Africa, despite a certain reluctance, it has maintained the role, in both formal and informal ways, of being "regional leader." Nevertheless, conflict resolution and political liberation in the African continent and regional integration and political co-operation in West Africa bring Nigeria up against a variety of extra-African interests and institutions; super and great powers (especially France's close ties with Ivory Coast and Senegal) and a range of international organisations are also involved in such issues. East-West conflicts and intra-Western tensions (including intra-EEC struggles) as well as corporate and religious (e.g., over Israel in the Middle East and Libya in the Sahel) concerns are all reflected in the range of such ostensibly "African" problems; and so they constrain Nigeria's own definition and implementation of its several African roles.

First, at the *continental* level, Nigeria's policy of supporting Pan-African unity and diplomacy has led it into active involvement in a range of OAU questions. Its encouragement of an African Common Market was market by the April 1980 economic summit and declaration in Lagos. Its concern over the festering civil war in Chad generated numerous meetings and proposals, including the dispatch of an ill-fated Nigerian "expeditionary force" to Ndjamena in 1979-80, which pitted Nigeria against Gaddafi's Libya. But with the ebb and flow of interrelated Sahelian struggles, Nigeria's oft-imagined regional security role was revived in late 1981 when 2,000 troops along with a Nigerian commander flew back to Chad to head-up an OAU peace-keeping force assembled to replace the Libyans, providing the security framework within which Habre finally replaced Oweddi despite Nigeria's reservations and threats to pull out once again.

President Shagari followed in the footsteps of Balewa, Gowon, and Obasanjo in serving as a Pan-African mediator, particularly on the Chad and Sahara issues just as his predecessors had been involved in Congo/Zaire/Shaba conflicts, Kenya/Ethiopia/Somalia tensions, and various Maghreb and Mashreq disputes.

Second, at the level of *Southern Africa,* Nigeria's support for antiracist African nationalism has put it more directly in opposition to various Western countries and corporations, although shared commercial interests once again moderate antagonisms. Nigeria's support of the liberation movements has overall been quite muted - especially in the comparable Balewa and Shagari periods - and it has emerged as a "helpful fixer" between the Western " contact group" and the Front Line States over a series of multilateral negotiations. In general, it has supported political rather than economic change (i.e., nationalism rather than socialism), although its recognition of the MPLA regime in Angola was, probably mistakenly, generally taken to be a move towards a more radical stance (Daddieh and Shaw 1983). Its assistance in the Lancaster House negotiation and agreement over independence for Zimbabwe, however, revealed the essential continuity in

Nigeria's Southern African policy — formal freedom without structural change. Yet the combined insensitivities of the Reagan and Thatcher administrations may further strain Nigeria's tolerance of Western perfidy, notwithstanding their common conservative inclinations, in terms of "national security" and laissez-faire economics.

And third, at the *West African* level, Nigeria's advocacy of regional integration is based on a pair of interrelated concerns: (i) regional cooperation for development (ECOWAS and river basin development), and (ii) regional cooperation to reduce extra-regional penetration (aid to Ghana, Guinea and Liberia and plans for regional collective security). Clearly, these two factors of development and vulnerability are interrelated. Nigeria's interest in its own economic, especially industrial, fortune since 1970 has coincided with its interest in reducing foreign, especially European, involvement in national and regional economies; hence the careful balancing of attempts at regional self-reliance (such as ECOWAS and collective security) with efforts at global restructuring (such as the Lome Conventions and PanAfrican peace-keeping capability, both involving revisions in EurAfrican linkages in favour of African interests). Nigerian diplomacy in West Africa — and hence its relationship with the EEC — has come to reflect those national interests which favour such regional and global reforms, as Olatunde Ojo (1980, 601) indicates in his insightful analysis of the domestic and bureaucratic politics involved:

> Domestically, one of the factors in Nigeria's active role in the formation of ECOWAS was and is the country's desire to become the industrial heart of West Africa with all the political power that this may bring, not only within Africa but also in the world at large. A concomitant of this is the desire to undermine or erode French economic and political influence which has sometimes been inimical to Nigeria's interests in the sub-region. The need to utilise Nigerian petroleum revenue, while it lasts, and to provide alternatives to oil dependence later came to reinforce commitment to ECOWAS. As it became clear that this task of reducing dependence could not be solved in isolation, the commitment to the success of ECOWAS became irrevocable.

But the status of intermediary is never certain. Particularly in the post-military, post-Bretton Woods period of pluralist politics domestically and protectionist politics globally, Nigeria's oil revenues and effective resources have been unstable. Subsequent difficulties over independence in Namibia or over the roles of Tanzania in Uganda, Libya in Chad, or Senegal in the Gambia (all of which Nigeria opposed, apparently out of fear of the three former states "annexing" the later trio in various "federal" arrangements) have revived worries about being either over-committed or under-powered. As Stephen Wright (1981,1686) indicates, Nigeria's grip on events has been uncertain even in relation to ostensibly weaker neighbours:

> The recent border clashes with Benin and Cameroon, the mistakes and failure to act effectively in Chad, and the refusal to intervene in Equatorial Guinea in the late 1970s, all are issues which have troubled Nigeria and which have not received the appropriate response.

In response to such apparent setbacks, Olajide Aluko (1981a,31,33) amongst others has called for a new calculus in foreign relations to avoid two particular errors based on economic and psychological miscalculations or misperceptions, namely

> to cast for Nigeria a role in world affairs that is clearly beyond our means...[and] the psychological error made by most Nigerians in and outside government that because of the size, population, and the agricultural and mineral resources in the country we are destined to lead Africa.

On one level, this debate over foreign policy could be cast in terms of *scope* of the "national" interest:

> ...in the Nigerian context there has been some contention about whether the focus should be egocentric, that is to say purely Nigerian, whether it should serve the West African region, Africa as a whole, or at its broadest, the interests of the black people throughout the world. (Wright 1981, 1685)

However, at another level, the debate is about the *bases* of the national interest. Any examination of these necessitates a slight diversion into the central characteristics of the national political economy. For an intermediate middle power like Nigeria has a distinctive position in the global economy as well as in the world diplomatic and strategic systems; this too may serve to explain some of its limitations and frustrations.

d) The Character of Nigeria's Political Economy

Nigeria's claim to being a middle power is one aspect of its incorporation into the international economy, which is essentially capitalist. Its espousal of a *laissez faire* system (reinforced because of regime changes and external constraints in the first half of the 1980s) serves to secure its position as an intermediary between "centre" and "periphery" – a part of the "semi-periphery". But "peripheral capitalism" also generates a range of contradictions which cluster around the tension between international and national interests. It also tends to reinforce patterns of dependence, at least until a degree of industrialisation secures an element of autonomy.

There are, then, limits on the extent to which Nigeria can claim to be a Newly *Influential* Country, let alone a Newly *Industrialising* Country (NIC). As Peter Evans (1979,299) indicates in his comparative analysis of this set of middle powers, "Nigeria is not only one of the least industrialised countries in the group but also one whose primary qualification for semi-peripheral status is its oil wealth. Brazil and Nigeria represent opposite poles within the range of Third World countries that might be considered members of the 'semi-periphery'".

Nigeria's claim to be a middle power is clearly stronger in terms of influence rather than of industrialisation, notwithstanding limits on the former. And its claim to be a NIC is really a function of the underdevelopment of its immediate region rather than of the development of its political economy. As Peter Evans notes, Nigeria's transition away from classic dependence seems to be assured primarily because of its *relative* position in region and continent.

However, the tenuousness of Nigeria's status as a NIC is also related to the character of its political economy. For while as a part of the semi-periphery, its economy is controlled by a coalition of international capital, local capital, and state capital – the "triple alliance" at the centre of Evans (1979,11) analysis – the first partner, transnational capital, is still dominant. Unlike the Nigerian case, Brazil's local capital has become hegemonic, suggestive of the rise of a "national bourgeoisie." Given continued dependence on petroleum exports and industrial imports such a bourgeoisie remains embryonic in Nigeria (Beckman, 1985 and Schatz 1977), with important implications for foreign policy.

The frustrations which Nigerian decision-makers articulate may in part be due to this continued reliance on transnational capital and to the limited evolution of a national bourgeoisie. Nevertheless, the trend towards the status and substance of a NIC at the semi-periphery is apparent.

To be sure, there are severe limits on the degree to which the military's programmes of indigenisation and now privatisation can by itself create or advance a national bourgeoisie; nevertheless, one is emerging in Nigeria as at least some of the oil revenue is used to prime indigenous entrepreneurs rather than multinational corporations.

Despite continued dependence, local interests have done rather well through the indigenisation exercise (Ake, 1986).

However, the OPEC windfall only lasted for a few years; "black gold" has not brought infinite income let alone exponential development. Instead, outward-oriented growth has been reinforced rather than reduced, with foreign loans coming to replace inadequate oil revenues. As the critical International Labour Office (ILO) report suggests in its advocacy of *First things First: meeting the basic needs of the people of Nigeria* (1981,v,4,5) from a comparative perspective:

> There is still much acute poverty in Nigeria...Since oil is a non-renewable resource, the governments of large oil-exporting countries had set the diversification of production and exports as a major objective. Yet the opposite had happened...despite considerable expenditures on education, the economies concerned were not noticeably more independent of the need for foreign technologies and equipment: on the contrary, they had become less self-reliant. Meanwhile, their populations became increasingly dependent on imports of consumer goods, even food...

> There is little evidence that Nigeria's big expenditure has made much impact on the conditions of the majority of the population. The distortions experienced by the other oil exporters seem to have been repeated in Nigeria.

This extended yet reinforced pattern of dependence is but the fundamental feature of Nigeria's incorporation within the world system; it affects all other aspects of political economy and foreign policy. First, as the ILO report itself makes clear, since the early 1970s

> ...several structural changes in the economy have occurred which have resulted in a *worsening of income distribution*. These transformations are all directly and indirectly linked to the oil boom and have culminated in a rapid increase in the urban economy...Altogether there are over three times as many poor families in rural areas as in urban areas (1981,220,231;emphasis added).

Second, Nigeria has been becoming very dependent on *food imports*, especially wheat and rice, despite its history of feeding itself. Third, following the indigenisation decrees, as already indicated, there is a growing tension between the more national and the more comprador elements within the *Nigerian bourgeoisie*. Fourth, many multinationals operating in Nigeria also have branches in *South Africa*, an apartheid regime that the government is determined to overthrow; will "national interest" constrain international goals? Fifth, Nigeria is a country divided not only by region, ethnicity, and class but also by *religion*; how will an officially non-sectarian administration deal with those issues - such as relations with Israel and Libya - with religious overtones? And sixth, in West Africa will Nigeria's role be that of *regional leader* or of regional dominator? Is its position in ECOWAS that of disinterested advocate or of "subimperial" power? In short, is Nigeria's Afrocentricity exercised on its own behalf or on behalf of Western countries and corporations?

This set of underlying issues, reflected in particular debates over Cameroon and Chad, led Aluko (1981a,12) to become increasingly critical as the new decade dawned about Nigeria overestimating its power and overstretching its scarce resources:

> The catalogue of errors in our foreign policy is long... The first is the failure of our leaders especially the post-1975 ones to appreciate severe external and internal constraints on their freedom of choice and therefore strike a foreign policy that will be Nigeria-centered; that is it will be self-seeking in the sense that its primary preoccupation should be the promotion of the country's security and the well-being of the people...

This rather "idealist" perspective by contrast with his earlier "realist" assertions is suggestive of the trend towards debate and revisionism in studies of Nigerian foreign policy, a final model of explanation or rationalisation to which we now turn.

e) Realism, Idealism and Radicalism

There is, then, a growing debate in and around Nigeria about the character and direction of the country's external politics and policies, reflective of the expansion of a "foreign policy community" inside Nigeria itself. (Shaw and Fasehun 1980). These alternative views about the bases, effects, and limits of Nigeria's political economy in the world system can be categorised, as already suggested, into three types: the idealist versus the realist (disagreement over contemporary and future capabilities and influences) and the realist versus the radical (disagreement over historical, current, and projected structures and relations). The majority of analysts, as befits a state with relative "power" at the semi-periphery, are realists (Stremlau 1981); only a minority are either idealists or radicals, with the latter minority position becoming more widespread than the former.

Characteristic of the dominant *realist* position as well as reflective of differences within this "paradigm" is the work of Bolaji Akinyemi and Olajide Aluko, at least until Aluko's inaugural lecture. Both of these leading scholars — it is not coincidental that they have been Director-General of the Nigerian Institute of International Affairs and Professor of International Relations at the University of Ife, respectively — take it to be axiomatic that Nigeria is powerful and influential. They may be in disagreement about some of the causes of this power and influence — political leadership, bureaucratic style, military might, or economic resources — but they exhibit few doubts about the overall character of Nigeria's external stature and status. In this shared assumption they reflect the perspective of most Nigerian scholars and statesmen as well as that of most students of Nigeria, who see Nigeria as a Newly *Influential* Country, as Africa's great power, and as a successful example of "development." If any scepticism about Nigeria's standing has been expressed by realists it has usually been about (i) how long oil (and gas) reserves will last, (ii) how long the civilian government would last, and (iii) how long contemporary confusion and chaos in the infrastructure will last. In general, though, such difficulties are taken to be surmountable given Nigeria's financial and entrepreneurial resources. In short, the mood is very optimistic and rather heady despite current setbacks.

By contrast, the two minority positions are considerably less optimistic and popular. The *idealist* view is less developed and debated than the radical one and is not identified with the work of any single scholar. Rather, there are elements of idealist views inside the writings of several Nigerian scholars such as Mazi Ray Ofoegbu (1978) and Aluko; what should be the bases and directions of Nigerian foreign policy? For instance, Aluko has recently lamented the deficiencies in Nigeria's economic, strategic, and political structures and argued for greater attention being given to the national interest rather than to regional and/or continental affairs. He proposes a careful balancing of means with ends rather than a reckless pursuit of grandeur. In general, the realist and idealist perspectives on Nigerian foreign policy are not very far apart. Rather, the latter consists of redefinitions of or revisions to the former. That is, *if* Nigeria is to be influential in the future, *then* it must reform its political economy and federal bureaucracy to make its goals more readily realisable — possibly doing what the ILO advocates, putting *First things First*. The idealistic impulse is more nationalist and isolationist than the radical stance, seeking to put the Nigerian state (i.e., bourgeoisie) first, even if not the Nigerian people. The idealism concentrates on the quest to balance ends and means not on the identification of "good" goals: a mix of modesty and maturity with underlying patriotism. In some ways, the idealist position is preemptive of the radical one; it anticipates future (positive) relations as a way of responding to current (negative) criticisms.

By contrast, the other minority position - that of the *radicals* - is much less optimistic and idealistic. Instead, it sees Nigeria potentially as a Newly *Industrialising* Country confronting all sorts of contradictions and constraints such as those suggested above; the future is less clear and more problematic - the working out of various contradictions - than in either of the other two perspectives. Rather, both indigenous and foreign analysts in this genre see Nigeria as an essentially dependent state, albeit one at the semi-periphery rather than at the periphery; its place in the world system and its emergent class society - in Evan's terms the triple alliance - will constrain both its present and future influence.

So, instead of an assured future, Nigeria's growth and influence are seen to be rather unstable and unsustainable; the favourable conjuncture of forces that generated the oil boom may not be repeatable. However, as a state at the semi-periphery, Nigeria did experience rapid, if uneven, growth in the 1970s. Nevertheless, the projection of oil-based boom into the future remains problematic because of both internal contradictions and external changes, particularly domestic tensions and international demand.

Such radical analysis clearly remains the minority school of opinion, yet one that is increasing in forcefulness as Nigeria's rapid growth generates further uneven development. Moreover, its persuasiveness is reflected in the fact that the major debate now is between realists and radicals; the idealist perspective is usually mobilised only in defence of the realist position rather than in its own right. One positive and immediate result of this growing debate is that both realists and radicals have had to reconsider their assumptions and evidence, especially the political and economic bases of foreign policy (Shaw and Aluko, 1983).

This re-evaluation has been stimulated not only by setbacks to Nigeria's foreign policy goals, brought about by either inadequate resources or overly ambitious intentions, but also by changes in the world system since the mid-1970s. Ironically, Nigeria has benefited significantly, at least in the short-term, from the high price of oil: but in the longer-term the shake-down resulting from the demise of the Bretton Woods system may yet retard its prospects. As already suggested, protectionist pressures in the North may come to disturb the close relationship between centre and semi-periphery to the detriment of the latter; notwithstanding Andrew Young's (1981) advocacy of an Americo-Nigerian alliance (Mazrui 1982), the logic of the semi-periphery may disappear as inflation and recession lead to pressure for "re-industrialisation" within the OECD. However, if sufficient global growth is generated, only the periphery and not the semi-periphery will suffer, especially if, as in the case of Nigeria, the semi-periphery produces petroleum products and consumes industrial products.

This vestigial confidence, a confidence expressed each time the Nigerian economy goes into a temporary nosedive, is based on the remains of "modernisation theory" as applied to the giant of Africa. This "theory" still serves dominant interests in the national economy just as it advanced colonial interests previously. As Segun Osoba suggests in his early critique of the state of Nigerian foreign policy studies:

> This ideology, initially inspired by the departing colonial authorities and later dressed up in academic respectability by Western and some Nigerian scholars, became the colossal myth used to gloss over all the ugly contradictions in Nigeria's domestic and foreign policies (1980, 209).

Osoba, writing initially in the 1960s, is critical about such a mode of analysis because (i) it originated from foreign and not indigenous scholars and (ii) it represented rather superficial scholarship. He is quite correct in arguing for more radical analysis of structure rather than of forms, along the lines proposed in the two preceeding sections of this chapter. But while his critique of foreign students of Nigerian foreign policy may have been justified in the sixties, it is clearly inappropriate for the seventies. For the main source of conservative, realist, and idealist opinion is now internal; by contrast, much revisionist and radical scholarship is foreign in origin (Williams 1976). Osoba's opposition to expatriate analysts should surely be focused on indigenous students, with their outward-oriented perspectives and borrowed, somewhat outdated, assumptions:

> They could not resist the strong, but baneful, temptation of being ideological flag-bearers for their respective countries. Because their countries had economic, ideological and political reasons for wanting Nigeria's foreign policy to be Western-oriented, they tend to shower encomiums on Nigeria for her coolness to the communist countries and for her enthusiasm for a Western alliance (1981, 211).

If it is now impossible to accept Osaba's criticism of foreign scholars for being conservative, one may welcome his lament for the superficiality of most studies of Nigerian foreign policy. His opposition to a "super-structural" level of analysis is supportive of the growing critique of non-radical studies and underlines the explanations offered above the unsatisfactory realist performance to date. In advocating a radical perspective, Osoba points to "the real issues" in foreign relations of economic production and exchange:

> Nigeria's position was not a unique one...most of the countries, referred to as the Third World, cannot, even with the greatest will the the world, pursue thoroughly independent and nonaligned foreign policies, insulated from the manoeuvres and manipulations of the big powers on the international scene (1980,214).

The revisionist mood in Nigerian foreign policy circles serves to popularise such a position. The renewed advocacy of more nationalist, as opposed to Afrocentric or intermediary, roles under pressure of economic and strategic difficulties may, of course, be quite compatible with a trend towards national, as opposed to transnational or state, capital – towards a renegotiation within the triple alliance. While Nigeria cannot readily escape from the legacy of a decade of oil boom, it can move to contain certain expectations and excesses. Austerity is the motif of a chastened regime with restricted room for manoeuvre. "Green revolutions" and industrialisation with indigenisation need now to be advanced with greater determination if the slowdown is to be turned to good advantage – the renewed nurturing of Nigerian capitalism (Schatz 1977 and 1982).

f) Conclusion: the future of the Nigerian state

The ultimate test of the three foreign policy "schools" identified above is, of course, whether they chart the future with any accuracy. Given recent events, the realist group sees itself to be under criticism: hence its shift towards revisionism as represented by the idealist and nationalist elements. By contrast, the responsive idealist and radical viewpoints have yet to be tried by history. Each of them contains implicit projections as well as prescriptions – Nigeria's future "foreign policy."

First, in general, the realists remain optimistic, considering any problem with oil exports, external payments, industrial imports or food production merely temporary and superable difficulties. Nigeria is clearly destined, according to this perspective, to become the leading diplomatic, economic, and strategic force on the continent — an "interdependent" actor. Second, the idealists are also reasonably confident that Nigerian decision-makers will, under the combination of internal pressures and external problems, come to reassess priorities so arriving at a more sustainable definition of the national interest even if the country's "mission" in Africa is reduced in scale — an "independent" actor. And finally, the radicals expect that a series of tensions — Nigeria versus larger and smaller states, national versus transnational bourgeois fractions, and bourgeois versus proletarian and peasant interests — will intensify before the country begins to transcend its continuing "dependent" position.

Of course, all of the latter set of contradictions could become more antagonistic in the foreseeable future, albeit in different degrees, if the place of the semi-periphery is squeezed between protectionist centre and self-reliant periphery. Tenuous NICs like Nigeria are both products of and subject to changes in the contemporary system — middle power ambitions with at best incomplete industrial capabilities. And the social relations, not merely the sequential chronology, of any period or regime are affected, even mediated, by such external links and limits. Internal hegemonies are inseparable from external happenings. So Nigerian "foreign policy" is not only a question of diplomacy and strategy but also an integral aspect of external incorporation and orientation. Hence, it is salient in the domestic and international milieus and it is relevant for internal and external scholarship — a truly problematic power, as indicated in our concluding chapter.

8 Nigeria restrained: foreign policy under changing political and petroleum regimes

The entire dynamic foreign policy concept, as Nigeria has employed it to date, reflects a certain unreality, not only about the Nigerian ability to force changes in Africa but also about the desired changes.
— R. O. Ogunbambi (1985:12)

Nigeria did seem to win a special place in the US firmament and the American popular consciousness. On a continent so full of violence and radicalism, Nigeria came to seem from afar like a calm, trustworthy, even conservative nation. For all its domestic turmoil, it did not have a significant movement that advocated a Marxist or even a mainstream socialist solution to the country's problems.
— Sanford J. Ungar (1985:155)

The nature of the crisis which the Nigerian state was undergoing when the military overthrew the Shagari government was such that it could be categorised as organic...the December 1983 coup was not just a military intervention in the usual conventional sense, but rather a decisive political intervention by an armed fraction of the Nigerian dominant classes aimed at saving the state (in this case, a 'stunted' one, ie. of the neo-colonial genre) from imminent collapse.
— Herbert Ekwe-Ekwe (1985:617 and 618)

> The foreign policy of the Federation of Nigeria is in certain respects atypical, in others fairly representative, of...African states...On many African and international issues, its policy has been surprisingly modest and restrained. This is a quite remarkable position, considering the fact that...several Nigerian leaders pioneered in the African nationalist awakening.
> – James S. Coleman (1963: 379)

In just twenty-five years since independence, Nigeria has experienced a meteoric rise and fall in its foreign policy status and success (see Shaw & Aluko (eds), 1983); the continuing decline in the price of petroleum highlights the precipitousness of this fall from grace. In its wake, national regimes have been removed, civilian and military alike, and foreign policy analyses have been revised. The fanciful notion, apparently held by scholars as well as statesmen, that Nigeria was Africa's great power and was prepared to follow declarations with actions, has been discarded almost as quickly as it was discovered (see previous chapter). The last decade has thus witnessed a rapid sequence of political and intellectual assertiveness followed by a new mood of reevaluation, redefinition and retreat (see part one).

a) Political Economy and Foreign Policy: from rentier to debtor state

Yet there was a remains an element of truth in claims for Nigeria's distinctiveness: it is still primus inter pares in West Africa and an influential actor in continental and global affairs. But it did exaggerate its potential and overextend its capacity in the late-1970s and early-1980s (Baker, 1984). Thus the current period of revisionism should not overlook the continuing as well as changeable bases of Nigeria's political economy and foreign policy. Unlike so much of the continent in crisis, Nigeria has both ebullience and resilience: Nigerian capitalism remains resourceful and potentially resurgent. The new modesty in Nigeria's stance may be welcome by neighbours and supporters alike but it should not lead to an underestimation or misperception of Nigeria's not inconsiderable power and potential, both now and in the future.

The seemingly dramatic sequence in Nigeria's foreign policy fortunes and economic frustrations since the start of the 1980s are essentially functions of changing internal (political) and external (financial) regimes: the return of the generals and the demise of petro-naira. But underlying apparent constraints and cycles is a large and active political economy. Nigeria's agricultural base has been overshadowed and undermined by the preoccupation with petroleum but it has not been altogether ruined. The inherited colonial commodity structure of cocoa, palm-oil and groundnuts may have shrunk but food production and distribution remain fundamental bases of the national economy. Likewise, under the imperative of foreign trade restrictions, local manufacturing may yet come to rely on internal rather than imported inputs. In short, Nigeria's massive market of about 100 million still offers potential opportunities and profits not found elsewhere on the continent. And the ubiquitous informal economy, without its smuggling and black marketeering elements, could be recognised as one engine of exchange and survival, particularly if its female bases were appreciated.

Windfall results from the petro-naira "bubble" generated fanciful notions of instant industrialization and continental dominance at the level of the state. But these were always elusive because at the level of individuals, private enrichment took precedence over collective goods. Traditional forms of inducement escalated into unprecendented plunder: "dash" became rape. The leadership aspirations of the country were undermined by the consumption habits of its countrymen. For a brief decade - 1971 to 1981 - Nigeria attracted an unending stream of merchant venturers and a few Nigerians exported the proceeds of the loot. Meanwhile, indigenous capacities were diminished and international involvements were short-lived. With the inevitable bursting of the bubble in the early 1980s the rentier state became a debtor state and the soldiers returned to abort the second Shagari Presidency (Falola & Ihonvbere, 1985).

The Second Republic, from 1979 to 1983, marked the zenith and decline of Nigeria's aspirations to become, overnight, both Newly Industrializing and Newly Influential Country (NIC). But the erstwhile "Brazil of Africa" had not properly laid the foundations for its elevation into a NIC despite the relative subordination of its surrounding territories (Shaw & Fasehun, 1980). Nigerian capitalism was too rapacious and impatient: the technocratic fraction of the indigenous bourgeoisie which sought to invest in infrastructure, technology and basic needs never had a chance in opposition to bureaucratic, comprador, military and political fractions. And even the petty bourgeoisie was mesmerized by dreams of petro-naira contracts and affluence. The future would obviously take care of itself, so the fourth five year plan announced, if the price of oil just remained around $40 a barrel. The 1985-6 15-month economic emergency and dramatic late-1986 naira devaluation indicate just how inappropriate was that assumption.

Even sweet Bonny Light never reached this apex so Nigeria's grandiose schemes were never feasible, no matter whether significant percentages of each contract had or had not gone

Table Eleven

Nigeria's Oil Production in Million Barrels a Day

	1975	1976	1977	1978	1979	1980	1981	1982	1983	1984	1985
January............	2.0	2.0	2.2	1.6	2.4	2.2	2.1	1.8	0.8	1.4	1.4
February...........	1.8	2.1	2.2	1.6	2.4	2.1	1.9	1.4	0.7	1.5	1.7
March..............	1.7	2.0	2.3	1.5	2.4	2.2	1.9	0.9	0.9	1.6	1.7
April..............	1.6	2.1	2.3	1.7	2.4	2.2	1.6	0.9	1.2	1.4	1.6
May................	1.5	2.1	2.2	1.7	2.4	2.1	1.3	1.3	1.6	1.2	1.4
June...............	1.6	2.1	2.2	1.9	2.4	2.2	1.4	1.6	1.5	1.3	1.2
July...............	1.6	2.0	2.1	1.9	2.4	2.1	0.8	1.3	1.7	1.1	1.0
August.............	1.8	1.9	2.0	2.1	2.2	2.0	0.7	1.1	1.3	1.1	1.3
September..........	1.9	2.0	2.0	2.1	2.1	1.6	1.1	1.2	1.2	1.4	1.5
October............	1.9	2.1	2.0	2.1	2.1	1.9	1.3	1.5	1.3	1.4	0.7
November...........	2.0	2.2	1.9	2.3	2.2	2.1	1.6	1.4	1.3	1.5	1.8
December...........	2.0	2.2	1.9	2.4	2.2	2.0	1.8	1.2	1.3	1.7	1.7
YEAR'S AVERAGE.....	1.8	2.1	2.1	1.9	2.3	2.1	1.5	1.3	1.2	1.4	1.4

Source: FT estimates.

into European bank accounts or exhorbitant local costs. The obverse of Nigeria's massive market is the demand for basic services, which the state was always unable to satisfy. Despite partisan and ethnic claims to the contrary, social services have never been free or extensive in Nigeria in pre- or post-independence eras. Bourgeois inclinations moderated redistributive measures and reinforced competitive, acquisitive urges: private rather than public good has always been the game in Nigeria. The most visible indicators of such individualistic values were the dramatic arson fires set along the Marina in the old External Affairs and new international telecommunications buildings, intended to destroy incriminating evidence of embourgeoisement. In general, personal aggrandisement took precendence over collective advancement.

The corruption of Nigerian society, reinforced by the trauma of civil war, intensified because of the petroleum boom and partisan tension. The Gowon and Obasanjo periods were hardly pristine yet the scope and scale of private plunder then was miniscule compared to the sacking of the public purse under the hapless Shagari regime, an era of personal jets and fortunes. The size of the acquisitiveness and aggrandisement became apparent with the revelations of the Irikife Commission on oil revenues and Johnson Matthey banking inquiry. The precipitous decline in oil prices undermined the logic of corruption and accumulation; networks and coalitions based on the trickle-down of dash quickly disintegrated to be replaced in the second set of national elections in mid-1983 by wide-spread rigging. Buhari inherited a disillusioned populace and an exhausted exchequer on new year's eve 1984. But his reformism was not enough; even Shagari had attempted to deflate expectations of further growth before his ignominous removal. It took a second palace <u>putsch</u> to bring "king-maker" Babangida to power in mid-1985 - a man in Murtala's mould? - to take a grip on the constraints and challenges of debt.

b) Debates and Directions

The distinctive political economy of Nigeria, from boom to bust, has been placed on centre stage by recent radical analysis (see introduction and Falola & Ihonvbere, 1985 and Ekwe-Ekwe, 1985). Prior to the oil era there was little such critical discussion or organisation, notwithstanding the searing experience of a civil war. But in the decade of the 1970s, as the economy appeared poised for "take-off", as tertiary education mushroomed, and as national pride expanded, a few sceptical voices began to be raised: Did Nigeria really have the resources and the resilience to become a NIC? Was

Nigerian capitalism capable of transcending its colonial, comprador origins? Was oil power a feasible foreign policy stance in the new international division of labour? And could capitalist black Nigeria confront capitalist white South Africa given that both were central to multinational corporations' African activities? In short, could an extroverted economy sustain an activist diplomacy? (see Ogunbadejo, 1980 and Wright, 1981). As the 1980s dawned, the "nationalists" were still assertive, the "realists" sceptical and the "materialists" critical (Shaw & Fasehun, 1980). The balance in this debate was already moving away from the nationalists and towards the realists and materialists as the period of austerity and instability dawned (Shaw & Aluko (eds), 1983: 1-20).

Studies of Nigerian foreign policy and political economy reflect the state's international salience and internal divisiveness: they are important and intense. They are also largely indigenous, reflective of the multiplication and expansion of Nigeria's universities and research institutes in the last 10 to 15 years. Like the national political economy and culture, most have been orthodox in their mode of analysis: diplomatic history, international relations, strategic studies and decision-making still dominate the field of Nigerian foreign policy (Aluko, 1981 a and b). However, as i) the limits of power (as concept and currency) became apparent, ii) the national economy went into decline so alternative approaches were recognised (see Ake (ed), 1986 and Falola & Ihonvbere, 1985). This revisionist mood has drawn strength from the international trend towards political economy, whether materialist or not, as well as from the national tendency towards reevaluation.

Yet the continued resilience of the dominant, nationalist genre is symbolised by the elevation of one of its major advocates, Bolaji Akinyemi, to the post of foreign minister under Babangida. One of Nigeria's leading scholars and advisers (see Akinyemi, 1978 and 1979), who as Director of the prestigous Nigerian Institute of International Affairs (NIIA) for eight crucial years (1975-1983) advised and criticised leaders and diplomats from Murtala to Buhari, he now has the opportunity to reorient foreign policy in very different circumstances. Akinyemi has often advocated more assertiveness in external relations, being particularly insistent that Nigeria should i) put Africa first and ii) challenge the West more (in Oyediran (ed), 1978: 106-114 and 1981: 105-114). Not that he preferred more radical economics or non-aligned politics, just greater visibility and influence.

But it may be difficult to repeat the diplomatic victories associated with Angola (see Daddieh & Shaw, 1984) and Zimbabwe as the global context has changed and the liberation of both Namibia or South Africa is more problematic. Further, in regional affairs, Nigeria has sustained a series of bloody noses, from Chad to the Cameroons, as well as administered arbitrary expulsion notices to "aliens" in 1983 and 1985. Thus Akinyemi may have to revise his optimistic estimations about the salience of the oil weapon as well as refrain his personal outspokenness given the disciplined hierarchy of military government.

Akinyemi's elevation and redesignation remains symbolic, however, of the acceptability and respectability of the realist (and orthodox) paradigm in Nigerian foreign policy. His predecessor as foreign minister, Ibrahim Gambari, was also drawn from and has returned to orthodox adaceme (see Gambari, 1980) incidentally succeeding, briefly, Akinyemi as Director of the NIIA in 1983. And the Murtala/Obasanjo foreign minister – Joe Garba – is back at the UN. In short, despite differences in emphasis and style, Nigeria does have a foreign policy elite which moves in and out of universities, institutes like the NIIA in Lagos and National Institute (for Policy and Strategic Studies) at Kuru, and governments. Characteristic of such an informed, attentive public was the April 1986 national conference on foreign policy options to the year 2000 held at Kuru, a successor to the earlier Adedeji review panel.

Also symptomatic of the acceptability of orthodox social science is the high proportion of establishment scholars in the 17-person "Political Bureau" set up in early 1986 to organise a further national debate, following that on finance, on the return to civilian rule by 1990. Unlike the large mid-1970s Constitutional Drafting Committee, the mid-1980s group is less broad based; there is little danger of a critical Osoba-Usman "minority report" this time. Likewise, notwithstanding the widespread availability of more radical analysis, it has yet to achieve a degree of acceptance, especially perhaps in a renewed military era (see chapter five and Ohiorhenuan, 1984).

Thus, despite the intense "IMF debate", the immediate trend in Nigeria is towards revived capitalism rather than innovative socialism. The climate of austerity has led to renewed emphasis on agriculture and local inputs and on production rather than consumption or defence; it has yet to recognise women's work and the informal sector. The mood favours privatisation and retrenchment rather than parastatals and mega-projects (see chapter four). In the process of reorientation, the poor as well as the rich will suffer as deregulation and desubsidisation lead to higher costs, smaller incomes and fewer services. Yet support for Babangida's reformism has been more resilient than for Buhari as the latter was seen to be too beneficient towards Shagari's entourage and too disrespectful of human rights.

The August 1985 coup was a reaction against repression as

well as against recession; Nigerians are as laissez-faire in politics and debate as they are in economics and exchange (see Shaw, 1985 and Wright, 1987). Their democratic (as well as anarchistic!) inclinations cannot be contained for long by either soldiers or politicians. This poses problems for orderly process but also ensures opposition to intrusive praetorians. Renewed liberalisation in economics thus balances continued liberalism in politics: the "Kaduna mafia" constitutes both checks and balances on political and economic pressures (Ekwe-Ekwe, 1985).

c) From Oil Power to Naira Devaluation

Yet although Babangida's reformism may contain some of the excesses of previous regimes - mega-projects, state proliferation, capital city and massive corruption - it cannot quickly escape the legacy of misgovernment and misjudgement (see part one). Deflationary pressure has moderated popular expectations arising from the petro-naira dream, but it cannot eliminate them entirely. Moreover, the mix of aristocracy and meritocracy, let alone influence and corruption, is too immediate to control bourgeois urges. Nigeria is a class as well as ethnic society, a correllate of capitalism as well as regionalism. Class inequalities may become more intense as deflation and population increase along with urbanisation and unemployment. While the illusion of expansion continued, antagonisms could be moderated by promises and hand-outs. Now that contraction is all too apparent - "oil doom" rather than boom - such social controls may be less effective. The several Maitaitsine riots in the northern half of the country may thus constitute not so much moslem fanaticism as popular reaction. Nigeria's substantial but disorganised military and police resources may thus be called upon increasingly to contain proletarian and peasant alienation as well as criticisms from intellectuals, retired generals and the <u>ancien regime</u>. Conversely, the unreliability of state services combined with difficulties of urban life may combine to deproletarianise and deurbanise some marginal social elements. A return to the land for personal survival may also advance national self-reliance and social order, reducing pressure on and by the state: a distinctive variety of informal rather than official Third World deregulation.
    Meanwhile, although Nigeria has steadfastly declined unacceptable IMF conditions it has never abandoned capitalist principles and predilections. The balances between state and private sectors and among bureaucratic, national and comprador fractions may shift but the "mixed economy" has greater longevity than any national constitution (see Beckman, 1982 and 1985 and Lubeck, 1986). The early-1986 budget revealed

determination to balance accounts as well as interests: IMF terms without the loans. If Nigeria can administer and absorb its own medicine, as indicated by the introduction of the Second Foreign Exchange Market (SFEM) in late-1986, it may yet become less extroverted: not so dependent on either oil exports or imports of food, manufactures and inputs. Moreover, a less overheated economy may direct more attention to repair and rehabilitation than to inappropriate and grandiose projects while needing less labour migration and capturing more local multiplier effects. And any deemphasizing of the import-export sector will reduce the prospects for corruption, particularly smuggling and black marketeering.

In short, de facto devaluation and desubsidisation may give the political economy a necessary breathing space to moderate expectations, repair much damage and restructure social and economic relations. In turn, these changes may yet provide a more realistic and sustainable basis for foreign policy interests into the next century (see Shaw & Aluko (eds), 1983: 191-204).

d) Resilience Without Arrogance

The new realism in political economy apparent in Babangida's first months may spill-over into foreign policy aspirations and analyses. If Nigeria can take its own medicine - economic and political, social and psychological - then it may yet be able to lay the foundation for a successful post-petroleum period (see Diamond, 1985/6). In this eventuality, its external as well as internal goals may become more modest, but also more attainable. The petro-naira era had generated inflation in both economy and diplomacy: Africa's great power was to lead the continent towards liberation and integration. Instead, it has witnessed the slowing-down even reversal of change in Southern Africa along with ambigious progress towards regionalism in West Africa. These tendencies were always present, masked momentarily by the oil boom. The bursting of the bubble has led to renewed recognition of the essential characteristics of Nigeria's political economy: a distinctive mixed economy along with an irrepressible openness of politics, media and expression. Wars against indiscipline can never work for long in Nigeria's ebullient social culture; austerity can only briefly dampen the national spirit.

Yet sustained revival of economy and diplomacy can only be effected if the dynamism of Nigeria's political economy is directed away from corruption and towards production (Rimmer, 1986). Such a basic reorientation would require a transformation in national policies and alliances. For underlying the outward-orientation is the continuing dominance of comprador elements – the ubiquitous import-export traders and agents. If the military, along with more nationalistic and technocratic elements in the local elite, can contain this group and encourage national rather than international capital and accumulation (see Beckman, 1985 and Ohiorhenuan, 1984) then the economy may be able to sustain itself, achieving eventually that elusive "take-off" point promised many years ago by Walt Rostow and other modernisation theorists: the NIC dream. If, however, the Babangida regime controls the economy only long enough for another period of spend-thriftness then the unending cycle of importation, corruption and accumulation abroad will remain unbroken: the foreign exchange nightmare. The Mohammed/Obasanjo interregnum pointed the way which Babangida seems determined, in different circumstances, to take. But any premature return to either civilian or comprador rule will lead to the evaporation of gains and a return to cynicism and confrontation. Radical forces may yet be embryonic in laissez-faire Nigeria but the mixture of austerity for most and affluence for the minority will help generate if not orchestrate the oft-predicted revolutionary pressures (Ake, 1978 and 1986). The real choice for Nigeria, then, is not between civilian and military rule nor between socialism and barbarism but rather between different capitalisms: more or less successful, more or less indigenous, and more or less corporatist (Shaw & Ihonvbere, 1987).

e) Nigeria Towards the Twenty-First Century

Nigeria's longer-term future has suffered from inflation of both aspiration and situation. Even before the oil decade, it was one of Africa's few major actors and even without the petro-naira period it would have wielded a certain influence, if it had been judicious in balancing capabilities with targets (Aluko, 1981a). But just as the economy had to go into a real tail-spin before austerity and emergency were declared so diplomacy had to be discredited before the dawning of any "new realism". If Nigeria's current modesty of style and goal are maintained then it may once again achieve acceptability and visibility. However, if personal or national aggrandisement are rekindled prematurely then Nigeria's credibility may be undermined for many years to come. The more realistic elements in the military, industry, universities, parties and other sectors need to take the more chauvinistic groups in hand; a not inconsiderable task.
The internal bases of foreign policy as well as external ambitions and conditions will determine Nigeria's success rate. In the remaining decade-and-a-half of the century

these domestic capabilities will depend in part on external terms of trade. But the salience of those can be minimized if more autonomous development directions are adopted along the lines of the ILO's <u>First Things First</u> (1981): more rural, agricultural, basic needs oriented development which also produces more inputs for the presently stymied manufacturing sector.

The internalization of Nigeria's inherited extroverted economy - a slow but sure path to development - affords greater prospects for sustained expansion and influence than any short-lived OPEC windfall. Of course, another Middle East War might revive the price and demand for oil but, until the year 2000, projected structural changes in the world economy - a post-industrial, post-petroleum period - will likely keep both down. The conjuncture of internal inflation and instability with external contraction and devaluation has been difficult yet ultimately therapeutic. It may constitute a new basis for a set of innovative external as well as domestic relations, notably those with the EEC and the US, on the one hand, and with Africa on the other (Shaw & Aluko (eds), 1983 and Ungar, 1985: 150).

The real issue remains, however, whether Babangida can succeed where Mohammed was prevented: the transformation of Nigeria's political economy from oil dependence to national independence. Self-reliance or continued vulnerability to international forces, fancies and futures? Will Africa's ambitious Newly Industrializing or Influential Country of the 1970s become a Newly Insignificant Country in the 1990s? The new realism about both national economy and foreign policy satisfies at least one prerequisite:

> On its 25th anniversary, Africa's most populous nation - and potential superstate - has precious little to celebrate. Like most of the continent, Nigeria is economically broke, politically unstable and tribally divided. But unlike much of Africa, its leaders are at least prepared to concede this reality. ("Editorial" <u>Globe & Mail</u>, 10 October 1985)

As the late James Coleman (1963:379) noted in his pioneering study of Nigeria's foreign policy, Nigeria's "comparative 'moderation'" was always a source of disappointment to nationalist "patriots who had hoped that their country would assume a more 'dynamic' role of leadership in African and world affairs, a role they believed it was destined by size and population to play." On the other hand, external forces constrained this activism and external interests encouraged the conservatism, merely reinforcing dominant political and intellectual forces. Jim Coleman's (1963:380) caution expressed in the early 1960s is still relevant 25 years later.

That is, although new elites in the Third World have enjoyed "considerable autonomy and freedom of action in their conduct of foreign relations" their choice is limited:

> ...Nigeria's foreign policy is affected by such basic factors as Nigeria's geography, the character of the Nigerian population, as well as the relevant aspects of Nigeria's history, early as well as recent, her economy, and her political system.

The salience and ranking of such factors remain issues in contemporary Nigerian foreign policy analysis and political economy praxis: a luta continua!

References

Achebe, Chinua (1982). <u>The Trouble with Nigeria</u>. Enugu: Fourth Dimension.
Adomolekun, Ladipo (1985). <u>The Fall of the Second Republic</u>. Ibadan: Spectrum.
Adedeji, Adebayo & Timothy M. Shaw (eds) (1985). <u>Economic Crisis in Africa: African perspectives on development problems and potentials</u>. Boulder: Lynne Rienner.
Ake, Claude (1978). <u>Revolutionary Pressures in Africa</u>. London: Zed.
---------- (1981). "Off to a good start but dangers await ....". <u>West Africa</u> 3330, 25 May: 1163.
---------- (1981). <u>A Political Economy of Africa</u>. London: Longman.
-------(ed) (1985). <u>Political Economy of Nigeria</u>. London: Longman.
Akeredolu-Ale, E.O. (ed) (1982). <u>Social Development in Nigeria: a survey of policy and research</u>. Ibadan: University Press Limited for NISER.
Akinyemi, Bolaji A. (ed) (1978). <u>Nigeria and the World: readings in Nigerian foreign policy</u>. Ibadan: OUP for NIIA.
------------------ (1979). "Mohammed/Obansanjo foreign policy". In Oyeleye Oyediran (ed) <u>Nigerian Government and Politics under Military Rule, 1966-1979</u>. London: Macmillan. 150-168.

Akpan, N.U. (1982). Public Administration in Nigeria, pp. 59-81, London: Longman.

Alavi, Hamzu (1972). "The State in post-colonial societies: Pakistan and Bangladesh"

Aluko, Olajide (1981a). "Necessity and freedom in Nigerian foreign policy". Inaugural Lecture, University of Ife 17 March.

Aluko, Olajide (1981b). Essays in Nigerian Foreign Policy. London: George Allen & Unwin.

Amu, Lawrence A. (1982). "Oil glut and the Nigerian economy". Lecture at the Administrative Staff College of Nigeria, October.

Andrae, Gunilla & Bjorn Beckman (1985). The Wheat Trap: bread and underdevelopment in Nigeria. London: Zed.

Arnold, Guy (1977). Modern Nigeria. London: Longman.

Atanda, J.A. & A.Y. Aliyu (eds) (1985). Political Development: Proceedings of National Conference on Nigeria since independence. Volume 1. Zaria: Panel on Nigeria since Independence History Project.

Ayu, Iyorchia, D. (1966). Essays in Popular Struggle: Fela, students' patriotism and the Nicaragua revolution. Oguta: Zim Pan-African.

Bach, Daniel C. (1986). Le Nigeria Contemporain. Paris: Editions du CNRS.

Baker, Pauline H. (1984). "A giant staggers: Nigeria as an emerging regional power" in Bruce E. Arlinghaus (ed) African Security Issues: sovereignty, stability and solidarity. Boulder: Westview: 76-97.

Barber, Karin (1982). "Popular reactions to the petro-naira" Journal of Modern African Studies 20(3). September: 431-450.

Barbour, K. Michael et al (1982). Nigeria in Maps. London: Hodder & Stoughton.

Beckman, Bjorn (1981). "Imperialism and the 'national bourgeoisie" Review of African Political Economy 22, October-December: 5-19.

-------------- (1982). "Whose State: state and capitalist development in Nigeria" Review of African Political Economy 23, January-April.

-------------- (1985). "Neo-Colonialism, Capitalism, and the State in Nigeria" in Henry Bernstein and Bonnie K. Campbell (eds) Contradictions of Accumulation in Africa: studies in economy and state. Beverly Hills: Sage: 71-113.

Berry, Sara S. (1985). Fathers Work for their Sons: accumulation, mobility and class formation in an extended Yoruba community. Berkeley: University of California Press.

Bienen, Henry & V.P. Diejomaoh (eds) (1981). The Political Economy of Income Distribution in Nigeria. New York: Holmes & Meier.

Biersteker, Thomas J. (1978). <u>Distortion or Development? Contending perspectives on the multinational corporation.</u> Cambridge: MIT Press.

Bernstein, Henry & Bonnie K. Campbell (eds) (1985). <u>Contradictions of Accumulation in Africa: studies in economy and state.</u> Beverly Hills: Sage.

Caccia, Goffredo (1983). "Nigeria: oil plot or oil glut?" <u>Journal of African Marxists</u> 3: 78-92.

Carlsson, Jerker & Timothy M. Shaw (eds) (1987). <u>Newly Industrializing Countries and the Political Economy of South-South Relations.</u> London: Macmillan.

Chikelu, G.P.O. et al (1985). "Implementation of the Lagos Plan of Action: Africa, Nigeria and Sierra Leone" <u>Dalhousie African Working Papers</u> Number 6, May.

Coleman, James S. (1963). "The foreign policy of Nigeria" in Joseph E. Black & Kenneth W. Thompson (eds) <u>Foreign Policies in a World of Change.</u> New York: Harper & Row: 379-406.

Daddieh, Cyril Kofie & Timothy M. Shaw (1984). "The political economy of decision-making in Africa: the cases of recognition of Biafra and MPLA". <u>International Political Science Review</u> 5(2) (January 1984): 21-46.

Decalo, Samuel (1976). <u>Coups and Army Rule in Africa: studies in military style.</u> New Haven: Yale University Press.

Diamond, Larry (1985/6). "Nigeria Update" <u>Foreign Affairs</u> 64(2), Winter: 326-336.

Diejomaoh, Victor P. (1972). <u>Rural Development in Nigeria.</u> Ibadan: Ibadan University Press.

---------------------- (1982). "Nigerian social science research priorities for development," <u>Afrika Spectrum</u> 17(2): 151-161.

Dudley, Billy (1973). <u>Instability and Political Order: politics and crisis in Nigeria.</u> Ibadan: Ibadan University Press.

-------------- (1982) <u>An Introduction to Nigerian Government and Politics.</u> London: Macmillan.

Economist (1984). <u>The Political Economy of Nigeria.</u> London.

Economist Intelligence Unit (1982). <u>Nigeria: economic prospects to 1985. After the oil glut.</u> London: EIU Special Report Number 123.

Ekekwe, Eme (1986). <u>Class and State in Nigeria.</u> London: Longman, 1988.

Ekwe-Ekwe, Herbert (1985). "The Nigerian Plight: Shagari to Buhari" <u>Third World Quarterly</u> 7(3), July: 610-625.

Evans, Peter (1979). <u>Dependent Development: the alliance of multinational, state and local capital in Brazil.</u> Princeton: Princeton University Press.

Ezegbobelu, E.E. (1986). <u>Development Impact of Technology</u>

Transfer. Theory and Practice: a case of Nigeria, 1970-1982. Frankfurt: Peter Lang.

Fadahunsi, Akin (1979). "A review of the political economy of the industrialisation strategy of the Nigerian state, 1960-1980". African Development 4(2/3), April-September.

Falola, Toyin (ed) (1986). Britain and Nigeria: exploitation or development? London: Zed.

Falola, Toyin & Julius O. Ihonvbere (1985). The Rise and Fall of Nigeria's Second Republic, 1979-1983. London: Zed.

Fashoyin, Tayo (1981a). Industrial Relations in Nigeria. London: Longman.

--------------- (1981b). "State regulation of trade disputes in essential services in Nigeria" Industrial Relations 36(1): 207-222.

--------------- (1986). Incomes and Inflation in Nigeria. London: Longman.

Forest, Tom (1982). "Recent developments in Nigerian industrialisation" in Martin Fransman (ed) Industry and Accumulation in Africa. London: Heinemann: 324-344.

----------- (1986). "The political economy of civil rule and the economic crisis in Nigeria 1979-84" Review of African Political Economy 35, May: 4-26.

Freund, Bill (1978). "Oil boom and crisis in contemporary Nigeria" Review of African Political Economy 13, May-August: 91-100.

Gambari, Ibrahim (1980). Party Politics and Foreign Policy: Nigeria under the First Republic. Zaria: Amadu Bello University Press.

Gramsci, Antonio (1980). Prison Notebooks. New York: International.

Holsti, Kal (1972). International Politics: a framework for analysis. Englewood Cliffs: Prentice Hall.

Hoogvelt, Ankie (1980). "Indigenisation and technological dependence" Development and Change 11(2), April: 257-272.

Huntington, Samual P. (1968). Political Order in Changing Societies New Haven: Yale University Press.

Ihonvbere, Julius O. (1982). "The political economy of the rentier state: oil and class struggles in Nigeria" Canadian Association of African Studies Toronto: May.

----------- & Timothy M. Shaw (1987). "Nigerian oilworkers in contextual and comparative perspective" in Roger Southall (ed) Labour Unions in Asia and Africa: contemporary issues. London: Macmillan: 80-108.

Ikoku, S.G. (1985). Nigeria's Fourth Coup d'Etat: options for modern statehood Enugu: Fourth Dimension.

International Labour Office (1981). First things first: meeting the basic needs of the people of Nigeria. Addis Ababa: Jobs and Skills Programme for Africa.

Iyayi, Festus (1986). "The primitive accumulation of capital in a neo-colony: the Nigerian case" Review of African Political Economy 35, May: 27-39.

Janowitz, Morris (1977). Military Institutions and Coercion in the Developing Nations Chicago: University of Chicago Press.

Joseph, Richard (1983). "Class, state and prebendal politics in Nigeria" Journal of Commonwealth & Comparative Politics 21(3), November: 21-38.

Kayode, M.O. & Y.B. Usman (eds) (1985). Economic and Social Development of Nigeria: proceedings of national conference on Nigeria since independence, Volume 2. Zaria: Panel on Nigeria since Independence History Project.

Kirk-Greene, Anthony and Douglas Rimmer (1981). Nigeria since 1970: a political and economic outline. London: Hodder & Stoughton.

Kitching, Gavin (1980). Class and Economic Change in Kenya: the making of an African petite-bourgeoisie. New Haven: Yale University Press.

Kraus, Jon (1982). "Nigeria under Shagari" Current History 81(473).

Lenin, V.I. (1971). Collected Works. Moscow: Progress.

Lubeck, Paul M. (1980). "Labour in Kano since the petroleum boom" Review of African Political Economy 13, September-December: 37-46.

Lubeck, Paul M. (ed) (1986). The African Bourgeoisie: capitalist development in Nigeria, Kenya and the Ivory Coast. Boulder: Lynne Rienner.

Madunagu, Edwin (1982). Problems of Socialism: the Nigerian challenge. London: Zed.

Mazrui, Ali A. (1982). "Nigeria and the United States: the need for civility, the dangers of intimacy," Orbis 25(4) (Winter): 858-864.

--------------- (1986). The Africans: a triple heritage. London: BBC.

Mejak, Miran (1983). "Nigeria's foreign policy: commitment to non-alignment and African unity," Review of International Affairs 34 (20 February): 18-20.

Nigeria: the effects of population factors on social and economic development 1985. Lagos: Federal Ministry of Health and National Population Bureau, April.

Nigeria Year Book, 1986 Lagos: Daily Times.

Nigeria: yesterday and today (1985). Lagos: National Commission for Museums and Monuments.

Nnoli, Okwudiba (1978). Ethnic Politics in Nigeria. Enugu: Fourth Dimension.

--------------- (ed) (1981). Path to Nigerian Development. Dakar: Codesria.

Nwankwo, Arthur (1981). Can Nigeria Survive? Enugu: Fourth Dimension.

Nwanwene, Omorogbe (1973). "Administrative implications" Quarterly Journal of Administration. 7(2), January: 121-145.

Nwosu, E.J. (ed) (1985). Achieving Even Development in Nigeria: problems and prospects. Enugu: Fourth Dimension for EDI, University of Nigeria.

Nzimiro, Ikenna (1975). "The political and social implications of multinational corporations in Nigeria" in Carl Widstrand (ed) Multinational Firms in Africa. Uppsala: Scandinavian Institute of African Studies: 210-243.

O'Connell, James (1971). "Political constraints on planning: Nigeria as a case study in the developing world" Nigerian Journal of Economics and Social Studies 13(1), March: 39-57.

Oculli, Okelo (1979). "Dependent food policy in Nigeria, 1975-1979". Review of African Political Economy 15/16, May-December: 63-74.

Odetola, T.O (1975). "Economic development and the structure and process of economic decision-making" Nigerian Journal of Economic and Social Studies 17(1), March: 139-150.

Ofoegbu, Mazi Ray (1978). "Towards a new philosophy of foreign policy for Nigeria". In A. Bolaji Akinyemi (ed) Nigeria and the World: readings in Nigerian foreign policy 116-135.

Ogunbadejo, Oye (1980). "Nigeria's foreign policy under military rule, 1966-79" International Journal 35(4) (Autumn): 748-765.

Ogunbambi, R.O. (1985). "The dilemmas of Nigeria's African policy" Journal of African Studies 12(1), Spring: 10-13.

Ogunsanwo, Alaba (1986). Our Friends; Their Friends: Nigeria's external relations, 1960-1985. Yaba: Alfa Communications.

Ohiorhenuan, John F.E. (1984). "The political economy of military rule in Nigeria" Review of Radical Political Economies 16(2/3), Summer and Fall: 1-27.

Ojo, Olatunde J.B. (1980). "Nigeria and the formation of ECOWAS," International Organization 34(4) (Autumn): 571-604.

------------------ (1984). "Nigeria" in Timothy M. Shaw & Olajide Aluko (eds) Political Economy of African Foreign Policy: comparative analyses Aldershot: Gower: 190-220.

------------------ (1987). "Nigeria: the political economy of dependent industrialisation and foreign policy". In Jerker Carlsson & Timothy M. Shaw (eds) Newly Industrialising Countries and the Political Economy of South-South Relations. London: Macmillan 121-150.

Okigbo, P.N.C. (1982). Nigeria's Financial System. London: Longman.

Okorma, N.S. (nd). A Guide to WAI. Port Harcourt: Green International.

Olaniyan, Richard (ed) (1985). *Nigerian History and Culture.* London: Longman, 1985.

Olatunbosun, Dupe (1975). *Nigeria's Neglected Rural Majority.* Ibadan: OUP for NIIA.

Olofin, S.O. et al. *Modelling Nigeria's Economic Development* Ibadan: Ibadan University Press, 1985 for Centre for Econometric and Applied Research.

Oni, Ola (1975). "A critique of development planning in Nigeria". *Review of African Political Economy* 4, November: 87–95.

───────── and Bade Onimode (1975). *Economic Development of Nigeria: the Socialist alternative.* Ibadan: Nigerian Academy of Arts, Sciences and Technology.

Onimode, Bala (1977). "A critique of planning concepts and methodology in Nigeria" *Review of Black Political Economy* 7(3), Spring: 296–308.

───────────── (1982). *Imperialism and Underdevelopment in Nigeria.* London: Zed.

Onokerhoraye, Andrew G. (1984). *Social Services in Nigeria.* London: Kegan Paul International.

Osoba, Segun (1972). "Ideology and Planning for national economic development, 1946–72" in Mahmod Tukur & Tunji Olagunju (eds) *Nigeria: in search of a viable polity.* Zaria: ABU Press.

───────────── (1977). "The Nigerian power elite, 1952–1965" in Peter C.W. Gutkind & Peter Watermann (eds) *African Social Studies – a radical reader* New York: Monthly Review: 368–382.

───────────── (1978). "The deepening crisis of the Nigerian national bourgeoisie" *Review of African Political Economy* 13, May–August: 63–77.

───────────── (1980a). "Considerations on some conceptual and ideological aspects of Nigerian underdevelopment in historical perspective" *University of Ife History Seminar Series,* January.

───────────── (1980b). "The economic foundations of Nigeria's foreign policy during the First Republic, 1960–1965." In I.A. Akinjogbin and S.O. Osoba (eds) *Topics on Nigerian Economic and Social History.* Ife: University of Ife Press: 209–233.

Oyavbaire, S. Egite (1985). *Federalism in Nigeria.* London: Macmillan.

Oyediran, Oyeleye (ed) (1978). *Survey of Nigerian Affairs, 1975.* Ibadan: OUP for NIIA.

───────────────────── (1979). *Nigerian Government and Politics Under Military Rule, 1966–79.* London: Macmillan.

───────────────── (ed) (1981). *Survey of Nigerian Affairs,* 1976–77. Lagos: Macmillan for NIIA.

Oyejide, T.A. et al (1985). *Nigeria and the IMF.* Ibadan: Heinemann.

Review of African Political Economy (1986). "Oil, Debts and Democracy in Nigeria" 37, December: 1-105.

Rimmer, Douglas (1986). "The overvalued currency and over-administered economy of Nigeria" African Affairs 84(336), July: 435-446.

Samoff, Joel (1982). "On class, paradigm and African politics" Africa Today 29(2), Second Quarter: 41-50.

Sano, Hans-Otto (1983). The Political Economy of Food in Nigeria, 1960-1982. Uppsala: Scandinavian Institute of African Studies. Research Report Number 65.

Schatz, Sayre P. (1977). Nigerian Capitalism. Berkeley: University of California Press.

--------------- (1981). "Nigeria's petro-political fluctuation," Issue II (Spring and Summer): 35-40.

--------------- (1982). "The Nigerian economy since the great oil-price increases of 1973-74," Africa Today 29 (Third Quarter): 33-42.

Shagari, President Alhaji Shehu (1981). "Annual foreign policy address," Nigerian Forum 1 (August): 46-50.

Shaw, Timothy M. (1980). "Review article. Foreign policy, political economy and the future: reflections on Africa in the world system," African Affairs 79(315) (April): 260-268.

--------------- (1983a). "Nigeria in the international system." In The Political Economy of Nigeria, edited by I. William Zartman. New York: Praeger: 207-236.

--------------- (1983b). Africa's International Affairs: an analysis and bibliography. Halifax: Centre for Foreign Policy Studies.

--------------- (1985). "Nigerian coups and foreign policy" International Perspectives November/December: 17-19.

--------------- (1986). "The Dialectics of Regionalism: EurAfrica and West Africa" in Amadu Sesay (ed) Africa and Europe: from partition to inter-dependence or dependence? Beckenham: Croom Helm: 222-245.

--------------- (1987). "Nigerian Restrained: foreign policy under changing political and petroleum regimes" The Annals 489, January 40-50.

--------------- and Julius Ihonvbere (1987). "Nigeria" in Julius Nyang'oro & Timothy M. Shaw (eds) Corporatism in Africa. Boulder: Westview.

--------------- and Olajide Aluko (eds) (1983). Nigerian Foreign Policy: alternative perceptions and projections. London: Macmillan.

------------------------------- (eds) (1984). Africa Projected: from recession to renaissance by the year 2000? London: Macmillan.

--------------- and Orobola Fasehun (1980). "Nigeria in the world system: alternative approaches, explanations and

projections" *Journal of Modern African Studies* 18(4), December: 551-523.
Shenton, Robert M. (1986). *The Development of Capitalism in Northern Nigeria* London: James Currey.
Sklar, Richard S. (1963). *Nigerian Political Parties* Princeton: Princeton University Press.
Stremlau, John S. (1981). "The fundamentals of Nigerian foreign policy," *Issue* II (Spring/summer): 46-50.
Stohr, Walter B. & D.R.F. Taylor (1981). *Development from Below or Above?* Chichester: John Wiley.
The Nigerian Economic Society (1986). *The Nigerian Economy: a political economy approach* London: Longman.
Tijjani, Aminu & David Williams (eds) (1981). *Shehu Shagari: my vision of Nigeria.* London: Frank Cass.
Turner, Terisa (1976a). "Multinational corporations and the instability of the Nigerian state" *Review of African Political Economy* 5, January-April: 39-45.
———————— (1976b). "The transfer of technology and the Nigerian state" *Development and Change* 7:353-390.
Ungar, Sanford J. (1985). *Africa: the people and politics of an emerging continent.* New York: Simon & Schuster.
Usman, Bala (1979). *For the liberation of Nigeria.* London: New Beacon.
Vayrynen, Raimo (1979). "Economic and military position of regional power centres," *Journal of Peace Research* 16(4): 349-369.
Wallerstein, Immanuel (ed) (1975). *World Inequality.* Montreal: Black Rose.
Walsch, Gretchen (1983). "Review of Mark W. DeLancey, *African International relations*," *Canadian Journal of African Studies* 17(1): 144-145.
Waterman, Peter (1983). *Aristocrats and Plebians in African Unions? Lagos port and dock workers organisation and struggle.* The Hague: Institute for Social Studies.
Williams, David (1982). *President and Power in Nigeria; the life of Shehu Shagari.* London: Frank Cass.
Williams, Gavin (1976a). "Taking the part of peasants' rural development in Nigeria and Tanzania" in P.C.W. Gutkind & I. Wallerstein (eds) *The Political Economy of Contemporary Africa.* Beverley Hills: Sage, 131-154.
———————— (ed) (1976b). *Nigeria economy and society.* London: Rex Collings.
———————— (1980). *State and society in Nigeria.* Idandre: Afrografika.
WIN Document: conditions of women in Nigeria and policy recommendations to 2000 AD (1985). Zaria: WIN.
Women in Nigeria (1986). London: Zed.
Wright, Stephen (1981). "Limits of Nigeria's power overseas" *West Africa* 3339 (27 July): 1685-1686.

────────────────── (1986a). *Nigeria: a survey of political issues, trends and consequences*. London: EIU.

────────────────── (1986b). "Nigeria: rising hopes but declining fortunes" in Colin Legum (ed) *Africa Contemporary Record, Volume 18, 1985-86*. New York: Africana, 1986.

Young, Andrew (1981). "The United States and Africa: victory for diplomacy," *Foreign Affairs* 59(3): 648-666.

Zartman, I. William (ed) (1983). *The Political Economy of Nigeria*. New York: Praeger.

Ziemann, W. & M. Lanzenporfer (1977). "The State in Peripheral Societies". *Socialist Register*. London: Merlin: 143-177.

Index

Accumulation, 7,8,11,18,3
  34,39,40,41,44,51,52,55,60,
  67,68,73,76,77,78,80,87,89,
  90,91,94,95,111,112,114,119–
  120,122,124,126,128,133,167,
  187,192
Africa, 4,8,23,24,53,59,60,63,
  73,78,129,130,131,135,141,
  143,151,158,159,162,165,166,
  167,168,170,171,172,173,181,
  184,185,188,193; see also
  Southern Africa, West Africa
Agriculture, 2,7,9,11,41,42,44,
  68,69,71,76,78,79,80–87,96,
  97,99,101,103,107,108,109,
  125,141,158,184,189,193;
  neglect of 9,44,107;see also
  food, peasants
Aid 39,40,76,78,92,93,96,97,
  123,149,151,152,156,172
Alienation, 10,190
Aliens 6,112,189;see also
  migration
Alliances, see coalitions
Angola 168,170,171;MPLA
  168,170,171,188;see also
  FLS,Southern Africa
Austerity 8,9,12,14,17,18,
  52,57,61,133,188,189,192;
  see also development,de-
  regulation
Autonomy 5,39,40,64,122,
  167,174,194; see also
  state

Babangida, Ibrahim 23,31,
  110,134,135,167,187,189,
  190,191,192;see also military,regime
Basic (Human) Needs 8,11,
  14,27,29,52,63,110,111,
  167,193;see also development,poverty
Benin 149,173;see also
  ECOWAS,West Africa
Biafra 31,96,155,159;see
  also civil war,East,
  regions
Bourgeoisie 2,5,6,7,9,10,
  11,12,14,15,17,24,25,27,
  31,32,34,35,36,37,38,39;
  bureaucratic 5;comprador

205

42,44,46,56,58,62,69,92,106,
111,121,126,136,150,151,155,
176,185,190,192;metropolitan
123,124,126,136;national 41,
47,56,58,59,65,86,91,111,131,
148,174,175,181,190
Brazil 33,35,36,57,158,174,185;
see also Latin America, triple alliance
Britain 31,76,94,96,112,127,
135,141,154,155,156,157,158,
160;see also capitalism,colonialism;Europe
British Petroleum 33,47,157-
158,168;see also Britain,oil,
Shell
Buhari, Muhammadu 23,31,110,134,
135,187,189;see also military,
regimes

Capital 6,9,10,11,14,17,22,33,
35,39,40,41,42,43,44,47,48,
49,50,51,52,54,55,56,60,63,
68,78,87,90,91,92,94,96,99,
102,104,112,114,116,119,125,
126,127,131,132,133,136,141,
148,150,153,174,180,192;foreign 9,10,14,17,22,33,35,39,
40,41,42,43,44,49,50,51,52,
54,55,56,60,78,87,90,91,92,
96,99,102-104,114,116,125,
126,127,131,132,133,136,141,
148,150,153,174,180,192;
indigenous 54,60,114,133,174,
180,192;see also bourgeoisie,
capitalism,state,triple
alliance
Capitalism 2,5,6,8,9,10,11,12,
13,17,18,21,23,24,25,27,29,
31,32,33,34,40,45,50,52,57,
58,60,62,65,73,77,79,82,87,
89,90,91,96,100,102,111,112,
114,115,117,128,131,136,141,
151,168,174,180,184,185,188,
189,190,192;international 31,
45,52,60,65,75,100,124,174,
192;Nigerian 10,32,50,58,60,
62,87,180,184,185,192;see
also capital,corporations,
state

Cities 80-87;see also urban
-rural
Civilians 1,2,5,9,10,11,22,
23,25,34,48,50,97,101,
104,107,108,109,117,135,
136,153,165,166,177,192;
see also military,regime
Civil society 120
Civil war 6,15,17,31,76,96,
134,136,145,148,152,155,
156,159,161,187;see also
Biafra,ethnicity,post-war
Class 2,3,4,10,11,13,14,21,
27,29,31,32,33,34,35,37,
38,39,40,42,48,50,51,52,
53,57,58,59,65,68,73,74,
75,80,89,90,93,94,102,
105,110,111,113,114,115,
116,119,120,121,122,124,
125,126,128,131,132,135,
140,141,156,167,178,183,
190;ruling 42,57,59,80,
114,119,120,121,128,135,
183;struggles 3,4,48,50,
73,75,90,94,102,105,110,
115,116,121,122,124,128,
132,141;see also bourgeoisie,peasants,proletariat,workers
Coalitions 2,3,4,9,11,12,
13,14,23,27,33,34,36,38,
40,41,44,49,50,56,60,64,
74,95,167,174;see also
class
Cocoa 31,67,185;see also
commodities,exports
Coercion 9,18,46,50,120,
133;see also military,
repression
Colonialism 5,11,37,75-76,
80,84,116,122,123,124,
125,129,144,151,154,179;
see also Britain,independence
Commodities 42,74,79,80,167,
185
Communism 11
Conjuncture 3,7,42,57,59,
105,168,178;see also

revolution
Constitution 2,9
Construction 7,44,45,158
Consumption 36,38,69,185; see also accumulation
Contraction 1,2,3,6,7,18,49, 60,168,190,193;see also austerity
Contradictions 2,4,5,6,7,8,10, 11,13,14,15,17,18,23,24,27, 31,33,35,36,38,40,41,48,51, 52,58,59,60,63,64,71,89,95, 96,99,112,113,116,129,130, 137,167,168,179;see also class
Cooperatives 67
Corporations 12,17,18,36,43, 54,60,61,69,71,78,104,105, 106,114,154-155,170,171,174, 175-176,188;multinational 71, 78,174,176,188;see also capital,sectors
Corporatism 8,10,14,18,31,64, 112,128,136,192;see also coalitions
Corruption 7,10,31,40,46,48, 50,55,91,96,97,98,99,105, 110,116,128,134,137,187,190, 191,192
Coups d'etat 15,111,119-130, 129-137,189;causes of 129-130;see also hegemony,military
Crisis 1,23,165;see also conjuncture
Cuba 158-159

Debt 166,185,187;see also austerity,devaluation
Decolonisation 5,39,93,123; see also colonialism,independence
Democracy 5,7,48,63,90,112, 117,121,141,143,190;democratisation 7;see also repression
Dependence 15,23,24,35,36,39, 40,42,47,53,54,57,60,61,73, 74,79,93,102,104,123,136, 137,140,141,145,152,166, 170,174,175,181,193;on oil 42,57,79,102,136,137,145; on West 152
Deregulation 8;see also devaluation
Deprivation 7;see also oil, states
Devaluation 7,8,14,23,74, 134,185,190,191,193;see also debt,IMF,structural adjustment
Development 3,12,13,14,15, 18,21,25,27,31,33,48,50, 58,65,69,73-78,89,90,93, 96,100,112,114,115,116, 134,141,166,177,193;strategy 3,58,69,73-78,115-116;see also planning, self-reliance
Dialectic 2,19,24,37,52,58, 65,166;see also contradictions
Discipline 8;see also indiscipline
Distribution 12,15,25,27, 29,41,60;see also accumulation,production

East (of Nigeria) 132;see also Biafra
Economic Community of West African States (ECOWAS) 6,17,46,55,57,147,149, 150,160,161,162,168,172, 176;see also West Africa
Economist Intelligence Unit (EIU) 25,27
Economy 9,13,18,24,42,45, 48,60,62,67,90,94,97,98, 107-108,110,124,126,137, 151,179,185,188,191,192, 193,194;see also political economy
Education 46,50,68,85,90, 97,98.101,103,104-105, 109,113,115,124-125,128, 175;see also BHN,students
Employment 42,45,78,79,81,

86,101;see also trade unions, unemployment,workers
Environment 2,18,45
Ethnicity 7,10,11,21,27,29,36, 37,38,40,47,58,62,63,104,128, 132,187,190;see also regions
Europe 31,34,168,172;see also capitalism
European Economic Community (EEC) 170,171,172,193
Export-Oriented Industrialisation 58;see also exports
Exports 15,17,42,74,78,79,96, 111,131,142,167,174,175,191; see also imports,terms of trade

Factions 7,9,14,15,33,40,50, 53,91,111,115,119,121,134, 136;see also bourgeoisie, class,fractions
False consciousness 120;see also class
Farmers 43,44,47,51,80-84,108; see also peasants
Fascism 10,14,59,63,112,118; see also corporatism
Federalism 10,25,29,36,43,76, 94,96;see also regions
Food 7,22,39,41,42,43,44,46, 68,71,80,83,83,107,111,136, 180,185,191;imports 44,46, 71,111,175,191;policies 43, 44,68,82,83,136;see also agriculture,peasants
Foreign exchange 13,15,17,42, 55,57,96,108,145,191,192; see also debt,devaluation
Foreign policy 2,5,6,17,105, 136,139-163,165-181,183-194; see also Africa,Southern Africa,West Africa
Fractions 3,4,7,9,11,12,14,18, 22,27,32,33,34,40,44,49,50, 53,57,58,59,63,91,111,119, 121,136,183;see also bourgeoisie,class,factions
France 148,149,155,158,159, 171;see also Europe,EEC, francophone states
Francophone states 17,147, 148,149;see also Benin, Ivory Coast,West Africa
Front Line States 17,170, 171;see also Namibia, Southern Africa

Gender 10,18,185;see also women
Ghana 145,172;see also aliens,West Africa
Gowon, Yakabu 31,96,97,134, 135,171,187;see also coups d'etat,military
Green revolution 43,50,68, 180;see also agriculture, food,ideology
Groundnuts 67,185

Hegemony 2,10,15,18,31,33, 39,41,49,50,51,52,56,96, 102,119-124,181;counterhegemony 121,128;crisis of 2,10,41;Gramsci 119-123;see also bourgeoisie, class,state

Idealism 170,176-178,179, 180-181;see also foreign policy,radical,realism
Ideology 4,25,31,50,90,91, 92,96,98,104,111,112,113, 117,125,132,133,139,154, 162
Imports 43,44,46,55,82,83, 101,102,146,160,174,175, 191;food 83;see also exports,terms of trade
Import-substitution 15,17, 18,62;see also industrialisation
Independence 2,5,8,10,15, 37,41,42,54,67,76,80,94, 104,113,116,123,124,126, 131,139,141,145,152,154, 184;see also colonialism, decolonisation
Indigenisation 6,15,18,22,

27,31,32,33,34,51,53,54,56,
59,61,62,100,101,104,115,
123,136,174,175,180;see also
bourgeoisie,capitalism
Indiscipline 12,14,97,105,134,
191;war against 12,14,191;
see also discipline
Industrialisation 9,15,17,18,
27,30,35,40,44,57,76,93,98,
101,104,109,126,167,168,174,
180,185;see also export-
oriented industrialisation
Inequalities 27,29,36,42,91;
see also contradictions,
poverty
Inflation 45,46
Informal sector 2,8,185,189;
see also smuggling,women
Instability 10;see also coups
d'etat
International Division of
Labour 9,14,39,49,73,75,91,
93,104,116,123,124,127,129,
135,139,154,161,188;see also
capitalism
International Labour Office
(ILO) 9,15,25,27,107,175,
193;see also UN
International Monetary Fund
(IMF) 53,90,189,190,191;see
also capitalism,structural
adjustment,World Bank
Investors 6,9;indigenous 6;
foreign 6,9;see also accumulation,capital
Israel 17,171,176
Ivory Coast 3,36,42,62,68,149,
171;see also ECOWAS,franco-
phone states

Japan 31,34;see also capitalism

Kenya 3,24,36,56,59,60,62,68

Labour 6,22,40,41,45,46,48,49,
52,63,68,71,81,84,104,112,
136;control 45,46,48,49,136;
see also proletariat,trade
unions,workers

Land 12
Latin America 14,36,62
Liberation Movements 160,
161,162,171-172;see also
Southern Africa

Marketing boards 82,83,95,
127;see also agriculture
Marxism see materialism
Materialism 4,13,18,24,31,
59,188;see also radical
Mexico 36;see also Brazil,
Latin America,NICs
Migration 45,80,113,149,
166,191;see also aliens,
rural-urban
Military 1,2,5,6,9,10,13,
14,19,22,25,34,38,40,51,
53,54,96,97,100,102,104,
105,117,120,121,122,125,
127,128,129-137,143,147,
151,153,155,156,160,162,
165,166,167,174,183,189,
192;interventions 129-
137,183;see also civil-
ians,coercion,regime,re-
pression
Mixed economy 11,31,54,91,
92,190,191;see also cap-
italism
Mode of production 2,3,4,
5,8,10,13,29,124,130,136
Modernisation 3,5,23,25,36,
37,73,115,166,179,192;see
also orthodox
Mohammed, Murtala 31,58,
134,135,167,168,192;see
also military

Namibia 151,153,168,170,
172,188;see also Southern
Africa
National interest 173,174,
176,177,181
Nationalisation 17,32,33,
53,54,63,104,114,115,157;
see also capitalism,in-
digenisation
Nationalism 35,37,52;eco-

209

nomic 52;see also decolonisation,independence
National Party of Nigeria (NPN) 12,110;see also parties
Neo-colonialism 5,34,60,63, 183
Neo-Marxism see materialism
Neo-Materialism see materialism
New International Economic Order 170;see also UN
Newly Industrialising Country (NIC) 7,8,36,165,168,174, 178,185,187,193;see also industrialisation,power
Newly Influential Country 7, 165,174,177,185,193;see also foreign policy
Nigeria Labour Congress (NLC) 48,49,110;see also proletariat,trade unions,workers
Nigerian National Petroleum Corporation 36,51,55,57,61, 145;see also oil,OPEC
Non-Alignment 145,154,167,180; see also Third World
Non-bourgeoisie 10,11,14,15, 18,23,49,57,58;see also class, peasants,proletariat,workers
North (of Nigeria) 29,84,132, 190
Nuclear 80

Obasanjo, Olusegun 31,58,105, 168,171,187,192;see also military
Oil 1,2,5,6,7,8,9,11,12,13,15, 17,18,19,22,23,27,28,39,40, 41,42,43,45,46,47,48,49,51, 52,53,54,55,57,58,67,69,71, 76,78-80,81,83,85,96,97,98, 101,102,105,106,108,109,112, 134,139,140,143,145,147,150, 151,152,153,155,156,158,159, 160,161,162,163,166,167,169, 172,174,177,178,180,184,185, 186,187,188,189,190,191,193; boom 5,6,7,9,11,12,15,18,27, 41,43,45,46,49,54,55,58,67, 71,83,97,136,140,143,151,152, 178,180,190,191;companies 48,145,151,157-158,161, 180;diplomacy 2,17,147, 160,172,188,189;glut 49, 57,167,184,187,190;production 109,145,167,169, 186;rents 6,7,8,40,53, 108;revenue 7,9,78,101, 109,134,139,150,155,156, 159;see also petro-naira
Organisation of African Unity (OAU) 143,145,152, 153,159,160,171;see also Africa
Organisation of Islamic Countries 57;see also religion
Organisation of Petroleum Exporting Countries (OPEC) 2,31,36,45,55,57, 61,62,68,76,96,140,149, 167,175,193;see also oil
Orthodox 1,2,3,23,51,52,57, 166,189;see also radical

Palm Oil 67,166,167,185;see also agriculture,commodities
Paradigm 4,65;see also idealist,radical,realism
Parties 5,9,12,13,18,23,37, 57,62,97,109,112,121,132, 192;see also civilians
Patriarchy 8,11
Patron-client relations 11, 12,37,56,128;see also ethnicity
Peasants 7,12,21,23,29,41, 43,50,51,60,65,67,71,78, 82,84,87,89,93,110,112, 120,125,132,133,134,135, 181,190;see also agriculture,women
Periphery 2,5,8,12,13,14, 15,18,19,25,31,35,40,52, 62,75,79,89,90,116,119, 120,123,124,127,129,133, 139,141,143,161,166,174, 178,181;see also semi-

periphery
Petro-Naira 5,7,11,17,22,29, 37,73,110,184,185,190,191, 192;see also oil
Planning 11,14,27,32,46,50,52, 73,74,75-78,80,86,89-117,127; theories of 90;see also development
Political culture 129
Political economy 1,2,3,4,5,8, 10,13,22,23,24,25,29,31,35, 36,44,45,54,56,57,64,67,69, 75,105,117,139,150,166,168, 170,173,175,176,184,187,188, 191,194;mode of analysis 2, 4,5,139;see also radical
Political science 5,35;see also social science
Politicians 9,12,190;see also civilians
Population 9,81,97,107,140, 143,160,161,166,175,190,194
Populism 31,48,51,57,59,65;see also corporatism,ideology
Post-colonial state 8,11,37,38, 39,40,43,49,52,58,67,76,78, 93,122,123,124,126,127,128; see also colonialism,independence,state
Post-war 6,31,36,37,94,96,98, 110;see also Biafra,civil war
Poverty 6,10,52,175;see also BHN
Power 7,8,39,51,120,128,140- 141,154,165,167,170,176,184, 188;see also foreign policy
Praetorian 19,31,130,190;see also military
Pre-colonial 8,39,51,167;see also Britain,colonialism
Privatisation 5,6,9,11,14,15, 23,33,43,57,74,134,189;see also structural adjustment
Production 4,7,8,12,15,18,24, 27,38,39,41,55,60,186,191; see also accumulation,consumption
Proletariat 27,45,87,181,190; see also class,workers, trade unions

Radical 1,2,3,4,5,18,21,23, 24,25,27,29,57,65,90,117, 161,166,170,176-178,179, 180-181,189,192;in foreign policy 176-178,179, 180-181;see also idealism,orthodox,realism
Realism 168,170-171,176- 178,179,180-181,188,189, 191,192,193;see also idealism,radical
Regime 4,8,10,25,34,50,51, 58,81,113,117,139,162, 165,168,181,190;see also coups d'etat
Regionalism 62,190,191
Regions 10,22,27,29,58,76, 94,95,96,104,132;see also ethnicity,states
Relations of production 4, 13,47,60,73,75,77,87,124, 126,135;see also capitalism
Religion 7,11,22,27,40,47, 50,58,104,128,176
'Rentier' state 1,2,3,4,8, 13,22,27,29,31,33,36,38, 39,40,41,55,58,60,61,62, 64,68-69,71,73,167,185; defined 69;see also capitalism,mode of production,oil
Repression 31,40,58,62,63, 190;see also coercion, military
Revenue 41,42,45,48,49,55, 68,69,78,79,80,83,96,97, 100,108,109,110,140,143, 151,167;see also regions, states
Revolution 59,62,63,65,128, 133,192;see also conjuncture,coups d'etat
Rhodesia (Zimbabwe) 152, 157,171,188;see also Southern Africa

Rural decay 41,43,45
Rural-urban 1,12,15,42,43,45,
　68,69,71,73,75,76,79,80-87,
　107,110,113;see also cities,
　peasants

Saudi Arabia 140;see also OIC,
　OPEC
Sahel 171
Sectors 7,9,29,40,42,53,77,92,
　96,97,98,100,101,107,111,125,
　190;modern 9;private 7,77,92,
　96,98,100,190;public 7,53,92,
　97,98,111,190
Self-reliance 3,23,27,74,76,90,
　97,104,181,190,193
Semi-periphery 8,13,18,19,22,
　25,27,29,31,33,35,39,48,49,
　53,57,58,59,154,166,174,176,
　178-179,181;see also NIC,
　periphery
Shagari, Shehu 10,38,43,46,55,
　101,107,109,151,153,160,162,
　168,171,183,185,187,189;see
　also civilians
Shell 47;see also BP,oil
Slaves 31
Smuggling 12,46,50,110,185,
　191;see also informal sector
Social formation 2,3,13,21,31,
　52,119,127,133;see also mode
　of production
Socialism 3,12,23,24,33,58,59,
　62,64,77,90,93,116,121,171,
　183,189,192
Social science 1,5,21,23,65,
　113,114,189;see also
　political science
South (of Nigeria) 29
South Korea 53,57
South Africa 6,17,151,152,153,
　157,176,188;see also Namibia
Southern Africa 6,17,55,151,152,
　153,156,160,162,170,171-172,
　191
Soviet Union 155,156,157,158
State 2,3,5,6,7,9,10,12,15,18,
　33,34,36,38,40,41,43,45,46,
　47,48,49,51,52,53,55,56,60,
　61,68,79,86,87,89,91,102,
　116,119,124,132,141,143,
　150,166,177;state crea-
　tion 5,190;strong 132;
　weak 132
State capitalism 52-53,58;
　see also capitalism
State farms 7,42,44,45,82,
　83;see also agriculture,
　green revolution
States 6,7,10,18,22,27,36,
　46,63,97,99,103;non-oil
　states 7;oil states 7;
　regions 6,10;creation of
　18,63,97
Strike 47,51,133;see also
　NLC,trade unions,workers
Structural adjustment 14,
　53,74,90;see also IMF
Structural change 12,48,65,
　193
Students 29,43,48,51,65,
　104-105,110,112,132,133,
　134,135;see also education
Subimperial 8,13,176;see
　also NIC,semi-periphery
Subimperialism 136,139,141,
　145-150
Substructure 4,13,23,24,25,
　166
Superstructure 4,13,23,24,
　37,121,127,131,166,168,
　180

Tanzania 3,4,24,65,83,172;
　see also FLS,Southern
　Africa
Technology 114,141,145,161,
　175
Terms of trade 7,193;see
　also exports,imports,oil
Third World 52,62,119,129,
　160,161,174,190,194;see
　also non-alignment
Trade unions 6,29,47,48,51,
　110,112,132,134;see also
　proletariat,workers
Triple alliance 33,35,36,
　47,49,50,52,53,54,55,60,

61,62,65,174,178;see also
Brazil,bourgeoisie,capital,
state

Unemployment 6,46,55,102,113,
190
United Nations 151,153,189
United States 83,111,135,156,
158,160,162,168,183,193;
see also West
Unity Party of Nigeria 12;
see also parties

West 35,96,105,111,114,115,
135,141,151,152,153,155,
156,159,170,171,176,179,188;
see also capitalism,
corporations
West (in Nigeria) 132
West Africa 136,145-150,170,
172-173,184,191;see also
Africa,ECOWAS
Women 2,8,12,43,48,49,51,78,
80,92,93,110,133,135,189
Workers 6,9,11,14,18,21,23,38,
41,45,46,47,48,49,50,60,65,
69,71,78,89,92,120,128,133,
134,145;in oil industry 69;
see also NLC,proletariat,
trade unions
World Bank 43,45,53,58,61,80,
81,83,84,85,87,90,92;see also
IMF

Zimbabwe see Rhodesia